ROGER MARIS

◀◀◀◀◀ AND A ▶▶▶▶▶

CAST OF HUNDREDS

GREGORY ROM

For my family and friends
who all helped to make this book happen.

www.gregoryrombooks.com

Printed in the United States of America

ISBN-13: 978-0-9815653-6-1
ISBN-10: 0-9815653-6-0

First Edition

Published by: Over the Moon Books
www.overthemoonbooks.com

Cover design & layout by: Nubson Design.
www.nubson.com
design@nubson.com

Cover illustration by: Adam Anderson

Personal Acknowledgments

This author is indebted to many kind people who offered their guidance and encouragement during my project. As a first-time author, I needed all the help and encouragement I could get. There are many others not named here who also expressed interest and encouraged me in my work.

My sister-in-law Karen Johnson of Knoxville, Tennessee provided much deserved criticism and assistance in her reading of an early draft of the book's introduction. She helped me realize how much I still needed to learn about the formal use of the English language.

Minnesota educators and authors Joe and John Gindele related their experiences to me, offered valuable advice about publishing, and answered all of my questions to the best of their ability. Even though, as they admit, they are not great sports fans, their sincere interest in my project was appreciated by me.

Mark Cox, an extremely bright and thoughtful baseball fan, especially of the Minnesota Twins and University of Minnesota Golden Gophers, patiently read through an entire draft of the document, as the text was nearing completion, and provided many helpful suggestions.

My young editor, Jennifer Shaw did a fine job in the editing process. In addition to helping me better construct some of my sentences, she encouraged me to fully take credit for my work.

I am indebted to the *Forum of Fargo-Moorhead* for providing the photographs of Roger Maris which appear in the book. Thanks go to Forum sportswriters Kevin Schempf and Jeff Kolpack. The words "pennant pursuit" which I used many times in the text to describe the pennant races, were consistently used by the Forum many years ago in the daily publishing of the baseball standings.

My publisher Avery and Amy Nubson of Nubson Design and Over the Moon Books of Fargo-Moorhead provided able and professional assistance throughout the publishing process. Their cover design and supervision of the book's layout is superb. The drawing of Roger Maris appearing on the front cover is an adaptation of a photograph also provided by the *Forum of Fargo-Moorhead*. Credit for the drawing goes to talented artist Adam Anderson of Beulah, North Dakota.

The photograph of the author in the Fargo-Moorhead Red Hawks baseball cap on the back cover was taken on a fine Autumn day in 2013 by fellow church-member and friend Dar Daily of Plymouth, Minnesota.

Finally, none of this would be at all possible without the steadfast and unwavering love and support of my wife Mary. She cheerfully endured weeks and months of my endless thinking and talking about this project, sometimes even in my sleep. The first autographed copy will be hers to keep.

Contents

INTRODUCTION

When I retired at the age of 62, I began to question what I was going to do with my time. I have occasionally imagined myself as a writer and I did some thinking about a book idea. What could I possibly write about that might be interesting, informative, and entertaining to even a small audience? My idea was to write about baseball history in a way that would appeal especially to baby-boomers like myself.

I was born in 1950, so my twelve years of public school in the Moorhead, MN schools ran from 1957 through my high school graduation in 1968. This was a unique time in baseball history. It was a time of monumental change for the game. After the 1957 season, the Brooklyn Dodgers and the New York Giants packed up their clubhouses and moved to Los Angeles and San Francisco, respectively, making the game a truly coast-to-coast experience. In 1961 the American League expanded from eight to ten teams and the National League followed suit the very next year for the 1962 season.

Then in just a few more years, the 1968 season was the last baseball season which concluded at the end of the regular season by going directly into the World Series with the postseason a maximum of seven games in length. Each game was a drama of unparalleled excitement which riveted the attention of the baseball world. One could say it was the last true baseball season in the traditional sense -- in the way the game had been played out since 1903, the year of the first World Series, two generations in the past. The next year in 1969 both leagues split themselves into two divisions and the playoffs began. Baseball was never again to be the same.

My birthplace, Fargo, North Dakota, was also the hometown of Roger Maris. Baseball fans in this sparsely populated and mostly rural area followed his career with avid interest. It just so happens that his twelve years in the Major Leagues corresponded exactly with my twelve years of school from 1957 through 1968. I was paying close attention to his many accomplishments even in the four years before his memorable 1961 season when he almost miraculously surmounted the cherished single-season home run record of the Yankees legendary Babe Ruth. In this twelve-year span, Roger Maris played in seven World Series -- five with the New York Yankees and then closed out his career in two more with the St. Louis Cardinals in 1967 and 1968.

So, I asked myself, was it just a peculiar coincidence that my twelve years in school exactly corresponded with the Major League Baseball career of Roger Maris? Or is it just possible that some unseen spiritual guidance was leading me on the way to write a narrative history about the game of baseball and its many games, players, and personalities during those years when so many things began to change in the midst of growing up?

This book is dedicated primarily to my parents who were fans of baseball, not in the sense of cheering wildly for every base hit or even every victory by a favorite team, but in the sense that they had a basic understanding of the game. They had played baseball and softball at amateur levels and had a good appreciation for the skills and dedication of the professional athletes that made the game joyful to watch. Many times in the summer the three of us would go sit along the third base line to attend the minor league games of our local team the Fargo-Moorhead Twins as they went up against their Northern League rivals from Aberdeen, Duluth-Superior, Eau Claire, Grand Forks, St. Cloud, Wausau, or Winnipeg.

The Major League Baseball season runs a full six months from the beginning of April through the end of September, from spring and continuously on into the fall. When the two leagues expanded from eight to ten teams, the schedule increased from 154 to 162 games. The American League did this in 1961 followed by the National League in 1962. As the seasons progressed, I considered certain games to be milestone games. A milestone game was a game where the first team in either league reached win number 10, 20, 30, etc, up to 100 wins. If we follow these milestone games during the course of the long baseball season, the story is told of how the year unfolded. Which teams got off to a good start? Which teams started to make their move as the weather heated up in the summer? Which teams got hot and which teams slumped as the season moved on to its conclusion after Labor Day? This narrative is a historical perspective upon baseball history for twelve years.

The results of all the games played, so many years ago, are well known. I do not strive to create suspense, but if there was tension or uncertainty at the time, this may be conveyed by my story. I do ask for a leap of faith to indulge my fantasy to attend, experience, and then describe the ball games that took place. It is my contention that many years later, I am revisiting the baseball games of those years to attend and experience them in a spiritual sense. Please be mentally prepared to make a return visit to the nineteen-fifties and sixties to simply be entertained by going back all the way to 1957.

The game of baseball consists of nine innings which can be further divided into three early innings, three middle innings, and three late innings. Out of the nine innings, there are two that stand out in importance in many individual games. These two are the first inning and the ninth inning. The players have to be able to come out onto the field both physically and mentally ready to play the first inning. If they are not well prepared, bad things may result, and they may be down a run or several runs as soon as the game gets under way. When the early innings stretch into the middle innings, the game will find a pace and character of its own and then journey to a conclusion in the late innings, perhaps with no clear winner until the ninth and final frame. All this unfolds before the crowd, normally, in a period of from two to three hours and is ideally staged on a warm and sunny afternoon. If the game is so tight that it remains all tied up at the end of nine, then extra innings will be required to decide the result. All of these game details are summarily reported in the box score. The box score is the summary of the game reported in a daily newspaper in a two to five inch column format. It shows among other things, the score by innings, the winning and losing pitchers, hits by each player, which players had doubles, triples and home runs, the position played by each player, the time of the game, and the game attendance. I ask for patience as I describe the unfolding of these twelve memorable seasons and the individual games and the players that made a difference.

A LITTLE BASEBALL HISTORY - THE HOME RUN

The home run is the most exciting play in baseball. In a single swing of the bat the baseball is powerfully hit, the hitter trots around the bases, steps on home plate, and a run is scored. If runners are on base, then two, three or even four runs may score, all in one magnificent play. The game of baseball was first played in the nineteenth century. The National League began in 1876 during which the league leader, with five home runs was George Hall of the Philadelphia Athletics. The American League began play in 1901. The first World Series contested between the American League and the National League was in 1903. The Major League leader in home runs exceeded 20 or more only five times from 1876 through 1918. These were Ned Williamson of Chicago with 27 in 1884, Sam Thompson of Philadelphia with 20 in 1889, Buck Freeman of Washington with 25 in 1899, Wildfire Schulte of Chicago with 21 in 1911, and Gavvy Cravath of Philadelphia with 24 in 1915.

All this ended with the arrival of George Herman (Babe) Ruth of the Boston Red Sox, who led the American League in home runs in 1919 with 29. Then, before the beginning of the 1920 season, Boston sold Babe Ruth to the New York Yankees. With the Yankees, the Babe went on to make home run history with 54 in 1920, 59 in 1921, a record 60 in 1927, and 54 in 1928. In his 22-year career which ended in 1935, Ruth hit 714 home runs with a batting average of .342. He left an indelible mark on baseball, not the least of which was Yankee Stadium, the "House that Ruth Built" in the Bronx, New York City. The 1957 baseball season would be the 30th anniversary of Ruth's record season of 1927. Through the remaining days of the Roaring Twenties, the Depression, the darkest days of the Second World War, and into the post-war years of "Ozzie and Harriet," the single-season home run record had remained steadfastly unchanged at the magic number 60. It had been challenged most notably by Hack Wilson of the Cubs with 56 in 1930, Jimmie Foxx of the Athletics with 58 in 1932, Hank Greenberg of the Tigers with 58 in 1938, Ralph Kiner of the Pirates with 54 in 1949, and more recently by Mickey Mantle of the New York Yankees with 52 in 1956. The record of 60 had been approached, but never equaled or exceeded.

I invite baseball fans to be ready to come along to attend the baseball games which will tell the amazing story of the twelve seasons. I shall describe the results of each game in varying detail depending upon the circumstances. However, there are many details which I shall not attempt to tell. Some of these are as follows.

First, I shall describe single games. In baseball, the teams usually play each other over three or four days in a series of three or four games in length. However, I have time and space to attend and describe only one game at a time. The basic unit of measurement of a team's success is single games won and lost. If there is a doubleheader scheduled, I usually arrive for the second game only. On a few occasions, I may describe the general results of a critical series, but normally I attend and describe individual single games.

Second, I do not know if the games were played during the day or at night and I also do not know about the weather. I prefer baseball under a bright blue sky. In April and September the conditions were probably cooler. For the games played in July and August, it was probably hot. The box scores do not tell about the time of day or the weather conditions. I shall describe a couple of games that were shortened by rain, but these were official games at least four and one-half innings in length.

Third, although home runs are often of paramount importance to produce the game outcomes, there are many details about the home runs which are not usually known. In most cases, it is not known if the baseball was hit to left, center, or right field and it is not known if the baseball barely cleared the outfield wall or if it was a tape measure blast.

Fourth, this is not a book about baseball strategy. There are elements of baseball strategy which are barely touched upon, if at all. I do not talk much about the right-handed versus left-handed aspects of the game. I also do not talk much about the decision to pinch-hit or not, which managers face in every game.

Fifth, the defensive aspects of baseball regarding plays in the infield and outfield are not mentioned very often. Every baseball game is affected by defensive play; however, these details are not apparent from the box scores, except for statistics on errors and unearned runs. In contrast to defensive plays in the field, much attention is paid to the art of pitching. Every play in baseball starts with the pitcher.

The events described in this narrative happened some fifty years ago. It was a different world in the nineteen-fifties and nineteen-sixties. People then still talked about the Second World War, which was simply called the War. Communism was perceived as a threat and so the Cold War was being staged with the Soviet Union. Across the Pacific Ocean, Red China was also a Communist menace. This was the time of Presidents Eisenhower, Kennedy, and Johnson. The nation followed Sputnik and the launch of men into space during an epic race to the moon. The civil rights movement made headlines, especially across the South. President Kennedy was assassinated in Dallas. The U.S.A. struggled with its perceived need to forestall Communist expansion into Southeast Asia in Vietnam and the perceived need for the expansion of government social programs to fight poverty here at home. A few of the baseball games described on this journey to the ballparks across America took place at the very time of an important event in the world beyond the realm of baseball and so I have inserted brief references to some of these events in the narrative history. The news of these events appeared in the very same newspapers which reported the baseball box scores of the day, whether reported in the *New York Times*, *Chicago Tribune*, or *St. Louis Post-Dispatch*. Now, it is the twenty-first century. Changes, like the following, have taken place in baseball since the era of the nineteen-fifties and sixties.

First, in those years there was a balanced schedule in both leagues and there was no interleague play in the regular season. In a balanced schedule each team plays all of the other teams in its league an equal number of times. Regular season interleague play began in 1997. In those years of 1957 through 1968, interleague play only took place in the World Series and the All-Star game. These interleague games were watched very closely by fans when they did occur. Along with the balanced schedule of games, there were many more scheduled doubleheaders, especially on Sunday afternoons in the summer months.

Second, the two leagues had no divisional setup. There was only one pennant race in each league for fans to follow. The two league pennant races could be followed more closely by the media and with greater interest by the fans. Because there were only two races to follow, far greater attention could be focused on each one and since there were no playoffs, the pennant races literally meant everything for the whole season. The World Series was the only postseason and it was a maximum of seven games in length. All World Series games were played during the day. The first World Series game played at night was in 1971.

Third, the American League had not yet adopted the rule of the designated hitter. It adopted the rule beginning with the 1973 season. The National League has thus far even today refused to go along.

Fourth, starting pitchers were generally allowed and expected to remain in the games longer. Complete game statistics over the years bear this out. The idea of removing the pitcher once he reached a certain pitch count was not yet considered standard protocol.

Fifth, free agency for the players had not yet become established practice. The players were under contract with a single team and stayed put unless they were traded, released, or sold.

The history of these twelve baseball seasons beginning in 1957 and ending in 1968 is not solely about home runs or mostly about Roger Maris. The game is about much more than the most exciting play on its stage and about much more than its home run record holder. Its drama had a cast of twenty teams and hundreds of players who sometimes won and sometimes lost. The previous season of 1956 had ended in the fall, as it always did, with the last game of the World Series -- which went the full seven games, as it often did. In that last World Series game at Ebbets Field in Brooklyn on October 10, 1956, the powerful Yankees soundly defeated Brooklyn 9-0, ending the Dodgers single-year reign as World Series champions, with a three-hit shutout pitching performance by Johnny Kucks and two home runs from Yogi Berra. The Bronx Bombers could celebrate again. Then in the cold of winter, there was relative inactivity in baseball for November and December of 1956 and January 1957. Finally in late February, as it always happened, the teams of Major League players and hopeful prospects began to gather, mostly in Florida, for the ritual of spring training and the schedule of exhibition games, which followed in March. With those games completed, preparations made, and fundamentals adequately practiced, it was then time to head North and to play ball with something on the line.

Before traveling back in time to 1957, here are some thoughts about the organization of this historical narrative. The narrative is organized into separate chapters, each covering a season from 1957 through 1968. Each season includes accounts of fourteen games for a total of 168 games over the twelve-year time span. It includes primarily games played by the leading teams as each season progressed. Also included are a scattering of games of historical significance and a few games played by second division teams that otherwise would not have been covered. Care was taken so that over the entire twelve-year period there were accounts of 84 American League and 84 National League games for a total of 168. The descriptions and accounts of the games vary in content depending on the circumstances of each unique ballgame. Following the descriptions of the regular season games for each year, is a report on the American and National League individual and team leaders in major hitting and pitching categories. Also included is a report on winners of the Most Valuable Player, Rookie of the Year and Cy Young Awards.

After the account of each year's regular season, is a section about the World Series. Each Series begins with a comparison of the two team's individual players by position, starting pitchers, and managers. Then there is a brief description of how the two competing team's regular seasons progressed in terms of their won-lost records and their relative success against other teams in their League. The individual World Series games are described with a detailed report on the first game, the fourth game, and the final game of each Series. A more brief account is presented for the other games. A short summary follows the individual game descriptions. I attempt to place the Series outcome in some historical or philosophical baseball context and present a simple list of the final scores of each game of the Series.

Interspersed among all of this information are what I call interludes. The purpose of these interludes is to provide additional information about the most successful individual players of the twelve-year period and attempt to place them in more human historical baseball context. A majority of these individuals were selected by virtue of being included in the top-ten leaders in the categories of home runs, hits, stolen bases, pitching wins, or pitching strikeouts for the twelve-year period. In addition, a very small number of interludes are presented about other subjects or other players of special significance. An attempt was made to place the interludes about each player within or near to the particular year in which his contribution to the story was the most significant. Most of these players were active through nearly the entire twelve years, so the interludes tend to be more frequently placed in the later years of the period.

Finally, after the year-by-year presentation of all twelve individual baseball seasons is concluded, the historical narrative winds up with a discussion of the individual leading players over the period. This includes final interludes and a presentation of the twelve-year highlights for each of the 20 then existing baseball franchises. Here is presented an extremely condensed summary of the games included for each team over the years, together with attendance data and some concluding historical baseball perspective for each American League and National League team.

Roger Maris at Barnett Field in Fargo, North Dakota. Maris played for the Fargo-Moorhead Twins in the Northern League in 1953, the first of his four years in the minor leagues. The team was affiliated with the Cleveland Indians farm system. His rookie year in Major League Baseball was 1957.

MILWAUKEE TOASTS ITS BRAVES

By revisiting a selection of the games each year from 1957 through 1968, a grand tour of this twelve-year period in Major League Baseball is presented. By virtue of hindsight, the focus is on primarily the games of the leaders in the races for the pennant as the seasons progressed. Attention is also concentrated on a central character in baseball during this time, the amazing career of Roger Maris and the teams for which he played. Following Maris would prove not to be difficult because his teams were generally hotly involved in the pennant race.

In his very first Major League Baseball game, Roger Maris had three singles in five at bats and scored a run for the Cleveland Indians as they lost their home opener 3 to 2 in eleven innings to the Chicago White Sox in Cleveland on Tuesday, April 16, before an opening day crowd of 31,145. The opening day starter for Chicago, Billy Pierce (1-0), went the full eleven innings for the win giving up eight hits with nine strikeouts. Cleveland pitcher Herb Score (0-1) went the full eleven innings for the loss. He recorded ten strikeouts, gave up only seven hits, but walked eleven White Sox batters. Score was the American League Rookie of the Year in 1955. In 1956, he was a twenty game winner for the Indians but would win only two games in 1957. His quite promising career was badly damaged later in the year when he was struck in the face by a wicked line drive in a game against the New York Yankees.

At the old Polo Grounds in New York on Wednesday, May 1, 1957, the Milwaukee Braves defeated the New York Giants by a score of 5 to 1 in ten innings before a sparse crowd of only 5,961. The Braves' left-hander Warren Spahn won his fourth game of the season by scattering eight hits over ten complete innings. Spahn would go on to lead the National League in wins with 21 for the 1957 season. The game was tied at one run each after nine innings, but then the Braves scored four runs in the top of the tenth for the win. The game winner was a two-run homer by Frank Torre with one out.

With this win, the Braves extended their record to 10 wins and 2 losses and maintained a one game lead over the defending National League champion Brooklyn Dodgers.

The 1957 season would be the last for the Dodgers in Brooklyn and the Giants in New York. After this season, they would be moving all the way to the West Coast to take their places as the Los Angeles Dodgers and the San Francisco Giants. With such established star players as Duke Snider and Willie Mays making the transition, both teams would continue to play many vital and memorable baseball games in the National League in the years ahead.

The Brooklyn Dodgers were in Chicago to play the Cubs on Thursday, May 16. Before a crowd of only 3,105 at Wrigley Field, the Dodgers prevailed by a final score of 3 to 2. Brooklyn had five hits in the game compared to four for the Cubs. The winning pitcher for Brooklyn was 22-year-old left-hander Sandy Koufax (2-0). Koufax worked all nine innings, allowed two unearned runs, struck out thirteen, and had seven bases on balls. The loss for Chicago was charged to Moe Drabowsky (1-3), who in six innings gave up three runs on three hits and struck out eight. Drabowsky, born in Poland, would go on to have a seventeen-year career in baseball from 1956 through 1972. He accumulated a lifetime record of 88 wins, 105 losses, and an earned run average (ERA) of 3.71 runs per game. Brooklyn scored two in the fourth and one run in the sixth; the Cubs managed only one run in the fifth and one in the last of the eighth inning. The margin for the Dodgers was the solo home run hit by center fielder Duke Snider, his 5th, in the sixth inning. Snider had two hits in the game, as did Brooklyn right fielder Carl Furillo. Following this win, the defending National League champion Dodgers had 15 wins and 10 losses. With their fifth loss in a row, the Cubs were now 7-18.

After starting out the season with a mediocre 6 and 7 record, the Cincinnati Redlegs won 15 out of their next 17 games, ending with a doubleheader sweep of the Pittsburgh Pirates on May 19. Cincinnati won the first game with a score of 8 to 7. The Redlegs took the second game of the day at Crosley Field in Cincinnati by coming from behind with three runs in the seventh and one in the eighth for a 5 to 4 victory. Pittsburgh outhit the Redlegs in the game thirteen to six, but two errors resulting in three unearned Cincinnati runs was the difference. The winning pitcher in relief was Tom Acker who

2

earned his 5th win against 1 loss. Acker would go on to win 10 games for the Redlegs in 1957, mostly in relief. There were no home runs in the game. Cincinnati was now 21-9 for the season thus far and Pittsburgh dropped to 8-21. The doubleheader sweep established a two game lead over Milwaukee for the Redlegs.

Meanwhile in the American League, the Chicago White Sox enjoyed early season success with 18 wins and 7 losses. This was good for a two game lead over the Indians and Yankees both at 17 and 10. In the previous two years (1955 and 1956), the league pennants had been won by the Yankees and the Brooklyn Dodgers, with the Dodgers winning the World Series in 1955 and the Bronx Bombers in 1956. Both series of games went the full limit of seven contests. In the late forties and early fifties, these two teams had dominated the two leagues and the World Series with such legendary players as Mantle, Berra, DiMaggio, and Ford for the Yankees; and Robinson, Campanella, Snider, and Newcombe for the Dodgers. The Dodgers had been perennial losers to the Yankees in the World Series but had finally broken through with a victory by taking four out of seven games in 1955.

Back at this time, prior to modern expansion, there were only sixteen Major League teams with eight in each league. There was no interleague play except for the World Series and the All-Star game. The teams played a 154 game schedule and each played the other seven teams in its league twenty-two times with eleven at home and eleven on the road. This made for a lot of four game series and plenty of Sunday doubleheaders. There were no playoffs. Interleague play was not even remotely considered. The World Series, typically lasting only one week, was a spectacle in the eyes of the entire nation as the league pennant winners matched up. Every play was important because it affected the outcome of the game and every game was important because it affected the outcome of the Series.

On Wednesday, June 5, the White Sox defeated the Boston Red Sox at Comiskey Park in Chicago by a score of 6 to 2. There were no home runs in the game. The line score read 6 runs, 11 hits, 1 error for Chicago and 2 runs, 8 hits, 2 errors for Boston. Chicago veteran Dick Donovan (5-1) was the winning pitcher, giving up only single runs in the first and third innings. The game highlights included Chicago shortstop Luis Aparicio with his 7th stolen base of the season and veteran Red Sox left fielder Ted Williams with two

3

hits in the game, including his 11th double of the season. The Venezulan-born Aparicio would go on to lead the American League in stolen bases in 1957 with 28. With this win, the White Sox at 30-12 maintained a five game lead over the Yankees at 26-18.

In a return matchup of the June 5 encounter, the White Sox outscored the Red Sox at Fenway Park in Boston on June 26, by a score of 7 to 5. There were a total twenty-seven hits in the game with thirteen for Chicago and fourteen for Boston. The winner for Chicago was Jim Wilson (8-4) with a strong relief performance from Paul LaPalme, who recorded his 6th save of the year with a shutout ninth inning to preserve the win. The White Sox defense recorded three double plays in the game with 30-year-old second baseman Nellie Fox figuring in all of them. Fox, with one base hit in the game, would go on to lead the American League in total base hits with 196 for the 1957 season. Chicago at 40-23, needed the win to preserve a narrowing one-half game lead in the standings over the Yankees at 40-24.

With the season reaching the halfway point, the Yankees would go 10 and 2 over their next twelve games to open up a three game lead over the White Sox as of July 6. In the National League, a close race seemed to be developing with the St. Louis Cardinals in first place, but closely followed by Cincinnati, Milwaukee, the defending league champion Brooklyn, and the Philadelphia Phillies. These teams were all within four games of the lead. Only the Cubs, Giants and Pirates seemed out of contention. In a game on July 6, the Yankees managed their 50th win of the season over the last place Washington Senators, by a score of 10 to 6. There were 10,511 in attendance at Griffith Stadium in Washington. The Senators used five pitchers in the game against the Yankees who scored in each of the first six innings. Left fielder, Elston Howard had four hits and four runs batted in (RBI) in the game, including his 6th home run of the season in the second inning. On the positive side for the Senators, slugger Roy Sievers belted his 19th homer of the season also in the second. He would go on to lead the American League with 42 for the 1957 season. Yankees' pitcher Johnny Kucks (6-6) gave up three late Washington runs in the seventh, but reliever Art Ditmar notched the final eight outs of the game including four strikeouts to save it for New York.

The 1957 All-Star game took place on July 9, at Sportsman's Park in St. Louis, the Cardinals' home ballpark. Prior to the game, National League fans in Cincinnati unfairly stuffed the ballot boxes to elect a starting lineup composed of players nearly all from the Redlegs. Commissioner of Baseball Ford Frick responded by removing Gus Bell and Wally Post from the starting lineup and transferred voting to the players, managers, and coaches beginning with the next season. In the game itself, the American League came away with a very close 6 to 5 victory by holding off a late three-run rally by the National League in the ninth inning. The contest ended with a fine running catch by the White Sox outfielder Minnie Minoso off the bat of the Brooklyn Dodgers' Gil Hodges for the National League. The winning and losing pitchers, respectively, were the starters Jim Bunning of the Detroit Tigers and Curt Simmons of the Philadelphia Phillies. There were no home runs in the game. Attendance in St. Louis was 30,693.

After the All-Star break, the season resumed in the National League with the Milwaukee Braves playing the Pirates at Forbes Field in Pittsburgh. On Thursday, July 11, in a game in which both teams had twelve hits, the Braves defeated the Pirates 7 to 2 before a crowd numbering 17,278. In the field, Pittsburgh committed six errors which resulted in two unearned runs for Milwaukee. In the fourth inning, the Braves scored four runs and assumed a 4 to 2 lead in the game. Shortstop Johnny Logan hit his 5th home run of the season with a man on base which produced two of the fourth inning tallies. In a losing cause, Pittsburgh center fielder Bill Virdon had three hits in five at bats, including his 14th double and 6th triple of the season. The winning pitcher for the Braves was 27-year-old starter Bob Trowbridge (3-1), who pitched all nine innings, walked three, and struck out four. Trowbridge would go on to finish the 1957 season with 7 wins, 5 losses, and a 3.64 earned run average. The loss for Pittsburgh was charged to starter Bob Friend (6-10), who lasted seven innings and surrendered four runs on nine hits. After the win, Milwaukee's record improved to 45-35. Pittsburgh dropped to 31-50 for the season thus far.

The Yankees continued with their heavy hitting; and notched their 60th win over the second place White Sox with a 10 to 6 triumph at the Stadium in the Bronx on July 23. Art Ditmar (7-1) was the winner for New York in relief of starter Don Larsen, who went the first four and one-third innings. Ditmar, 28 years old, was in his first season with the Yankees after three years with the Athletics. He would go on to finish the 1957 season with a record of 8 wins and 3 losses. The White Sox assumed a 6 to 4 lead with four runs in the sixth inning, only to have the Yankees counter with five big runs in the seventh and then coast to the win. Thirteen bases on balls by the Yankees' hurlers contributed to a 3 hour and 20 minute game. For New York, center fielder Mickey Mantle slammed his 26th home run and also recorded a double, triple, and his 10th stolen base of the season.

Bob Turley (8-3) hurled a four-hit shutout over the Washington Senators for New York's 70th win of the season on August 6, at Yankee Stadium before a Tuesday crowd of 15,455. The time of the game was a quick 1 hour and 59 minutes. Turley would finish the regular season with 13 wins and 6 losses with a 2.71 earned run average. The losing pitcher for the Senators was Chuck Stobbs (5-15). The Yankees picked up single runs in the first, second, fourth, and fifth innings for the win. Right fielder Hank Bauer led off the game with his 19th home run of the season. This extended the Yankees lead over the White Sox to seven games. Meanwhile, over in the Senior circuit, Milwaukee and St. Louis kept pace with identical 63 and 42 records.

By the last week of August, the White Sox had moved up to within four and one-half games of New York in the American League pennant race. In a game at Comiskey Park on August 27, the Yankees scored three runs each in the top of the eighth and ninth innings for a 12 to 6 victory, their 80th win against 45 losses. By this time, the White Sox were the only American League team left in the race to potentially challenge New York. The Yanks pounded out sixteen hits to nine for Chicago during the game. The winning pitcher in relief for New York was Bob Grim (11-4). Offensively, the big blow for New York was a three-run homer by 32-year-old veteran catcher Yogi Berra in the eighth, his 20th of the year. Berra went four-for-five in the game with six runs batted in. In the National League, from August 6 through August 27, Milwaukee opened a seven and one-half game lead over the Cardinals by going 14-5 compared to a 7-13 record for St. Louis.

Black players were becoming more accepted in Major League Baseball by 1957 than in previous years. It is true that there were more black players with some teams than with others. About this time, the struggle of the civil rights movement in America was picking up momentum. On September 9, 1957, President Eisenhower signed into law the Voting Rights Act of 1957, which was aimed at ending barriers that had been erected, primarily in the South, to make it difficult for blacks to vote. This is generally considered to be the first civil rights legislation to be enacted by the U.S. Congress since the end of Reconstruction. The two teams in Major League Baseball with, perhaps, the most ties to the South were in Cincinnati, located on the border with Kentucky, and St. Louis, on the Mississippi River adjacent to Southern Illinois. On Sunday, September 8, the previous day, the two teams met in a game at St. Louis before a crowd of 19,684. The Cardinals edged out the Redlegs 4 to 3 with a late inning rally. For St. Louis, starter, Vinegar Bend Mizell worked the first eight innings, gave up three runs on seven hits, and left the game trailing 3-0. Cincinnati had scored three runs on eight hits including the 26th home run of the season by center fielder Frank Robinson in the sixth inning. The winning pitcher in relief was Larry Jackson (14-8), who hurled a scoreless ninth inning for St. Louis before the Cardinals won it with two runs in the last of the ninth. Starting pitcher, left-hander Joe Nuxhall (9-10), took the loss for Cincinnati. Nuxhall went eight innings and only two of the four runs he allowed were earned. The game's line score read 4 runs, 8 hits and 2 errors for St. Louis and 3 runs, 8 hits and 1 error for Cincinnati. The one error for Cincinnati was committed by pitcher Joe Nuxhall.

The Yankees won games number 90 and 91 of the season with a sweep of a doubleheader over Kansas City on Sunday, September 15. The first game was a 5 to 3 win for the Yankees followed by a 3-0 shutout over the Athletics in the second game. The 20,176 spectators gathered at Yankee Stadium saw a quickly played second game with not even one extra base hit for either team. For the Yankees, Don Larsen (9-4) scattered three hits and two walks for the complete game win. The Yankees managed eight base hits with only Mickey Mantle producing two of them. With only ten games to go in the season, the New York lead over Chicago was five and one-half games.

The regular season concluded on September 29, with the New York Yankees and Milwaukee Braves winning the league pennants by eight games each over the Chicago White Sox and St. Louis Cardinals, respectively. On the basis of their superior team experience, the Yankees seemed to be the favorite in the World Series; but the young Milwaukee team would prove to be a team to be reckoned with. The Braves last game of the season at Milwaukee saw them defeat the Cincinnati Redlegs by a score of 4 to 3. To give a few of their regulars some rest before the start of the Series, the Braves used 24 players in the game. The winning pitcher in relief for the Braves was Don McMahon (2-3). In thirty-two relief appearances in 1957, the 27-year-old rookie McMahon posted a 1.54 earned run average in 48 innings pitched. First baseman Joe Adcock had two hits in the game including his 13th double of the season to lead in that department. The line score was 4 runs, 6 hits and no errors for Milwaukee and 3 runs, 8 hits and 1 error for Cincinnati. The Redlegs concluded a winning season with 80 wins and 74 losses, which was good for fourth place in the National League final standings.

After flirting with .400, veteran Red Sox outfielder Ted Williams led the American League in batting with a .388 average. Mickey Mantle of the Yankees finished second with .365. In home runs, the league leader was Roy Sievers of the Washington Senators with 42, followed by the Red Sox legend Williams with 38. In a big league career spanning seventeen seasons, Sievers would total 318 home runs with at least 20 in each year from 1954 through 1962. Sievers led in runs batted in with 114, followed by Vic Wertz of the Cleveland Indians with 105. From a team standpoint, the Yankees led with a .268 team batting average and 723 runs scored. The Kansas City Athletics led in home runs with 166.

Pitchers Jim Bunning of Detroit and Billy Pierce of Chicago led the American League in wins with 20 each. Tom Sturdivant was the leading winner for the Yankees with 16. Bobby Shantz of the Yankees led in earned run average with 2.45. Two of the next three pitchers in this category were also with New York --Sturdivant with 2.54 and Bob Turley with 2.71. Detroit's Jim Bunning finished with 2.69. In strikeouts, Early Wynn of Cleveland led with 184, followed by Bunning with 182. In team pitching, the Yankees led the league in earned run average at 3.00, fewest hits allowed with 1,198, and strikeouts with 810. The White Sox led with 59 complete games and the Baltimore Orioles in fewest home runs allowed with 95.

In the National League, veteran Stan Musial of the St. Louis Cardinals won the batting championship with a .351 average. Willie Mays of the Giants was second with .333. Henry Aaron of the Braves was the leader in both home runs and runs batted in, with 44 and 132, respectively. Ernie Banks had 43 for the Cubs and Duke Snider had 40 for the Brooklyn Dodgers. Del Ennis of St. Louis was second in RBI with 105. In team batting, St. Louis took the batting honors with a .274 average. Milwaukee led in power numbers with 199 home runs and 772 total runs scored.

8

In pitching wins, three of the top five were Milwaukee Braves -- Warren Spahn 21, Bob Buhl 18, and Lew Burdette 17. Jack Sanford of the Phillies finished with 19 wins and Don Drysdale of the Dodgers with 17. Lefty Johnny Podres of Brooklyn had the lowest ERA with 2.66 followed by his teammate Drysdale with 2.69. Spahn also finished with 2.69 for Milwaukee. Jack Sanford led in strikeouts with 188. Team earned run average honors went to Brooklyn with 3.35. Brooklyn pitchers also had the most strikeouts with 891, and fewest hits allowed of 1,285.

Postseason award winners for 1957 for the American League were from the New York Yankees. Mickey Mantle was selected as the Most Valuable Player (MVP) and shortstop Tony Kubek was American League Rookie of the Year. Mantle had also been selected as the MVP for the American League for 1956. In the National League, Henry Aaron of the Milwaukee Braves was MVP. Pitcher Jack Sanford of the Philadelphia Phillies was Rookie of the Year. For 1957, the Cy Young Award went to the Milwaukee Braves' southpaw Warren Spahn. Until 1967, only one Cy Young Award winner was selected to honor the most outstanding pitcher in baseball.

It is difficult to describe the intense and stressful competition that took place on the baseball fields of play. Even the players that were just average or were mostly on second division teams were extraordinary. That is why I sometimes include references to the career or individual year accomplishments of selected players who participated. For every one player mentioned, there are countless others to whom credit is also due. They may not all have won a batting title or led in home runs, but their individual participation made everything else possible. Many hours and even years of work and play was needed to reach the Major League level.

The 1957 World Series was scheduled to open on Wednesday, October 2, at Yankee Stadium, home of the American League champion New York Yankees. Media speculation centered around a comparison of the two teams' primary position players and starting pitchers, as follows:

CATCHER - Milwaukee, Del Crandall, 27, and New York, Yogi Berra, 32. Crandall played in 118 games and hit .253 with 15 home runs. Berra was in 134 games and hit .251 with 24 home runs. Berra was a three time American

League Most Valuable Player Award winner (1951, 1954, 1955). Edge goes to the Yankees on the basis of experience.

FIRST BASE - Milwaukee, Joe Adcock, 30, and New York, Bill Skowron, 27. Because he had suffered a mid-season injury, Adcock appeared in only 65 games. He batted .287 with 12 home runs. Skowron, in his fourth year, batted .304 with 17 home runs in 122 games. This was the fourth consecutive season that his batting average was over .300. Yankees have the edge.

SECOND BASE - Milwaukee, Red Schoendienst, 34, and New York, Jerry Coleman, 33. Schoendienst led the National League in hits with 200. Coleman was in his last year in Major League Baseball. He batted .268 in 157 at bats. The Braves would seem to have the edge on experience and 1957 performance.

SHORTSTOP - Milwaukee, Johnny Logan, 30, and New York, Gil McDougald, 29. Logan had been with the Braves since 1951. In 1957 he batted .273 with 10 home runs. McDougald also had been with the Yankees since 1951. He hit .289 with 13 home runs for the year. No edge to either team.

THIRD BASE - Milwaukee, Eddie Mathews, 26, and New York, Jerry Lumpe, 24. Mathews had been a genuine star for the Braves since his rookie season of 1952. Mathews hit .292 with 32 home runs in 1957. In his second season with New York, Lumpe batted .340 in 103 at bats. Edge is to Milwaukee.

LEFT FIELD - Milwaukee, Wes Covington, 25, and New York, Tony Kubek, 22. Covington was in his second year with the Braves and hit .284 with 21 home runs. Kubek hit .297 in his first year with the Yankees with limited power. He was voted 1957 American League Rookie of the Year. Both were young talented players with limited experience. Rated even.

CENTER FIELD - Milwaukee, Henry Aaron, 23 and New York, Mickey Mantle, 26. Aaron hit .322 with 44 home runs in his fourth season with the Braves. Mantle broke in with New York in 1951. Mantle hit .365 with 34 home runs in 1957. Both were considered team leaders and capable of dominating the Series if things went their way. Rated even.

RIGHT FIELD - Milwaukee, Andy Pafko, 36, and New York, Hank Bauer, 35. The veteran Pafko had his most productive seasons with the Cubs in the late forties. He hit .277 for Milwaukee in 1957. Bauer, a member of the Yankees team since 1948, hit .259 with 18 home runs. Bauer had been more of an everyday player in 1957. He appeared in 137 games opposed to only 83 games for Pafko. The edge goes to New York on the basis of experience and the year's longevity.

STARTING PITCHING - For Milwaukee: Warren Spahn, 36, won 21, lost 11. Lew Burdette, 31, won 17, lost 9. Bob Buhl, 29, won 18, lost 7. For New York: Whitey Ford, 29, won 11, lost 5. Bobby Shantz, 32, won 11, lost 5. Bob Turley, 27, won 13, lost 6. All were veteran and extremely capable Major League pitchers. The staff aces, Spahn and Ford, were in their prime. Warren Spahn showed little signs of aging at age 36. It seemed there would be no edge to either ballclub.

MANAGERS - Milwaukee, Fred Haney, 61, and New York, Casey Stengel, 67. Haney became manager of the Milwaukee Braves midway through the 1956 season. As a player, Haney was active from 1922 through 1929 mostly with the Detroit Tigers. Casey Stengel began managing the Yankees at the start of the 1949 season. Stengel's actual name was Charles Dillon Stengel but he was simply known as Casey or "The Old Perfessor." He was in the major leagues for several different teams from 1912 through 1925. Stengel appeared in the 1916 World Series with Brooklyn and the 1922 and 1923 Fall Classics with the New York Giants.

Milwaukee won the pennant by eight games with a record of 95-59. The Braves were 9-2 in April and went 19-7 in August. They had a winning record against every team in the National League except for St. Louis, with which they split twenty-two games. The Yankees also won by eight games with a record of 98-56. In the middle of the season, New York came on strong and won 21 and lost 9 in both June and July. They had a winning record against all seven other American League teams. The Yankees were 19-3 against Kansas City. They were shut out only twice in 154 games.

For the city of Milwaukee, Wisconsin, 1957 was the culmination of several years of Braves progress in unseating the Brooklyn Dodgers as the National League powerhouse. The team had been the Boston Braves and they had moved west to Milwaukee beginning with the 1953 season. Over these few years, the Braves nucleus reached its prime while many of the Dodgers' players were moving past their peak. Yankee Stadium in New York would be the scene of games one and two and, if necessary, games six and seven. Located in the South Bronx, Yankee Stadium, often called "the House that Ruth Built," opened in 1923. Prior to this, the Yankees had shared the Polo Grounds with the National League New York Giants. In 1920 the Yankees acquired Babe Ruth from the Boston Red Sox and many years of Yankees success was underway. The Yankees won their first American League pennant the next year in 1921. With this new good fortune, the team opted to build its own ballpark. Outfield dimensions in Yankee Stadium tended to favor left-handed hitters, like the Babe, who could pull the ball sharply down the right field line.

In the first game of the 1957 World Series on October 2, the Yankees, living up to their reputation as Series veterans, defeated the Braves by a score of 3 to 1 at Yankee Stadium before 69,476. Southpaw Whitey Ford (1-0) pitched the complete game for New York giving up five hits and four bases on balls. For Milwaukee, left-hander Warren Spahn (0-1) started the game and lasted five and one-third innings, allowing one run in the fifth and two in the sixth to give the Yankees the lead. The New York nine-hit offense was paced by second baseman Jerry Coleman who had two hits, one of them a double, and had one RBI in the game. Right fielder Hank Bauer also doubled for New York. The Braves lone tally came in the top of the seventh as Wes Covington doubled and was driven in by Milwaukee leadoff man Red Schoendienst. Neither Henry Aaron (1 for 4) for Milwaukee or Mickey Mantle (2 for 4) for the Yankees turned out to be major factors in the game.

The next day, in the second game, the Braves evened the series with a 4 to 2 victory behind the pitching of Lew Burdette (1-0). On Saturday, October 5, the third game was played at Milwaukee County Stadium. The Yankees asserted themselves with a 12 to 3 blowout of the Braves, featuring two home runs by Yankees' rookie Tony Kubek, to take a two game to one lead in the Series. Kubek, who was born in Milwaukee in 1935, had hit only 3 home runs during the regular season in 431 official at bats. New York relief pitcher Don Larsen (1-0) was credited with the win. This was the first World Series game ever staged in Milwaukee and was attended by a crowd numbering 45,804.

Although it took ten innings, the Braves once again evened the Series at two each in the fourth game on Sunday, October 6. After spotting the Yankees a single run in the first inning, Milwaukee took a 4 to 1 lead in the fourth behind a three-run homer from Henry Aaron and a solo blast from Frank Torre. Warren Spahn took the 4 to 1 lead into the ninth inning only to have Yankees first baseman Elston Howard tie the game with a three-run home run. In the tenth, Spahn stayed on the mound and gave up a single lead run to New York. Then in the last of the tenth, the Braves managed three runs for a 7 to 5 triumph. The game ended on a two-run homer by Eddie Mathews off Yankees' relief pitcher Bob Grim (0-1) with one out. In the Braves critical second win in the Series, Spahn (1-1) pitched ten innings, gave up five runs, eleven base hits, and struck out two.

Milwaukee won game five of the Series on Monday by a score of 1-0 behind the fine shutout pitching of Lew Burdette (2-0). The Yankees managed only seven hits in the game. The only run of the game was driven in by first baseman Joe Adcock in the bottom of the sixth inning. After a day off for travel, the Series resumed with game six at Yankee Stadium on Wednesday, October 9. With Bob Turley (1-0) picking up the win, the Yankees prevailed in a close 3 to 2 contest that sent the Series into a deciding seventh game. This would be the third consecutive year that the Yankees were involved in a game seven.

The seventh game was played in New York on Thursday, October 10. In the normal rotation, Warren Spahn would have made his third start of the Series, but he was disabled by flu like symptoms. So the Braves went with Lew Burdette, winner of games two and five, against the Yankees' Don Larsen. Burdette (3-0) responded with a fine seven-hit shutout win over the Yankees, which decisively gave the Milwaukee Braves the 1957 World Series championship. The Braves scored four big runs in the top of the third inning to take the lead and then an insurance run in the eighth on a solo home run by catcher Del Crandall. In the losing effort, New York used five pitchers in the game with the loss charged to starter Don Larsen (1-1). The game was played in front of 61,207 fans at Yankee Stadium.

In seven games, Henry Aaron hit 3 home runs for the Braves and batted .393 for the Series. For New York, center fielder Mickey Mantle batted .263 and had 1 home run. In the fifth and sixth games of the Series, Mantle was not in the starting lineup and only appeared in game five as a pinch runner. As a team, the Yankees batted .248 compared to .209 for the Braves. Although Yankees' hurlers Whitey Ford, Bob Turley, and Don Larsen pitched credibly in winning one game each, there was little question that the Series belonged to Milwaukee pitcher Lew Burdette. In winning the second, fifth, and seventh games, he posted an earned run average of 0.67 in 27 innings pitched.

1957 WORLD SERIES SUMMARY

Game 1	At New York	Yankees 3, Braves 1
Game 2	At New York	Braves 4, Yankees 2
Game 3	At Milwaukee	Yankees 12, Braves 3
Game 4	At Milwaukee	Braves 7, Yankees 5
Game 5	At Milwaukee	Braves 1, Yankees 0
Game 6	At New York	Yankees 3, Braves 2
Game 7	At New York	Braves 5, Yankees 0

MILWAUKEE WINS THE WORLD SERIES BY 4 GAMES TO 3.

INTERLUDE - WARREN SPAHN

Taking nothing away from the success of Lew Burdette in the 1957 World Series, the ace of the Braves' pitching staff for many years was the left-hander Warren Spahn. He was born in Buffalo, NY on April 23, 1921. After service in World War II, he was with the Braves in Boston and Milwaukee from 1946 through 1964. Spahn won 20 or more games in thirteen different seasons and compiled an overall record of 363 wins and 245 losses with an earned run average of 3.09. The 363 lifetime games won make him the winningest left-hander in baseball history. In the twelve baseball seasons from 1957 through 1968, he won 160 games. In three World Series appearances (1948,

1957, and 1958), Spahn won 4 games, lost 3, and had an ERA of 3.05. He appeared in seven All-Star games with an ERA of 3.21 and was the winning pitcher for the National League in 1953.

Spahn would easily be considered one of the most disciplined and durable pitchers ever to play the game. His ability to continue pitching, at a relatively high level, well into his forties was a remarkable achievement. Spahn, for a pitcher, was also an excellent hitter. For his career, he had 363 hits which included 35 home runs and a batting average of .194.

INTERLUDE - EDDIE MATHEWS

Eddie Mathews was born October 13, 1931, in Texarkana, Texas. After his family moved to California, he attended high school in Santa Barbara, CA. Mathews was with the Braves, primarily at third base, in Boston, Milwaukee, and Atlanta for the 1952 through 1966 seasons. He concluded his career in 1967 and 1968 with Houston and Detroit. In the history of the Braves franchise, he is the only player to have played in all three Braves' city locations. He was a powerful left-handed pull hitter, who batted overall .271 with a total of 512 lifetime home runs. From 1953 through 1961, he hit at least 31 home runs each season. His immense popularity was such that Mathews was chosen to appear on the cover of *Sports Illustrated* for its very first issue, dated August 16, 1954.

In the twelve seasons from 1957 through 1968, Mathews accumulated 322 home runs, with a batting average of .268. In this period, he twice batted over .300, with .306 in both 1959 and 1961. In the nine years from 1957 through 1965, he hit at least 23 home runs each year with a peak total of 46 in 1959. Mathews played in the 1957 and 1958 World Series with Milwaukee and the Series in 1968 with the Detroit Tigers. His only home run in World Series competition won game four of the 1957 Series for the Braves. In the seventh game of the 1957 Fall Classic, Mathews recorded the final out against the Yankees on a force out that resulted from a ground ball hit to him at third base. Overall Mathews had ten hits in fifty World Series at bats for an average of .200. In ten All-Star game appearances, Mathews had only two hits in twenty-five at bats. However, both hits were home runs, one in 1959 and one in 1960.

Nearly 1957 All Over Again

ᔕᔑ

An exciting new era in baseball began on Tuesday, April 15, 1958, as the Los Angeles Dodgers squared off against the San Francisco Giants at Seals Stadium in San Francisco. On opening day, San Francisco shut out the Dodgers by a score of 8-0. The Giants hit safely eleven times versus six for the Dodgers. Ruben Gomez went all nine innings to notch the win, walking six and striking out six. The 31-year-old right-hander from Puerto Rico would go on to compile a record of 10 wins and 12 losses for 1958. In his career, his best year in the big leagues would turn out to be the Giants' World Series championship year of 1954 during which he won 17 games and had a 2.88 earned run average. In the opener, home runs for the Giants included solo shots by Daryl Spencer in the fourth inning and Orlando Cepeda in the fifth. The schedule called for the Dodgers and Giants to square off against each other in the first six games to start the season on the West Coast. The Giants took two of three in the first series and San Francisco followed again with two of three in the next series at Los Angeles.

On Friday, May 2, the defending American League champion Yankees defeated the Kansas City Athletics by a score of 8 to 1 at Yankee Stadium. It was a complete game victory for Bob Turley (3-0), who gave up one run, four hits, and three walks over nine innings. The only run scored by Kansas City came in the second inning on a solo home run by left fielder Bob Cerv, his 8th of the young season. For the Yankees, 28-year-old first baseman Bill Skowron notched his 3rd homer of the season in the third inning. Skowron drove in three runs for New York. He was also known as "Moose" Skowron and would hit 14 home runs for the Yankees in 1958. With this win, the Yankees were 10 and 4 for the season. In second place, with a record of 8 and 5, were the Washington Senators, a league also-ran in 1957. In the National League, defending World Series champion Milwaukee started only 8-7. Early spring pacesetters were the Chicago Cubs at 10-5 and the San Francisco Giants with 10 wins and 6 losses.

On Sunday, May 18, San Francisco swept a doubleheader from the Cubs at Wrigley Field in Chicago. Following a 7 to 3 win in the first game, the Giants continued playing well in the second game and shut out the Cubs 4-0 before a good crowd of 33,224. Stu Miller won his first game of the season with a complete game three-hitter. In 41 games for the Giants mostly in relief, Miller would finish with a 6 and 9 won-lost record and an earned run average of 2.47 in 182 innings. The loser for Chicago was right-hander Jim Brosnan (3-4). Two days later, on May 20, Brosnan was traded to the Cardinals for veteran infielder Alvin Dark. Hitting leaders for San Francisco were 25-year-old rookie third baseman Jim Davenport and journeyman second sacker Danny O'Connell each with three hits. There were no home runs in the game. With this win, the Giants extended their record to 21-11. Chicago fell to 15 wins and 18 losses.

The Cubs proceeded to Philadelphia to face the Phillies on Thursday, May 22, and mustered up enough hitting to gain a 7 to 4 win. The Cubs outhit Philadelphia twelve to ten in the game. In the first two innings, Chicago took a 5 to 1 lead with three runs coming in the second from a home run by Ernie Banks, his 8th of the season. Banks finished the game with three hits in five at bats and four runs batted in. The winning pitcher for Chicago was Moe Drabowsky (2-4), who lasted seven and one-third innings, allowed four runs on ten hits, and had eight strikeouts. Starter Jack Sanford (3-4) was the loser for the Phillies. In a losing cause for Philadelphia, third baseman Willie Jones hit his 4th home run of the year in the fourth inning and left fielder Chuck Essegian, his 3rd, in the eighth. Jones would end his fifteen-year baseball playing career, which was mainly with the Phillies, after the 1961 season with 190 lifetime home runs and a batting average of .258. The Cubs were now 17-19 for the year and Philadelphia was 15-18.

INTERLUDE - ERNIE BANKS

Ernie Banks played his entire Major League Baseball career on the North Side of Chicago with the Cubs, spanning the years from 1953 through 1971. In nineteen years, he amassed 2,583 base hits which included 512 home runs and a lifetime batting average of .274. He was especially known for his contagious enthusiasm for the game. In an era when doubleheaders were common, he would relish the thought of playing two. Banks was voted the

National League Most Valuable Player in 1958 and 1959. Statistically those were his two best years. Banks hit 47 home runs and batted .313 in 1958. In 1959, he had 45 home runs with a batting average of .304. He won those two MVP awards in spite of the Cubs' losing record in both years. In 1958, the Cubs were 72-82, and in 1959, they were 74-80. In thirteen All-Star games, Banks was 10 for 33, a .303 average with 1 home run.

Banks was born in Dallas, Texas on January 31, 1931, and was one of the most prominent black ballplayers that came into the Major Leagues in the early nineteen-fifties. In the years 1957 through 1968, Banks hit 381 home runs and had an overall batting average of .274. Despite his success as an individual ballplayer, it was his smiling face and genuine love for his sport that set him apart. Banks began his career as a shortstop, but beginning in 1962, he played mostly at first base. In his career, he started 1,226 games at first base and 1,121 games as a shortstop. In the nineteen-sixties, Banks and his two teammates, Ron Santo and Billy Williams, formed a trio of power hitters which greatly fortified the Cubs' lineup day-in and day-out against the other National League ball clubs. Santo had a fifteen-year career in baseball from 1960 through 1974, with 342 total home runs and a batting average of .277. Williams had a baseball career spanning the years from 1959 through 1976, with a lifetime total of 426 home runs and a batting average of .290.

The Chicago Cubs played their home games at Wrigley Field, one of the most historic ball parks in the Major Leagues. In this era of baseball, the Cubs at Wrigley Field were the only Major League team which chose to play every one of its home games during the day. In other words in those years, Wrigley chose to not have a lighted playing field. After many subsequent years, the first night game played at Wrigley was in 1988. The Cubs' ballpark is sometimes known as "the friendly confines of Wrigley Field." It has been home to the Chicago Cubs since 1916 and is located on Chicago's North Side in a community called Lakeview. The park's mailing address is 1060 W. Addison Street. Wrigley Field is known for its ivy covered brick outfield wall which was originally planted back in 1937. There are many other traditions at Wrigley Field that are carried out on a daily basis which help to make it a baseball icon in Chicago, if not also in American culture.

The Yankees' early season dominance in the American League continued into June. On Sunday, June 5, New York split a doubleheader with the Chicago White Sox at Yankee Stadium in the Bronx. New York won the opening contest 12 to 5. However, in the second game, the White Sox earned a win behind six-hit pitching from Ray Moore (2-1). Moore struck out seven and issued only one walk in the game. The losing pitcher for New York was Bobby Shantz (4-2). In the top of the first inning, White Sox catcher Sherm Lollar hit his 7th home run of the season with one on base for a two run lead. The only other runs in the game were in the ninth, when Chicago picked up one insurance run driven in by Lollar, and the Yankees scored twice but fell short in a 3 to 2 loss. Active on the base paths for the White Sox in the game was shortstop Luis Aparicio, who stole his 13th base of the season. After this Sunday split, the Yankees at 30-12 led second place Kansas City by seven games. In the National League, Milwaukee and San Francisco were in a virtual tie for first place five games ahead of the Cardinals and the Redlegs.

On June 24, the Yankees defeated the White Sox in Chicago by a score of 6 to 2. After three scoreless innings, the Yankees scored five runs in the top of the fourth to take control of the game. Bob Turley went six and one-third innings for his 11th win of the season with Ryne Duren going the final two and two-third innings for his 11th save of the season. Duren, a Wisconsin native, gave up no hits, struck out six, and walked only one White Sox batter for the save. Early Wynn (7-6) took the loss for Chicago. Fourth inning home runs were hit by Mickey Mantle (13), Jerry Lumpe (1), and Norm Siebern, his 3rd of the season. With the win, New York was 40-22 which gave them an eight game lead over second place Kansas City. In the National League, the Braves opened a three and one-half game lead over the second place St. Louis Cardinals.

The 1958 All-Star game was played at Memorial Stadium in Baltimore on July 8, before a crowd of 48,829. The American League came away with a 4 to 3 win by scoring single runs in the first, second, fifth, and sixth innings, with the go ahead run driven in by Gil McDougald of the New York Yankees. The winning pitcher was Early Wynn of the Chicago White Sox, and the loser was Pittsburgh's Bob Friend. Even though the game was a close one run contest, it lacked for excitement because there was not even one extra base hit in the entire game, double, triple, or home run. This was the second year in a row in which there were not any All-Star game round trippers.

After the All-Star break, the Yankees swept a doubleheader from the Indians on Thursday, July 10 at Yankee Stadium. New York won the first game over Cleveland by a 7 to 4 margin. In the second game, the Yankees won their 50th of the season with a 4 to 3 win. At this point, the Yankees were in front of second place Boston by eleven full games. After falling behind by three runs in the middle innings of game two, the Yankees rallied to score four in the eighth inning for the 4 to 3 victory. The winning pitcher for New York in relief was Bobby Shantz (5-3). The losing pitcher for the Indians, also in relief, was knuckleballer Hoyt Wilhelm (2-4). A three-for-three hitting performance by catcher Russ Nixon for Cleveland proved not enough. Pinch-hitter and third baseman, Jerry Lumpe, for New York had two hits and drove in two of the runs in the eighth inning come-from-behind rally.

The Yankees increased their dominating lead still further to thirteen full games over Boston after winning game number 60, on July 23, over the Detroit Tigers by a score of 16 to 4. In the process, they pounded out eighteen hits including home runs by Norm Siebern, his 9th, Mickey Mantle, 25th, and Yogi Berra, 15th. In a futile cause, Al Kaline had three hits and two runs batted in for Detroit. The winning pitcher for New York was starter Art Ditmar (6-1), who went eight and one-third innings. The loser for Detroit was starter Frank Lary (9-9). Frank Lary would go on to compile a lifetime won-lost record of 128-116 and a 3.49 earned run average. In 1958 Lary would end the season with 16 wins, 15 losses, and a 2.90 earned run average. A good crowd of 39,644 was on hand at Briggs Stadium in Detroit only to be disappointed by the result. Over in the National League, the eight teams were bunched much more closely. The Braves (50-38) had a one game lead over San Francisco in second place with Los Angeles in last place ten games out.

Six days later, on Tuesday, July 29, the Los Angeles Dodgers were in Milwaukee at County Stadium and beat the Braves 4 to 2. July 29, 1958, was historical because it marked the founding of the National Aeronautics and Space Administration (NASA) which would play an important role in future years in the civilian control and coordination of space exploration.

The Dodgers scored two runs in the sixth, two in the seventh, and then limited the Braves to only two runs in the last of ninth inning for the win. The winner for Los Angeles was Don Drysdale (5-10), who pitched eight and one-third innings, allowed two runs on seven hits, and struck out eight. Johnny Klippstein came on to record the last two outs in the ninth for his 4th save of the year. In the aborted ninth inning rally, Braves' left fielder Wes Covington hit his 18th home run of the season with the bases empty. The Dodgers' veteran Pee Wee Reese doubled in the sixth to drive in their first two runs. Reese was in the final year of a big league career for the Dodgers that stretched all the way back to 1940. Starting pitcher Jocy Jay (6-4) took the loss for Milwaukee. In five and one-third innings, Jay allowed two runs on two hits and three bases on balls. The victory for Los Angeles improved the Dodgers record to 44-52. With the loss at home, Milwaukee was now 52-42.

On Friday, August 1, the Yankees began a weekend series of games against the White Sox at Comiskey Park in Chicago. In a five-hit shutout, New York defeated Chicago 7-0 behind starter Bob Turley (16-4). The line score read 7 runs, 9 hits, 1 error for the Yankees and no runs, 5 hits and 2 errors for Chicago. The losing pitcher for Chicago was left-hander Billy Pierce (10-8). Pierce lasted seven innings and allowed three runs on five hits. The Yankees led the game 3-0 after seven innings and then added three runs in the eighth and one in the ninth for the seven run total. First baseman Bill Skowron hit his 9th home run of the season in the top of the second inning for the Yankees first tally. That proved to be all they needed. Skowron had three hits in the game and drove in four of the Yankees' runs. There were 38,832 at Comiskey to see the defending American League champions in action. With the win, New York improved to 66-34 for the season and the White Sox fell to a disappointing 49-51.

In a well-pitched ball game on both sides at Baltimore, the Yankees took win number 70 over the Orioles by a score of 3 to 1 on August 6. Catcher Elston Howard drove in the lead and winning two runs for New York in the sixth inning. In 1958 Howard would hit .314 with 11 home runs for the Yankees in 103 games. Pitcher Art Ditmar earned his 8th win against two losses for New York with the complete game five-hitter. The loser for the Orioles was 31-year-old veteran Jack Harshman (8-10). The win allowed the Yankees to maintain a huge sixteen game lead over the second place Boston Red Sox.

The Yankees picked up win number 80 against only 50 losses in a 7 to 6 game against eighth place Washington (54-74) on Sunday, August 31, at Griffith Stadium. Bob Turley went six and two-third innings for his 20th win of the season against 6 losses. The loss for the Senators went to Russ Kemmerer (6-14). The lead runs for the Yankees came in the fifth on a two-run home run by Hank Bauer, his 11th of the year. The Senators rallied in the bottom of the ninth with four runs but fell just short in the 7 to 6 one run defeat. Both teams had nine hits in the game, including for the Yankees the first triple of the year by Mickey Mantle.

With such a comfortable cushion, the Yankees seemed to coast in on cruise control during the month of September. By contrast, in the National League, the Milwaukee Braves had a somewhat smaller league lead. The Braves accomplished win number 90 against 60 defeats on Sunday, September 21, in Cincinnati with a hard fought 6 to 5 win. The veteran Warren Spahn (21-11) was the winner. Spahn pitched into the seventh before giving up five runs (only three earned) to the Redlegs. Reliever Don McMahon came on to finish the final two and two-third innings to notch his 8th save of the season. Milwaukee had scored four runs in the fifth and two runs in the seventh before the Cincinnati rally fell just short of tying the game. The starter, Brooks Lawrence (8-13), took the loss for Cincinnati. For the Braves, right fielder Henry Aaron hit home run number 30 in the seventh with one on base. Third baseman Frank Robinson started the late Redlegs' rally in the seventh with his 31st home run off Spahn with none on and none out. After this game, the Braves lead over the Pittsburgh Pirates in second place was five and one-half games with only four games to play.

On the last day of the regular season, Sunday, September 28, the Yankees hosted Baltimore in a doubleheader. After New York won the opener 7-0, the Yankees completed the sweep with a 6 to 3 second game win over the Orioles. The Yankees got off to a four run lead in the first inning and never trailed in the game. Mickey Mantle was three-for-four for the Yankees and 27-year-old third baseman Andy Carey was a perfect four-for-four with two runs batted in. There were no home runs in the game for the Yankees. In the ninth inning for Baltimore left fielder Leo Burke hit a solo home run, his 1st of the year. The winner for New York was right-hander Tom Sturdivant (3-6) and the loser for the Orioles was 19-year-old, second year player, Milt Pappas (10-10). In the game, Pappas went five innings as the starter. Only two of the six runs he surrendered were earned. Even though there were nineteen hits in the game, it was played in a snappy 2 hours even before a crowd of 17,763.

The seasons of 1957 and 1958 were dominated by the New York Yankees and the Milwaukee Braves. The Yankees won a total of 190 games which was eighteen more than the Chicago White Sox with 172. The White Sox featured speed and defense and managed to finish second in both years. The lowly Washington Senators were last in the American League with a mere 116 total combined wins in the two years. In the National League, Milwaukee had a two year total of 187 wins and the St. Louis Cardinals were next with 159. Milwaukee was the only National League team to play better than .500 ball in both 1957 and 1958.

In 1958, for the second year in a row, Ted Williams of Boston won the American League batting title with an average of .328. He was six points ahead of his teammate Pete Runnels with .322. Mickey Mantle of the Yankees led in home runs with 42, followed very closely by Rocky Colavito of the Cleveland Indians with 41. The runs batted in champion was Jackie Jensen of the Red Sox with 122. He was followed by Colavito with 113. Team batting statistics were mostly dominated by the champion Yankees. They led in batting average with .268, home runs with 164, and runs scored with 759.

In pitching, Bob Turley of New York was the league's only 20 game winner with 21. Billy Pierce of the White Sox was second with 17. Lefty Whitey Ford of the Yankees led in ERA with 2.01 followed also by Pierce with 2.68. In strikeouts, Early Wynn of the White Sox led with 179 followed closely by Detroit's Jim Bunning with 177. In team pitching, New York came in with the best ERA of 3.22 and fewest hits allowed of 1,201. Baltimore Orioles' pitchers led in fewest home runs allowed, 106, and fewest walks allowed, 403. The pitchers of the Detroit Tigers recorded the most strikeouts with 797.

National League batting honors in 1958 went to 31-year-old Richie Ashburn of the Philadelphia Phillies with a .350 batting average. Ashburn would retire from baseball after the 1962 season with a career batting average of .308 and 2,574 hits. He was followed by Willie Mays of the Giants with .347 and Stan Musial of the Cardinals with .337. Ernie Banks of the Chicago Cubs ran away with the home run title with 47 and was followed by Frank Thomas of the Pirates with 35. The leader in runs batted in was also Ernie Banks of the Cubs with 129 followed by Frank Thomas with 109. No one else in the National League broke the 100 mark. Team batting honors were shared by Milwaukee in batting average with .266, the Chicago Cubs in home runs with 182, and the San Francisco Giants with 727 runs scored.

In pitching, Bob Friend of the Pirates and Warren Spahn of the Braves each won 22 games. Lew Burdette of Milwaukee won 20. The season earned run average chart was topped by Stu Miller of San Francisco with 2.47, followed by Sam Jones of St. Louis with 2.88, and Burdette with 2.91. The strikeouts title was won in a landslide by Sam Jones with 225. Warren Spahn of Milwaukee was a distant second with 150. Milwaukee had the lowest team ERA with 3.22, and fewest hits allowed with 1,261. The L.A. Dodgers' pitching staff had the most strikeouts with 855.

The American League Most Valuable Player was Jackie Jensen of the Boston Red Sox, and Rookie of the Year was Albie Pearson of the Washington Senators. Jensen was 31 years old and was in his fifth year with Boston. In addition to leading the league in RBI, he also hit 35 home runs and batted .286. Pearson, 24 years old, hit .275 in 146 games for Washington. In the National League, the Cubs' Ernie Banks was voted Most Valuable Player and Orlando Cepeda of San Francisco was Rookie of the Year. At age 21, for the Giants, Cepeda batted .312 and hit 25 home runs in 148 games. The Cy Young Award for excellence on the pitching mound was won by right-hander Bob Turley of the Yankees.

For the second year in a row, the World Series contestants would be the New York Yankees and the Milwaukee Braves, with the Series to begin in the Braves National League home park. The teams featured lineups which were very quite like the ones from the previous year, with the exception that all of the players on both clubs were one year older.

CATCHER - New York, Yogi Berra, 33, and Milwaukee, Del Crandall, 28. Berra in 122 games had 22 home runs and batted .266. Crandall in 131 games hit 18 home runs with an average of .272. Both were experienced veterans having consistent years. No advantage for either team.

FIRST BASE - New York, Bill Skowron, 28, and Milwaukee, Joe Adcock, 31. Skowron hit .273 with 14 home runs. These numbers were somewhat down from his previous four years with the Yankees. Adcock appeared in 105 games with 19 home runs and hit .275. Again, both were proven ball players and are rated even.

SECOND BASE - New York, Gil McDougald, 30, and Milwaukee, Red Schoendienst, 35. McDougald hit .250 with 14 home runs in 138 games for the Yankees. He was a versatile defensive player who could also be an excellent shortstop. Schoendienst, showing a little age, appeared in 106 games for the Braves and batted .262. He was a reliable contact hitter in the leadoff position in the Braves' batting order. A very slight edge goes to New York.

SHORTSTOP - New York, Tony Kubek, 23, and Milwaukee, Johnny Logan, 31. Kubek hit .265 for the Yankees in his second year, which was down from his rookie season. In the 1957 Series, Kubek had played in left field, but shortstop was his preferred position. Logan's batting average had also fallen off compared to 1957 from .273 down to .226. Logan exhibited occasional power with 10 home runs for the season. There is not much advantage to either team.

THIRD BASE - New York, Jerry Lumpe, 25, and Milwaukee, Eddie Mathews, 27. Lumpe had an average of .254 in 81 games for the Yankees. Although Mathews' batting average dropped off to .251, he still hit 31 home runs and drove in 77 runs for the Braves in 1958. Mathews, who played in 149 games, continued to be a durable every-day player. Advantage to Milwaukee.

LEFT FIELD - New York, Elston Howard, 29, and Milwaukee, Wes Covington, 26. Howard was in his fourth year with the Yankees. He batted .314 with 11 home runs. He was a most versatile player because he also could catch and play first base. In 1958 Covington raised his average to .330 and hit 24 home runs. Both players are in their prime and rated even.

CENTER FIELD - New York, Mickey Mantle, 27, and Milwaukee, Bill Bruton, 33. It was Mickey Mantle's eighth year as a New York Yankee and his reputation as a baseball legend was blossoming more than ever. Mantle, number 7 in Yankee pinstripes, batted .304 with 42 home runs in 1958. Bruton hit .280 in his sixth season with the Braves. The spectacle of Mantle's greatness would be rated higher than the consistency of Bill Bruton. Advantage to the Yankees.

RIGHT FIELD - New York, Hank Bauer, 36, and Milwaukee, Henry Aaron, 24. Bauer had another consistent season for New York, hitting .268 with 12 home runs. Aaron, in his fifth Major League season, batted .326 with 30 home runs for the Braves. Advantage goes to the Braves.

STARTING PITCHING - For New York: Whitey Ford, 30, won 14, lost, 7. Bob Turley, 28, won 21, lost 7. Don Larsen, 29, won 9, lost 6. For Milwaukee: Warren Spahn, 37, won 22, lost 11. Lew Burdette, 32, won 20, lost 10. Bob Rush, 33, won 10, lost 6. Rush, formerly with the Cubs, was in his first year with Milwaukee. The other five pitchers had all appeared in the 1957 Series. All were extremely capable Major League pitchers. Burdette was the Series standout pitcher from the prior October. Rated even.

MANAGERS - New York, Casey Stengel, 68, and Milwaukee, Fred Haney, 62. Stengel had previously managed the Yankees to six World Series titles in 1949, 1950, 1951, 1952, 1953, and 1956. In his managing, Stengel liked to use all of his players in a platoon kind of system, in which the lineups were often changed more than usual from one game to the next, and in which the pitching staff was not overextended by being used for too many innings. Haney had previously served as manager of the St. Louis Browns from 1939 through 1941, and for the Pittsburgh Pirates from 1953 through 1955.

The Yankees finished the season ten games in front of the pack in the American League with 92 wins and 62 losses. During the last two months of the season, they were 27-28, one game under .500. They went 15-7 against both Chicago and Cleveland, but only won 10 and lost 12 against the Detroit Tigers. Milwaukee also finished 92-62 and took the National League by a margin of eight games for the second year in a row. The Braves started the season strong, seemed to coast through June and July, and then had their best month in August by going 23-11 (34 games in 31 days). They went 17-5 against Cincinnati but won just 8 games and lost 14 when playing the Los Angeles Dodgers.

It took 3 hours and 9 minutes and ten innings for the Braves to finally edge the Yankees 4 to 3 to open the 1958 World Series at County Stadium on

Wednesday, October 1. Milwaukee ace left-hander Warren Spahn (1-0) was the winning pitcher. He lasted all ten innings for a complete game and gave up four walks and eight hits to the Yankees. The three New York runs all came on home runs, a solo shot by Bill Skowron in the fourth inning, and a two-run homer hit by right fielder Hank Bauer in the fifth. The Braves scored two in the fourth and then tied the game at three runs each in the last of the eighth on a sacrifice fly by Wes Covington. Yankees' starter Whitey Ford pitched seven innings and was charged with the first three Milwaukee runs. Ford allowed only three base hits but walked eight. In the last of the tenth, a long single by center fielder Bill Bruton off reliever Ryne Duren (0-1) drove in the winning run for the Braves.

The next day the Braves routed the Yankees 13 to 5 to take a two game to none lead in the Series. Milwaukee erupted for seven runs in the very first inning off Yankees' starting pitcher Bob Turley (0-1). Lew Burdette (1-0) was the winner for the Braves. On Saturday, October 4, the Series resumed at Yankee Stadium in New York. For the Yankees, a strong performance from pitcher Don Larsen (1-0) shut out the Braves 4-0 on only six hits. The Series then stood at two games to one in favor of the Braves.

In game four played at Yankee Stadium on Sunday, October 5, the table turned and the Braves, behind their ace Warren Spahn (2-0), shut out the Yankees by a score of 3-0. It was Spahn's second complete game of the Series. The Yankees managed only two hits and two walks. Spahn recorded seven strikeouts. One of the two Yankees' base hits was a triple by Mickey Mantle, but it was to no avail. The Braves scored single runs in the sixth, seventh, and eighth innings. For the lead run in the sixth, Red Schoendienst tripled, as left fielder Norm Siebern lost the fly ball in the sun, and then scored on an error by shortstop Tony Kubek. Henry Aaron also had two doubles for the Braves. Although he pitched well, the Yankees' starter Whitey Ford (0-1) was tagged with the loss. The win put the Braves up in the Series three games to one and they seemed to be nearly on the verge of taking the prize for a second consecutive year.

To make a long story short, the determined Yankees stormed back to take both games five and six to tie up the Series at three games each and forced a seventh game. Game five in New York on Monday was a 7-0 four-hit whitewash by Yankees' pitcher Bob Turley (1-1). The Series then moved back to Milwaukee for game six played on Wednesday, October 8. The Yankees edged the Braves 4 to 3 in ten innings. The winner for New York was Ryne Duren (1-1) in relief, with the loss going to Warren Spahn, pitching with only two days of rest.

New York battled to win the decisive game seven in Milwaukee 6 to 2. The line score was Yankees, 6 runs, 8 hits, no errors and Milwaukee, 2 runs, 5 hits and 2 errors. The starting pitchers were Don Larsen and Lew Burdette. The score after five innings was Yankees 2, Braves 1. In the last of the sixth, Braves' catcher Del Crandall hit a solo home run off Bob Turley, who had relieved Larsen. This tied up the score 2 to 2. Then in the top of the eighth inning, New York broke the game wide open by scoring four runs, with three of them by virtue of a home run by first baseman Bill Skowron off Lew Burdette. The decisive win went to Bob Turley (2-1), who gave up only two hits and one run in six and two-third innings on the mound.

For the second time, New York and Milwaukee had played a close and hard fought seven game World Series. It seemed somehow fitting that each team had managed to win one of them. The 1958 Yankees became the first team since the Pittsburgh Pirates in 1925 to come back from a three games to one deficit to win the Series. For New York, right fielder Hank Bauer hit .323 for the Series with four home runs and eight runs batted in. Bill Skowron, Gil McDougald, and Mickey Mantle also each homered twice for New York. Bob Turley pitched well for New York, winning twice in games five and seven. The Braves used pitchers Spahn and Burdette extensively. Together they pitched 51 out of 63 total innings in the Series; but their luck and effectiveness against the tenacious Yankees' hitters finally ran out.

1958 WORLD SERIES SUMMARY

Game 1	At Milwaukee	Braves 4, Yankees 3
Game 2	At Milwaukee	Braves 13, Yankees 5
Game 3	At New York	Yankees 4, Braves 0
Game 4	At New York	Braves 3, Yankees 0
Game 5	At New York	Yankees 7, Braves 0

| Game 6 | At Milwaukee | Yankees 4, Braves 3 |
| Game 7 | At Milwaukee | Yankees 6, Braves 2 |

NEW YORK WINS THE WORLD SERIES BY 4 GAMES TO 3.

INTERLUDE - *GAME OF THE DAY*

The 1958 season ushered in Major League Baseball on the West Coast of the United States in Los Angeles and San Francisco. This outreach to other growing parts of the country was important to the future of the game. Otherwise, if fans did not reside in the big cities of the East and Midwest, there were not many opportunities to attend big league ball games in person. One option for fans which made baseball come alive for them was the Mutual Broadcasting System's *Game of the Day*, which aired nationally on the radio throughout the nineteen-forties and nineteen-fifties. Then, with the gradual advent of baseball broadcasts on television, the Mutual *Game of the Day* broadcasts ended in 1960. What remained of baseball on the radio was each Major League team generally broadcasted all of its games, home and away, on a flagship station with affiliated stations carrying the games throughout the team's market area.

1959 SEASON

L.A. STOPS THE GO-GO SOX

I f the 1957 and 1958 seasons seemed predictable and repetitive because of the domination of the Braves and Yankees, then the 1959 season would prove different and exciting with an unexpected outcome. In the American League, the Cleveland Indians began the season by winning ten of their first eleven games. Their tenth win came in a 6 to 4 win over the White Sox at Cleveland on Friday, April 24. After six innings, Chicago led 4 to 1, but the Indians tied the score with three runs in the last half of the seventh. The winning pitcher for Cleveland was Humberto Robinson (1-0), who pitched the final two scoreless innings in relief. Humberto Robinson was the first native Panamanian to play in the Major Leagues. In the last of the eighth, the Indians picked up two runs which gave them the win. Both teams came up with only six hits in the game. Catcher Russ Nixon, for the Indians, was two-for-three including his first triple of the season off Chicago starter Dick Donovan.

The next day, April 25, the Kansas City Athletics hosted the Detroit Tigers at Municipal Stadium in Kansas City. The Athletics held off a late Detroit rally in the eighth and ninth innings for an 8 to 7 win. This day in history marked the formal opening of the St. Lawrence Seaway, a joint undertaking of the United States and Canada, which connected the Great Lakes and the Atlantic Ocean. The winner for Kansas City was right-hander Ned Garver (2-1), who lasted seven and one-third innings and gave up four runs on ten hits. Dick Tomanek picked up his first save of the year for the Athletics by retiring the final two Detroit hitters in the ninth inning. The go-ahead runs for Kansas City came in the second inning on a three-run home run by left fielder Bob Cerv, his 2nd of the season. Right fielder Roger Maris had three hits in three at bats and also scored three runs in the game for Kansas City.

The loss for the Tigers was charged to starter Paul Foytack (0-2). In two and one-third innings pitched, Foytack allowed six runs on six hits. Both teams had thirteen hits in the game, but the Detroit rally fell one run short of forcing the game into extra innings. The one run victory evened Kansas City's record at 6 wins and 6 losses. Detroit dropped to 1 win and 11 losses for the 1959 season thus far.

On May 17, the White Sox defeated the Senators at Washington in the second game of a doubleheader by a score of 10 to 7. The Senators had picked up a win in the opener by 4 to 2. The second game featured twenty-eight hits, thirteen by Chicago and fifteen by Washington. Bob Shaw was the winning pitcher for Chicago. Shaw (3-0) went seven and one-third innings, gave up fourteen hits and six earned runs, but still prevailed for the win. Shaw would go on to post an 18-6 record with a good ERA of 2.69 for the 1959 campaign. Offensively, the Sox were led by second baseman Nellie Fox who had four hits in five at bats. For the Senators, 23-year-old rookie third baseman Harmon Killebrew homered in both the seventh and eighth innings, his 13th and 14th home runs of the season. Following this win, Chicago (20-12) actually trailed Cleveland in the standings by one-half game. In the National League, defending champion Milwaukee had the early season lead with a 19-10 record, and was trailed by the Giants and the Dodgers, two and one-half and three and one-half games behind, respectively.

One of the most unusual games ever in Major League Baseball history took place at Milwaukee's County Stadium on Tuesday, May 26, as 34-year-old left-hander Harvey Haddix of Pittsburgh pitched a perfect game for twelve complete innings, only to lose in the last of the 13th inning on a game-winning double by first baseman Joe Adcock with two out. With the loss, Haddix was 4-3 for the young season. For Milwaukee, right-hander Lew Burdette picked up the win by scattering twelve hits over thirteen complete innings. This memorable game was played in 2 hours and 54 minutes before a Braves' crowd of 19,194. In his career, Haddix pitched fourteen years in the big leagues for five different teams and compiled a record of 136 wins and 113 losses. Even with his lengthy and successful career, he is probably most remembered for this single thirteen inning loss on May 26, 1959.

At County Stadium in Milwaukee on June 3, the Braves outscored the San Francisco Giants 7 to 4 behind the pitching of Bob Buhl (4-3) and reliever

Don McMahon, with his 4th save of the season. Both teams showed off their power with three Braves' home runs and two by San Francisco. For the Giants, Orlando Cepeda hit number 10 in the sixth inning and Willie Kirkland his 5th in the eighth. For Milwaukee, Henry Aaron banged out his 15th of the season and Eddie Mathews hit two, his 18th and 19th of the season. The Braves picked up three in the sixth and three in the seventh to put the game away for their 30th win against 17 losses. The second place Giants dropped to 27-21. At this point, Chicago and Cleveland continued to set the pace in the American League and the surprising New York Yankees were 20 and 24.

Three weeks later, on June 24 at County Stadium, Milwaukee shut out the St. Louis Cardinals in a rain shortened game by a score of 4-0 before a crowd numbering 19,166. Major League Baseball rules require at least five innings to be completed to qualify a game as official. The time of the seven inning affair was 1 hour and 58 minutes. For Milwaukee, Joey Jay scattered eight hits and three walks for the win. It was his 3rd of the season versus five earlier losses. The Braves scored all four runs in the home half of the first inning, which featured Henry Aaron's 20th homer of the season with two men on base. The won-lost record for the Braves at this point was 40-28 which was two games ahead of the Giants and three ahead of the Los Angeles Dodgers. The race continued tight over in the American League with Cleveland leading and only six and one-half games separating all eight teams.

The year 1959 was the first of four years in which Major League Baseball scheduled and played two midsummer All-Star games. The first one took place at Forbes Field in Pittsburgh, on July 7, before 35,277 fans. It was a one run game won by the National League by a score of 5 to 4. The winning pitcher was Johnny Antonelli of San Francisco and the loser was Whitey Ford of the Yankees. Home runs were hit by Eddie Mathews of the Braves in the first inning and by Al Kaline of Detroit in the fourth. The winning run in the eighth inning was scored by Henry Aaron on a triple by Willie Mays off Ford.

In Pittsburgh eight days later, on July 15, the Pirates lost to the Dodgers at Forbes Field in a shutout 3-0. The strong right-hander Don Drysdale gave up only three hits, three walks and struck out seven for his 11th win against 6 losses. Drysdale also drove in two of the Dodgers' runs on a double and sacrifice fly, both off losing pitcher Bob Friend (4-11). After winning 22 games for the Pirates in 1958, Friend would go on to finish 1959 with only 8 wins. However, to this point the Pirates were having an improved season with a record of 48 and 42. The Dodgers with a record of 50-40 actually trailed San Francisco by one game in the standings. The Giants were at 49-37. Over in the American League, the Indians and the White Sox were in a virtual tie for the league lead, separated only by percentage points.

In the waning days of July, the White Sox got hot by winning nine of ten games. On August 1, they picked up win number 60 against 40 losses by defeating the still struggling Washington Senators by 2 to 1. This put Chicago two full games in front of Cleveland in the standings. After the Senators scored one run in the fourth inning, Chicago rallied to win the ballgame with two big runs in the last of the ninth. Both runs were driven in by 25-year-old Chicago center fielder Jim Landis with a ninth inning double, his 16th of the season. The starter for Washington, Camilo Pascual, gave up only one base hit and two walks in seven innings pitched. In 1959, for the Senators, the Cuban-born Pascual would win 17, lose 10, and post an earned run average of 2.64. The winner for Chicago in relief was Gerry Staley (3-3), who pitched one scoreless inning to pick up the win. Staley, a 39-year-old veteran in his thirteenth Major League season, would go on to pitch in 67 games for the White Sox in 1959, all in relief, and post a 2.24 earned run average.

The year's second All-Star classic was played on August 3, at the Memorial Coliseum in Los Angeles, home of the Dodgers, before 55,105. The American League evened up the series for the year with a 5 to 3 win. The relatively small confines of the Coliseum yielded five home runs in the game hit for the American League by Frank Malzone, Yogi Berra, and Rocky Colavito and for the National League by Frank Robinson and Jim Gilliam. The winning pitcher for the American League was Jerry Walker of the Baltimore Orioles, and the loser was the Dodgers' Don Drysdale.

Two days after the second All-Star game on Wednesday, August 5, the Cubs hosted the Philadelphia Phillies at Wrigley Field in Chicago. The Phillies started off with three runs in the first inning and one run in the second. After six innings, Philadelphia still led 4 to 3, but the game was tied up at four runs each after the Cubs scored one more in the stretch half of the seventh inning. There were home runs hit by Chicago's Ernie Banks in the sixth inning, his

30th, and catcher Sammy Taylor in the seventh, his 8th of the season. In a game that took 2 hours and 57 minutes, the Phillies won it in the top of the ninth with two runs to give them a 6 to 4 win. The line score read 6 runs, 12 hits, 1 error for Philadelphia and 4 runs, 6 hits and no errors for Chicago. Five Phillies' hitters had more than one hit, led by first baseman Ed Bouchee, who went three-for-five with two runs batted in. The winner for the Phillies was Gene Conley (10-7), who allowed three earned runs and five hits in eight innings pitched. The losing pitcher for the Cubs in relief was 32-year-old Bill Henry (6-5). Henry had a Major League pitching career from 1952 through 1969 for several different teams during which he won 46 and lost 50 with a 3.26 ERA. With the win, the Phillies improved to 44 wins and 60 losses. The Cubs record fell to 50-55.

On the South Side of Chicago, the White Sox continued to play well with 10 wins in 15 games ending with a 6 to 4 win over the Orioles at Comiskey Park on Tuesday, August 18. This brought them to a record of 70-45 and a four and one-half game lead over the Cleveland Indians. Gerry Staley (6-3) was again the winner in relief. Staley went the final three innings for the Sox, allowing only one hit and one walk. Chicago outhit Baltimore nine to eight. Nellie Fox hit his 29th double and Jim Landis his 20th double for Chicago. A crowd of 34,547 excited fans with White Sox pennant fever watched the game which took a lengthy 2 hours and 59 minutes. Shortstop Luis Aparicio was three-for-four but did not steal a base in the game. Over in the National League, a tight race was still in progress with San Francisco at 67-51 setting the pace. This amounted to a two game lead over the Dodgers and a four game lead over Milwaukee. The two races were more contested than either the 1957 or 1958 races, which had been so dominated by the Yankees and the Braves. The Yankees, in fact, were mired in third place on August 18, with exactly 59 wins and 59 losses.

INTERLUDE - LUIS APARICIO

Luis Aparicio was an outstanding shortstop in the American League for eighteen years from 1956 through 1973. Aparicio was born on April 29, 1934, in Venezuela. He played with the Chicago White Sox from 1956 through 1962 and again from 1968 through 1970. In between, he was with the Baltimore Orioles from 1963 through 1967, and he finally finished his career with the Boston Red Sox from 1971 through 1973. Throughout his baseball career, Aparicio defined what a shortstop should be with his fine defensive skills and speed on the bases. He was selected as American League Rookie of the Year in 1956, won nine Gold Glove Awards for his fielding, and led the American League in stolen bases nine times.

In his eighteen-year career, Aparicio had a lifetime batting average of .262. He accumulated 2,677 hits, 92 of which were triples, and 506 stolen bases with a stolen base success rate of .788. In the twelve seasons from 1957 through 1968, Aparicio stole 431 bases, which ranked second over this period. By looking at his career statistics, it is evident that he was an extremely durable player. He appeared in 2,599 games, with an average of 144 per year. Aparicio played in two World Series, for the 1959 White Sox and for the 1966 Orioles. Overall he averaged .286, but had only one stolen base in World Series competition. In All-Star game play, Aparicio had two hits in 28 total at bats for a batting average of .071. All through his career he was an excellent shortstop, but he is probably most remembered for his first seven years with the White Sox when he was one-half, combined with Nellie Fox at second base, of arguably the best defensive double play combination of this era.

On Sunday, August 30, Chicago (80-49) concluded a sweep of a four game series at Cleveland which extended their lead over the Indians to five and one-half games. In the second game of the Sunday doubleheader before a crowd of 66,586, it was Chicago with 9 runs, 11 hits, 2 errors to Cleveland's 4 runs, 9 hits and 2 errors. The White Sox jumped off to an early lead which was never relinquished with three runs in the second inning and two in the third. Pitching the first five innings to pick up the win was 23-year-old Barry Latman (8-5). In relief, Turk Lown pitched the final four innings of the game for Chicago giving up no runs and five hits for his 12th save of the season. There were two home runs in the game by Cleveland off Latman. In the fourth, Rocky Colavito hit a three-run homer, his 39th of the year and in the fifth, Woodie Held hit a solo shot for his 26th of the season. For Chicago, left fielder Al Smith notched his 12th of the season in the fifth inning. Al Smith would go on to play twelve years in the big leagues and finish with 164 career home runs. For ten straight years (1954 through 1963), he would hit at least ten home runs each year.

On September 15, the White Sox defeated the New York Yankees 4 to 3 at Yankee Stadium for win number 90 against 56 losses. At this point, the Yankees were mathematically eliminated. They were sixteen and one-half games behind Chicago with only eight games remaining in the season. Billy Pierce (14-14) went seven full innings for the win. The loser in relief was Whitey Ford (14-10). New York scored two in the first inning for a lead, but the Sox rallied for two in the eighth and one in the ninth for the victory. In defeat, the Yankees had two home runs by Mickey Mantle, numbers 30 and 31 for the season, which drove in all three Yankees' runs in the game. With the Yankees already out of the race officially, only 9,108 fans showed up to see the affair.

The National League regular season ended with the Los Angeles Dodgers and the Milwaukee Braves tied with identical records of 86 wins and 68 losses. The Giants had led in the standings on September 15. However, they lost eight of their last ten games to finish 83 and 71. National League rules called for a best-of-three game playoff between Los Angeles and Milwaukee to be held to decide the pennant.

The first playoff game took place at Milwaukee County Stadium on Monday, September 28. In a close game, the Dodgers defeated the Braves by a score of 3 to 2. The winning run came on a solo home run in the sixth inning by Dodgers' catcher Johnny Roseboro, his 10th of the season, to give the Dodgers the 3 to 2 advantage. The winning pitcher was 24-year-old right-hander Larry Sherry (7-2). Sherry hurled the last seven and two-third innings, giving up four hits and striking out four Braves' hitters. The loser for Milwaukee was right-hander Carl Willey (5-9), who pitched six complete innings and surrendered all three Los Angeles runs.

The playoff series shifted to Los Angeles the next day Tuesday, September 29, for the second game which also produced a one run Los Angeles win and gave them the National League pennant. The game proved to be a memorable twelve inning contest, which lasted a full 4 hours and 6 minutes before attendance of 36,528. The Braves' Lew Burdette, the 1957 World Series pitching hero, took a 5 to 2 lead into the last of the ninth; but the

Dodgers battled back and scored three runs to tie the game and send it into extra innings. The Dodgers won the game in the 12th inning with one run crossing the plate for a 6 to 5 comeback win. L.A. used six pitchers in the game with the winner being right-hander Stan Williams (5-5), who pitched the last three innings in no-hit scoreless fashion. The loser for the Braves was veteran pitcher Bob Rush. His season ended with a record of 5 wins and 6 losses. There were two home runs in the game. For Milwaukee, Eddie Mathews hit his 46th in the fifth inning and The Dodgers' Charlie Neal, hit his 19th of the season in the fourth.

Two players from the Detroit Tigers were tops in American League batting in 1959. Harvey Kuenn won the batting title with an average of .353, with his teammate Al Kaline next at .327. Pete Runnels of the Red Sox was third at .314. Rocky Colavito of the Indians and Harmon Killebrew of the Washington Senators tied in home runs with an American League leading total of 42 each. Two more members of the last place Senators hit at least 30. They were Jim Lemon with 33 and Bob Allison with 30. Jackie Jensen of Boston led in runs batted in with 112. He was followed closely by Colavito with 111, Killebrew with 105, and Lemon with 100. In team batting average, the Kansas City Athletics led the league with a team average of .263. The Cleveland Indians were tops in home runs with 167 and runs scored with 745. Overall team speed enabled the Go-Go White Sox to lead with 113 stolen bases and 46 triples.

Early Wynn of the White Sox led the American League in games won with 22. He was the league's only 20 game winner. In second place was Cal McLish of Cleveland with 19 wins. In earned run average, Hoyt Wilhelm of the Orioles was the best with 2.19. Camilo Pascual of Washington had 2.64 and Jim Perry of Cleveland had 2.65. The familiar leader in strikeouts was Jim Bunning of Detroit with 201 followed by Pascual with 185 and Early Wynn with 179. The pitching staff of the Chicago White Sox led in team ERA with 3.29. Cleveland Indians' pitchers allowed the fewest hits with 1,230. New York Yankees' hurlers led in strikeouts with 836.

Twelve National League players hit better than .300 in 1959. They were led by Henry Aaron of Milwaukee, with .355, followed closely by Joe Cunningham of the St. Louis Cardinals with .345. The league leader in home runs was also a member of the Braves, third baseman Eddie Mathews with 46. This was just one more than runner-up Ernie Banks of the Chicago Cubs with 45. Aaron finished third with 39. Banks of the Cubs led in runs batted in with 143. Frank Robinson of Cincinnati finished second with 125, and Aaron was also third in this category at 123. In team batting, the Cincinnati Reds led in several statistical categories including team batting average with .274, and total runs scored with 764. Milwaukee hitters were at the top in home runs with 177.

Three National League pitchers ended the season with 21 wins. They were Warren Spahn and Lew Burdette of the Braves, and Sam Jones of the San Francisco Giants. For the lowest earned run average, Jones with 2.83 narrowly was better than his Giants' teammate Stu Miller with 2.84. Bob Buhl of Milwaukee was next with 2.86. Don Drysdale of the Dodgers had the most strikeouts with 242. He was followed by Sam Jones with 209. Left-hander Sandy Koufax of the Dodgers finished third with 173. In team pitching, the San Francisco Giants ended with the lowest ERA of 3.47. The Giants also had the fewest base hits allowed of 1,279. Los Angeles Dodgers' pitchers led with 1,077 strikeouts.

Nellie Fox, second baseman of the pennant winning Chicago White Sox, was named the Most Valuable Player for the American League. Also from Chicago, Ernie Banks from the Cubs won the National League MVP award for the second consecutive year. The Cy Young Award for best pitcher in baseball went to 39-year-old and 22 game winner Early Wynn of the White Sox. Rookie of the Year honors in the American League was awarded to 25-year-old Bob Allison of the Washington Senators. Allison batted .261 with 30 home runs and led the American League in triples with nine. Over in the National League, the 1959 Rookie of the Year was the San Francisco Giants' Willie McCovey, who at 21 years of age, averaged .354 with 13 home runs. This marked two years in a row that this Award had gone to a member of the Giants (Orlando Cepeda for 1958).

After two years of being the runner-up to the Yankees, the Chicago White Sox had won their first American League pennant since 1919. With limited power, their team was built upon good pitching, speed, and superior defensive play on the field. The Dodgers would be playing in the Fall Classic representing the National League for the first time from the city of Los Angeles. The Series would open with the first two games in Chicago. Games three, four, and five would be played in the spacious Los Angeles Coliseum, with its seating capacity of over 92,000 fans. Figure 1 indicates the results by team for both American and National Leagues for 1957, 1958, and 1959. A two year total is presented for 1957 and 1958 to illustrate the domination of the Braves and Yankees during those two years. The 1959 season represented the unexpected decline of the Yankees. The White Sox, to their credit, were ready to claim the pennant when the opportunity presented itself. The Senior Circuit race in 1959 was captured by the Dodgers in two difficult one run playoff contests over Milwaukee. The Braves nearly captured the pennant for the third year in a row. The following is a list of key players for both the L.A. Dodgers and the Chicago White Sox by position for the 1959 World Series.

CATCHER - Los Angeles, Johnny Roseboro, 26, and Chicago, Sherm Lollar, 35. Roseboro was in his third year with the Dodgers. He batted .232 with 10 home runs for the year. Lollar had been in the Major Leagues since 1946 and had joined the White Sox in 1952. In 1959 he batted .265 and hit 22 home runs in 140 games. The edge goes to Chicago.

FIRST BASE - Los Angeles, Gil Hodges, 35, and Chicago, Ted Kluszewski, 35. Hodges had been with the Dodgers since 1947. His most productive years were in the early fifties. In 1959 he still managed to hit 25 home runs with an average of .276. Kluszewski was a 1959 late season acquisition from the Pirates. He was past his prime but in 31 games for Chicago, he had a batting average of .297. Both were players nearing the end of their careers. Rated as a slight advantage to Los Angeles.

SECOND BASE - Los Angeles, Charlie Neal, 28, and Chicago, Nellie Fox, 32. Neal was in his fourth year with the Dodgers, during which he hit .287 with 19 home runs in 151 games. Fox had been a reliable regular every-day player for the White Sox since 1950. He ended the season batting .306 for the year. He was a good contact hitter and struck out only 13 times in 624 at bats. Both were experienced players; but the edge goes to Chicago.

SHORTSTOP - Los Angeles, Maury Wills, 27, and Chicago, Luis Aparicio, 25. Wills had just completed his rookie year with the Dodgers in which he batted .260 in 83 games. Although two years younger, Aparicio was in his fourth year as the regular shortstop for Chicago. In 1959 he was the American League leader in stolen bases with 56 and had a batting average of .257 in 152 games. Rated as an advantage to the White Sox.

THIRD BASE - Los Angeles, Jim Gilliam, 31, and Chicago, Billy Goodman, 33. Gilliam had been a full time regular with the Dodgers since 1953. He had a .282 average in 145 games in the 1959 season. Goodman was a veteran major leaguer going back to 1947, mostly with the Red Sox. He had a batting average of .250 in 104 games in his second year with Chicago. Perhaps, a small edge to Los Angeles.

LEFT FIELD - Los Angeles, Wally Moon, 29, and Chicago, Al Smith, 31. Moon was in his first year with the Dodgers after five years with St. Louis. Moon hit .302 in 145 games for the season with 19 home runs. Smith was in his second year with the White Sox after five years in Cleveland. Smith batted .237 with 17 home runs in 129 games for Chicago. The edge goes to Los Angeles.

CENTER FIELD - Los Angeles, Duke Snider, 33, and Chicago, Jim Landis, 25. Snider was a veteran of World Series play. He had been with the Dodgers all the way back to 1947. Although his most active playing years were behind him, Snider still had an average of .308 and 23 home runs in 126 games. In his third year with Chicago, Landis batted .272 with 5 home runs in 149 games. Throughout his career, Snider was one of those players who seemed to rise to the occasion in big games. Advantage to Los Angeles.

RIGHT FIELD - Los Angeles, Norm Larker, 29, and Chicago, Jim Rivera, 38. Larker, a utility player in his second year with the Dodgers, hit .289 with 8 home runs. Rivera had been a member of the White Sox since his rookie year in 1952. His finest years had been in the mid fifties. In 1959 Rivera had a batting average of .220 in 80 games. No significant advantage goes to either team.

STARTING PITCHING - For Los Angeles: Roger Craig, 29, won 11, lost 5. Johnny Podres, 27, won 14, lost 9. Don Drysdale, 23, won 17, lost 13. For Chicago: Early Wynn, 39, won 22, lost 10. Bob Shaw, 26, won, 18, lost 6. Dick Donovan, 32, won 9, lost 10. Both teams had very capable pitching staffs even beyond these three. It seemed likely that the games would be close and well-pitched with the outcomes decided by key plays in the late innings. No apparent edge to either team.

MANAGERS - Los Angeles, Walter Alston, 48, and Chicago, Al Lopez, 51. Alston became manager of the Dodgers at the start of the 1954 season when the team was still located in Brooklyn. The 1959 World Series was his third. Lopez started as Chicago White Sox manager at the beginning of the 1957 season. Prior to this, he served as manager of the Cleveland Indians from 1951 through 1956. He had managed the Indians during the World Series of 1954.

Los Angeles, with a record of 88-68, won the National League in a two game playoff over Milwaukee. The Dodgers best months were April (11-6) and September (16-9). They finished the season 14-10 against Milwaukee and played .500 or better ball against the other teams except for a 9-13 showing versus Cincinnati. The Chicago White Sox captured the American League with a five game margin by winning 94 games versus 60 losses. During the long season, the White Sox did not have a losing month and played very effectively in July and August when they were a combined 41-16. They came through with a winning record against the other teams, except for Baltimore, against whom they evenly split 22 games. In games decided by one run, the White Sox were 35-15 for the 1959 season.

The Series opened on Thursday, October 1, at Comiskey Park in Chicago. The normally light hitting White Sox shut out the Dodgers 11-0. The White Sox started with two in the first, seven runs in the third, and two more in the fourth. Chicago first baseman Ted Kluszewski banged two home runs, one each in the third and fourth innings, and drove in five runs. Center fielder Jim Landis had three of the eleven hits for Chicago. He scored three runs in the game. The Dodgers used five pitchers in the game with the loss going to starter Roger Craig (0-1). The win went to Chicago starter Early Wynn (1-0), who pitched seven innings, struck out six, and yielded only six hits and one base on balls. Reliever Gerry Staley hurled the last two innings, giving up two more harmless hits to finish the shutout. The attendance at Comiskey was 48,013.

Games two and three of the Series were close, well-pitched, and were both won by the Dodgers so that L.A. led the Series two games to one. The second game on Friday wound up Dodgers 4 to the White Sox 3, with left-hander Johnny Podres (1-0) picking up the win. After a travel day, game three at the L.A. Coliseum took place on Sunday, October 4, with the Dodgers prevailing

3 to 1 behind the pitching of Don Drysdale (1-0). After the first three games, the White Sox led in total runs 15 to 7; but Los Angeles led in wins two games to one.

In the fourth game played Monday, October 5, before 92,650 fans, the Dodgers narrowly edged Chicago 5 to 4 to take a commanding three games to one lead in the Series. The Dodgers scored four runs in the last of the third inning only to have the White Sox tie the score in the top of the seventh inning by picking up four runs of their own. Catcher Sherm Lollar for Chicago hit a three-run homer in the seventh to tie the game. Then in the eighth, first baseman Gil Hodges homered for Los Angeles for what proved to be the fifth and winning run. Chicago used four pitchers in the game. Starter Early Wynn was knocked out of the box in the third inning with the loss charged to Gerry Staley (0-1) for yielding the go ahead run in the eighth. The win went to Dodgers' reliever Larry Sherry (1-0), who pitched the last two innings, replacing starting pitcher Roger Craig. Sherry had also been credited with saves of the second and third game wins for the Dodgers.

On the next day, the White Sox were able to extend the Series back to Chicago by winning 1-0 in the fifth game. Three pitchers combined for the shutout, with the win going to Bob Shaw (1-1) and the loss to L.A. starting pitcher Sandy Koufax (0-1).

After four games decided by a total margin of only five runs, the sixth game, back in Comiskey Park on October 8, turned out to be a 9 to 3 one-sided win in favor of the Dodgers giving them the World Series title four games to two. Starting pitchers were Johnny Podres for Los Angeles and Early Wynn for Chicago. There were four home runs in the game. For the Dodgers, Duke Snider hit a two-run homer in the third, Wally Moon, a two-run shot in the fourth (during which L.A. came up with six runs), and Chuck Essegian, a pinch-hit solo home run in the ninth inning. In a losing cause, Ted Kluszewski hit his third home run of the Series in the fourth inning to produce Chicago's only three runs of the ballgame. The final totals were 9 runs, 13 hits, no errors for Los Angeles and 3 runs, 6 hits and 1 error for Chicago. Larry Sherry (2-0) worked the last five and two-third innings allowing only four hits and one walk in relief of Podres for the win. The loss was charged to Early Wynn (1-1), who had been the winner of game one of the Series.

For the six game Series, both teams finished with identical team batting averages of .261. Twenty-four-year-old pitcher Larry Sherry worked in all four games the Dodgers won, saving the first two and winning the last two. In twelve and two-third innings pitched, Sherry had an earned run average of 0.71 runs per game. Four of the six games were extremely close affairs. The Dodgers, to their credit, came away winning three of them.

1959 WORLD SERIES SUMMARY

Game 1	At Chicago	White Sox 11, Dodgers 0
Game 2	At Chicago	Dodgers 4, White Sox 3
Game 3	At Los Angeles	Dodgers 3, White Sox 1
Game 4	At Los Angeles	Dodgers 5, White Sox 4
Game 5	At Los Angeles	White Sox 1, Dodgers 0
Game 6	At Chicago	Dodgers 9, White Sox 3

LOS ANGELES WINS THE WORLD SERIES BY 4 GAMES TO 2.

Yankees Stumble at Forbes Field

The first three seasons in Major League Baseball for Roger Maris were spent with the Cleveland Indians and the Kansas City Athletics. After spending his rookie season at Cleveland, Maris was traded to Kansas City on June 15, 1958. He played all of 1959 in Kansas City. In the offseason, he was traded to the New York Yankees on December 11, 1959. In his first three seasons, Maris hit 14, 28, and then 16 home runs for a three season total of 58. After their unusually mediocre season in 1959, the Yankees expected that adding Maris to their lineup would help them regain a competitive advantage.

Interlude - Rocky Colavito

Rocky Colavito was born in New York City on August 10, 1933. His big league career spanned the time from the very tail end of the 1955 season through 1968. He was a six foot three inches tall, right-handed batting outfielder. He broke in with the Cleveland Indians and had four productive seasons with them from 1956 through 1959. His seasons with the Indians peaked with 41 home runs in 1958 and 42 in 1959. Then on April 17, 1960, he was traded in a two player transaction to the Detroit Tigers for Harvey Kuenn, who possessed much less power but had been a consistent .300 hitter for the Tigers. Kuenn spent only one year with Cleveland and was then dealt to the San Francisco Giants. Kuenn retired after the end of the 1966 season with 2,092 total hits and a lifetime average of .303. In the 1959 season, Colavito's batting average had tailed off to .257 from .303 in 1958. Colavito played with the Tigers for four years from 1960 through 1963. His highest home run total during his Detroit years was in 1961 with 45. His three final productive years were 1964 with the Kansas City Athletics, and then 1965 and 1966 back with Cleveland.

Colavito was one of the most steady power hitters of the late fifties and early sixties. His home run total reached double figures for 11 consecutive seasons from 1956 through 1966. In his career, he totaled 374 home runs with a lifetime batting average of .266. He reached the 100 or more RBI plateau in six separate seasons with his highest in 1961 at 140. In the twelve years from 1957 through 1968, Colavito hit 353 home runs. He never had the opportunity to play in a World Series. However, he did appear in nine All-Star games for the American League in which he hit three home runs in 1959, 1961, and 1962.

The Pittsburgh Pirates started the 1960 season with 10 wins and 3 losses. On April 28, in a game at Connie Mack Stadium in Philadelphia, the Pirates won number 10 in a 3-0 four-hit shutout behind Bob Friend (3-0). Friend struck out eleven and issued only one walk in the game. The Pirates scored two runs in the second and one in the fifth off Philadelphia starter John Buzhardt (0-2). Right fielder Roberto Clemente had two base hits and drove in one run to set the pace for the Pirates nine-hit offense. Clemente would go on to bat .314 during the 1960 season in 570 total at bats. In his career, Clemente would play eighteen years, have a lifetime batting average of .317, and accumulate exactly 3,000 base hits. In the 1960 early season, the San Francisco Giants also started strong with a 9 and 5 record, only a game and one-half behind the Pirates.

On Sunday, May 1, at Memorial Stadium, the Baltimore Orioles played host to the New York Yankees. This was a dark day in the history of the Cold War between the United States and the country at that time known as the Union of Soviet Socialist Republics (U.S.S.R.). American pilot Francis Gary Powers was shot down over the Soviet Union and was captured. Powers admitted that he was on a photo reconnaissance flight for the U.S. Central Intelligence Agency. Known as the U-2 incident, this episode proved to be a very difficult period in relations between the United States President Dwight D. Eisenhower and the Soviet Premier Nikita Khrushchev. Meanwhile, in Baltimore in the top of the first inning, the Yankees scored three runs off Baltimore starting pitcher Chuck Estrada. The Orioles countered with two runs in the bottom of the second inning. Catcher Elston Howard hit his third home run of the season in the third inning to make it 4 to 2 for the Yankees. New York added one more in the fourth, and then in the last of the fourth, Baltimore erupted for six runs to take the lead 8 to 5. The Orioles added one run in the stretch half of the seventh and finally prevailed by 9 to 5, in a game that lasted 3 hours and 13 minutes. Chuck Estrada (2-0) went all the way giving up eleven hits and settling down for the win. Right fielder Al Pilarcik had three hits in five at bats to lead the Orioles' twelve hit batting assault. Pilarcik had a six-year Major League career from 1956 through 1961 mostly with the Orioles with an overall batting average of .256. The Yankees fell to 6-5 in the young season. Baltimore improved to a record of 7 wins and 6 losses with the win.

On Tuesday, May 17, the Giants picked up their 20th win in a game at Crosley Field in Cincinnati over the Reds by a score of 9 to 3. Pitcher Jack Sanford (4-1) of the Giants went all the way for the victory giving up six hits and three runs. The Giants led 7-0 after three innings of play and hit safely fourteen times but had no home runs. Sparking the San Francisco offense was leadoff man Jim Davenport, who had four hits and scored two runs. 1960 was the third year for Davenport with the Giants. He would go on to play thirteen seasons all with San Francisco and finish with a career batting average of .258. For the Cincinnati Reds, the losing pitcher was the starter Jim O'Toole (3-3). The only home run in the game was hit by Reds' catcher Ed Bailey, his second of the season. At this point, the Giants at 20-9 had a one game lead over Pittsburgh with a record of 19-10. Meanwhile in the American League, the Chicago White Sox (15-10) were one-half game ahead of both Cleveland and Baltimore in early season standings.

In a game played on Wednesday, June 8, at Wrigley Field in Chicago, the Pirates defeated the Cubs 5 to 3. Pittsburgh took a 5-0 lead into the late innings behind the pitching of 30-year-old Vinegar Bend Mizell; but Mizell (2-3) gave up three runs in the seventh and needed help from the bullpen. Reliever Roy Face went the final two and two-third innings, giving up only two Chicago base hits for his 7th save of the season. Home runs were hit by Pittsburgh's Bob Skinner, his 8th of the season, and Dick Stuart, his 4th. With this win, the Pirates improved to 30 wins and 17 losses which was good for a one game lead over second place San Francisco. In the American League, no clear leader had yet emerged from the pack. Cleveland and Baltimore were in a virtual tie for first place with the White Sox trailing by three full games and the New York Yankees by three and one-half.

One day later on Thursday, June 9, New York won their 25th game against 21 losses in a 5 to 2 decision over the Chicago White Sox at Yankee Stadium. The line score read 5 runs, 12 hits, no errors for New York and 2 runs, 8 hits and 1 error for Chicago. After three innings, the White Sox led 2 to 1. Then in the last of the fourth, Yankees' center fielder Mickey Mantle launched his 11th home run of the season with one runner on base, and put New York in front 3 to 2. The Yankees added two more runs in the sixth and held on for the win. Bill Skowron had three hits in four at bats for the Yankees, including his 15th double of the season. The winning pitcher in relief for New York was Johnny James (2-0), who gave up only one hit and one walk to Chicago in two innings pitched. In his very brief three-year pitching career, James won 5 games and lost 3 in 119 total innings pitched. Left-hander Frank Baumann (3-3) was the loser for Chicago. He was the starter for the White Sox and yielded the game winning hit to Mantle in the fourth inning.

Winning ten of their next fifteen games, Pittsburgh won game number 40 against 22 losses at Forbes Field on Friday, June 24, over the Cubs by a score of 4 to 1. For the Pirates, Vinegar Bend Mizell (4-4) pitched the complete game, allowing seven hits and striking out five. Mizell also drove in two of the four Pittsburgh runs. Right fielder Roberto Clemente had three of the Pirates' ten total hits in the game, which featured no home runs by either team. Second baseman Jerry Kindall had two hits for the Cubs and drove in their only run of the game. The losing pitcher for Chicago was 20-year-old left-hander Dick Ellsworth (3-5), who surrendered all four Pirates' tallies in six complete innings pitched. Ellsworth's baseball career would extend through 1971. He would retire with 115 wins and 137 losses, pitching for a total of five different teams. The win extended Pittsburgh's lead over Milwaukee to three and one-half games and to six and one-half games over the San Francisco Giants.

Major League Baseball took the All-Star break with two games played on Monday, July 11, and Wednesday, July 13, 1960. The National League swept both contests. During this same week in Los Angeles, the 1960 Democratic National Convention took place and nominated Massachusetts Senator John F. Kennedy for President of the United States. The convention ballot was taken on Wednesday and Kennedy's acceptance speech was on Friday. As for the baseball, in the first game at Municipal Stadium in Kansas City on July 11, the National League took a 5-0 lead after the first three innings and then held off a late American League rally for a 5 to 3 win. The winner was Bob Friend of Pittsburgh and the loser starter Bill Monbouquette of the Boston Red Sox. Pitchers Roy Face and Vern Law were also used in the game. This meant that three of the five National League pitchers were from the Pirates. Home runs were hit by Ernie Banks of the Cubs in the first, Del Crandall of the Braves in the second, and Al Kaline of the Detroit Tigers in the eighth inning. In the second game at New York's Yankee Stadium, on July 13, six National League pitchers combined to shut out the American League team 6-0. The winner was Vern Law of Pittsburgh and the loser Whitey Ford of the Yankees. The American League did manage eight hits but the game was highlighted by four National League home runs by Eddie Mathews, Willie Mays, Stan Musial, and Ken Boyer, respectively. This marked the sixth All-Star game home run for St. Louis Cardinals' star Stan Musial.

INTERLUDE - TONY TAYLOR

Tony Taylor was born in Cuba on December 19, 1935. He began his Major League playing career, primarily at second base, with the Chicago Cubs in 1958 and then was traded to the Philadelphia Phillies on May 13, 1960. His career lasted through the 1976 season all with Philadelphia, except for about a two and one-half year stint with the Detroit Tigers from 1971-1973. Taylor was a right-handed career .261 hitter who accumulated 2,007 hits over this nineteen years. His relative longevity allowed him to also accumulate 234 stolen bases. Ten times in his career he stole ten or more bases in a season with a peak of 26 in 1960.

In the years from 1957 through 1968, Taylor had 182 stolen bases and managed an overall batting average of .257. His three years with the highest average were 1959, 1960, and 1963 when he batted .280, .284 and .281, respectively. Taylor was selected in 1960 for the National League All-Star team and had one hit in his only time at bat in that year's second All-Star game at Yankee Stadium. Taylor was a member of the 1964 Philadelphia Phillies. This team came very close to winning the 1964 National League pennant, but faltered with a devastating ten game losing streak late in September.

The Pirates picked up their 50th win against 32 losses with a come-from-behind win over Cincinnati on Saturday, July 16. The Reds, behind pitcher Jay Hook, had a 5 to 3 lead after seven innings but lost it as the Pirates rallied with two runs in the last of the eighth inning and one in the last of the ninth. The walk-off home run to win the game in the ninth was number 13 of the season for pinch-hitter Dick Stuart. Bill Mazeroski also hit his 9th home run of the season in the eighth for the Pirates off Hook. The winning pitcher for Pittsburgh was 25-year-old rookie Earl Francis (1-0), who gave up only one walk in pitching the last two complete innings in relief. The win enabled the Pirates to maintain a three game lead in the pennant race over Milwaukee.

Pittsburgh went 10-8 over their next eighteen games and won game number 60 by a score of 1-0 over San Francisco on Friday, August 5, at Forbes Field. Vinegar Bend Mizell (8-5) pitched a complete game five-hitter and struck out three. Mizell was born in the small town of Vinegar Bend, Alabama which was the source of his nickname. His real name was Wilmer Mizell. In his baseball career, Mizell won 90 games and lost 88 with a lifetime ERA of 3.85 runs per game. The losing pitcher for the Giants was Sam Jones (13-11), who struck out eight but gave up six hits and three bases on balls. The game was scoreless after seven innings with the game's only run scored in the last of the eighth by Pittsburgh center fielder Bill Virdon. Virdon would go on to play for the Pirates up through the 1965 season with a career batting average of .267 and at least 100 base hits each year from 1956 through 1965. The Pittsburgh lead over second place Milwaukee was now four full games. In the American League, the Yankees led with a record of 57-40, which was two and one-half games over defending league champion Chicago and three full games in front of the Baltimore Orioles.

Continuing on in August, the Pirates remained hot by winning ten of their next thirteen and by sweeping both games of a doubleheader for their 69th and 70th wins at home against the Phillies on August 16. The first game was 11 to 2 for the Pirates, who also won the second game by a score of 4 to 3. The winner of game two in relief for the Pirates was Roy Face (7-6). Face went two scoreless innings to finish the game in relief of starter Joe Gibbon, who surrendered five hits and three runs in seven innings. In 1960 Face would appear in 68 games, all of them in relief. He would win 10 games, lose 8, and post an earned run average of 2.90 runs per game. The loser for Philadelphia was starter Robin Roberts (8-11), who pitched all eight innings, gave up twelve hits, and allowed the winning run scored by the Pirates in the bottom half of the eighth inning. Eventual batting champion shortstop Dick Groat went three-for-four for the Pirates. The second game was played in a snappy 2 hours even, before a Forbes Field crowd of 34,673. At this point, the Pirates' league lead over both Milwaukee and St. Louis was seven and one-half games.

On Saturday, August 27, the Washington Senators defeated the Detroit Tigers 4 to 1 at Griffith Stadium in Washington, the nation's Capital. First baseman Harmon Killebrew for the Senators homered in the first inning, his 23rd of the season, for a 1-0 lead. The lead stood up for the remainder of the game as Washington added one run in the fourth and two runs in the seventh to offset a single run by Detroit in the fifth inning. The Senators outhit the Tigers eight to seven. Two pitchers combined for the Senators victory. Don Lee (6-4) went the first six and one-third innings, scattering five hits for the win, and Ray Moore gave up two hits over the final two and two-third innings to earn his 12th save of the year. Bob Bruce (2-5), who pitched six innings and allowed two runs on five hits was the losing pitcher for the Tigers. With the win, the Senators improved to 63-60 for the season. They would go on to finish 10-21 for a season total of 73 wins and 81 losses for fifth place in the American League race. This was an improvement over the eighth place finishes of the prior three years. With the loss, Detroit dropped to 57 wins and 64 losses.

As the National League race moved into the final month, on September 4, at Forbes Field, Pittsburgh notched win number 80 against 50 losses over the Philadelphia Phillies by 5 to 3. The Phillies took an early second inning lead on a two-run homer by 24-year-old rookie center fielder Tony Gonzalez, his 8th of the season. The Pirates immediately countered with four runs in the last half of the second to take the lead in the ballgame for good. Home runs for Pittsburgh were hit by third sacker Don Hoak, his 14th, and right fielder Roberto Clemente, his 7th of the season. Game totals were 5 runs, 11 hits, no errors for Pittsburgh and 3 runs, 6 hits, no errors for the Phillies. Starter Vinegar Bend Mizell (10-7) recorded the win with the loss charged to Philadelphia starter Jim Owens (3-12). For the first place Pirates, the save went to Clem Labine who worked the last three and two-third innings in relief, giving up only one hit with five strikeouts. The 34-year-old veteran Labine was signed by the Pirates on August 16. This was his 4th save of the 1960 season. Neither Milwaukee or St. Louis had been able to gain ground on the Pirates through September 4. Their lead was still six and one-half games over second place Milwaukee. In the American League, the streaking Baltimore Orioles had won fourteen of their last eighteen games to take a slim two game lead over the New York Yankees. The White Sox were three and one-half games back.

At Connie Mack Stadium in Philadelphia on September 20, the Pirates, in the second half of a Tuesday doubleheader, won game number 90 over the Phillies 3 to 2. Pittsburgh also prevailed in the first game by a score of 7 to 1. In the closely contested second game, the Pirates came from behind with one in the seventh inning and one in the eighth for the win. The winning pitcher was Clem Labine (3-1), who worked the final three innings in relief of starter Harvey Haddix. Although he pitched all nine innings and gave up just three earned runs, Jim Owens (4-13) was the loser for Philadelphia. In the eighth inning, Pittsburgh journeyman catcher Hal Smith hit his 11th home run of the season for the winning run. The loss extended the Phillies' last place record to 53 wins and 93 losses which was 37 and one-half games back of the Pirates' leading 90-55. The Pirates were six games ahead of St. Louis with nine games left to play. The Pirates were in the middle of a September stretch in which they swept three doubleheaders in six days with two wins over the Reds at Cincinnati on the 18th, two over the Phillies at Philadelphia on the 20th, and two over the Cubs at Forbes Field on September 22. Meanwhile in the American League, the Baltimore Orioles slumped to fall four full games behind the Yankees in the standings. The Yankees were 12-4 over their most recent sixteen ballgames.

INTERLUDE - MILT PAPPAS

The Baltimore Orioles finished the 1960 season in second place with a record of 89 wins and 65 losses. That 1960 Orioles team had three young pitchers with high potential for the future. Milt Pappas, who was considered a control pitcher, had the most success over the next several years. Pappas was born on May 11, 1939, in Detroit, Michigan and broke into the Major Leagues in 1957, with Baltimore at the age of 18. In a 17-year Major League career, Pappas was with the Baltimore Orioles from 1957-1965, the Cincinnati Reds from 1966-1968, the Atlanta Braves from 1968-1970, and finally the Chicago Cubs from 1970 through 1973. Beginning with the 1958 season, Pappas had a streak of eleven consecutive years through 1968 during which he won ten or more games. In his pitching career, Pappas accumulated 209 wins, 164 losses, 43 shutouts, and a 3.40 earned run average. Although he was never a twenty-game winner in a single-season, he won 17 games twice with the Cubs in 1971 and 1972 and 16 games three times with the Orioles in 1963 and 1964 and with the Reds in 1967.

In the years 1957 through 1968, Pappas won a total of 150 games. He never had the good fortune to be on a pennant winning team, and therefore, never played in a World Series. He appeared in both of the 1962 All-Star games and was the starting pitcher for the American League in the 1965 All-Star game at Minnesota. In these three appearances, his earned run average was an unspectacular 12.00 runs per game. Pappas was involved in one of the most meaningful trades of the era after the 1965 season. He was traded along with two other players by the Baltimore Orioles to the Cincinnati Reds in exchange for outfielder Frank Robinson.

The two other young Orioles' pitching prospects at that time were pitchers Chuck Estrada and Steve Barber. Estrada was 22 years old in 1960. In his baseball career, which lasted through the 1967 season, Estrada won 50 games and lost 44. He was with Baltimore through the 1964 season before brief stints with the Cubs and Mets. Steve Barber was also 22 years old in 1960. He remained with Baltimore up through the halfway point of the 1967 season. He was then with several other teams through the 1974 season and finished with a lifetime total of 121 wins and 106 losses.

As the season drew to a close, it was apparent that the New York Yankees would be returning to the World Series to face the National League's Pittsburgh Pirates. Attention turned briefly to Fenway Park in Boston on September 28, for the Red Sox 5 to 4 win over the second place Baltimore Orioles before 10,454 fans. The Red Sox scored two runs in the first inning off Baltimore starter Steve Barber, who lasted only one-third of an inning. There were two home runs in the game. For Baltimore, catcher Gus Triandos hit his 12th of the season in the second with a man on to tie the game at two runs each. However, the memorable blow came in the last of the eighth inning with one out. Baltimore had a 4 to 2 lead behind 21-year-old reliever Jack Fisher. In what would be his last Major League at bat, the Red Sox Ted Williams stepped up to the plate and hit out his 29th of the season and home run number 521 of his illustrious career, which extended all the way back to 1939. Williams also ended his career with a .344 lifetime batting average. In the ninth, Boston picked up two more runs for the 5 to 4 win. The winner in relief for Boston was Cuban-born Jose (Mike) Fornieles (10-5). Fisher (12-11) ended up with the loss for the Orioles.

The regular season ended on Sunday, October 2, with the World Series pairing already established. At Yankee Stadium, the Yankees scored two runs in the last of the ninth to defeat the Boston Red Sox 8 to 7. The Yankees used five pitchers in the game, with the win going to Duke Maas (5-1), who pitched the final two innings. The Red Sox used three hurlers with the loss charged to lefty Arnold Earley (0-1), who was making only his second big league appearance. Reserve first baseman Dale Long knocked out his 3rd home run of the season with one aboard in the ninth for the walk-off game winner. Roger Maris concluded his first regular season with New York with two hits in three at bats including his 7th triple of the season and three runs batted in. It had been a close pennant race, but starting on September 1, the Yankees went 22-7 to finish the season 97-57. Over the same period, the second place Baltimore Orioles won 13 and lost 12 to end the year 89-65 which was eight games back in the final standings.

The American League batting champion for 1960 was Pete Runnels of the Boston Red Sox with .320. Al Smith of the White Sox was second at .315, and Minnie Minoso of the White Sox was third at .311. Mickey Mantle of the New York Yankees led in home runs with an even 40. Four other players hit at least 30. Roger Maris of the Yankees had 39, Jim Lemon of the Washington Senators had 38, Rocky Colavito of Detroit had 35, and Harmon Killebrew of the Senators finished with 31. Maris was tops in runs batted in with 112, followed by Minoso with 105, Vic Wertz of Boston with 103, and Jim Lemon with 100. In team batting average, the Chicago White Sox led the way with .270. The Cleveland Indians, however led the league with 1,415 base hits. Mantle and Maris set the pace, and the pennant winning Yankees led in home runs with 193 and total runs scored with 746.

No pitcher in the American League was able to win 20 games. Chuck Estrada of the Baltimore Orioles and Jim Perry of the Cleveland Indians were co-leaders with 18 wins. Bud Daley of Kansas City won 16. In earned run average, Frank Baumann of the White Sox was best with 2.67, followed by Detroit's Jim Bunning with 2.79. Bunning also struck out 201 to lead in strikeouts. He was followed by Pedro Ramos of the Senators with 160 and Early Wynn of the White Sox with 158. In team earned run average, the Yankees' pitching staff led with 3.52 earned runs per game allowed. The Baltimore staff gave up the fewest hits at 1,222. The Detroit pitchers, with Jim Bunning setting the pace, led the American League with 824 strikeouts.

Dick Groat, the Pittsburgh Pirates' shortstop, was National League batting champion with .325. Willie Mays of the Giants was second at .319 followed by Roberto Clemente of the Pirates at .314. Ernie Banks of the Cubs barely earned the title in home runs with 41, which edged out two Milwaukee Braves teammates, Henry Aaron with 40 and Eddie Mathews with 39. In runs batted in, Henry Aaron topped the list with 126 followed by Mathews with 124, Banks with 117, and Mays with 103. Overall team batting was led by league champion Pittsburgh with .276 and the Pirates were also the league leader with 1,493 base hits and 734 runs scored. Milwaukee dominated in power with 170 home runs.

In pitching games won, three National Leaguers won 20 or more times. Ernie Broglio of St. Louis and Warren Spahn of Milwaukee led with 21 each. Vern Law of Pittsburgh won 20. Mike McCormick of the San Francisco Giants finished with the best earned run average with 2.70. He was followed closely by Ernie Broglio of the Cardinals with 2.74 and Don Drysdale of the Dodgers with 2.84. Drysdale had by far the highest strikeouts total with 246. He was followed by his Dodgers' teammate Sandy Koufax with 197. Drysdale and Koufax led the Los Angeles Dodgers, and they dominated in team pitching with a 3.40 staff ERA. L.A. pitchers also allowed the fewest base hits with 1,218 and recorded the most strikeouts with 1,122. Pittsburgh Pirates' hurlers allowed the fewest number of home runs with 105.

The American League Most Valuable Player for 1960 was Roger Maris, the Yankees' new right fielder. National League MVP was shortstop Dick Groat of the Pittsburgh Pirates. Both helped lead their teams to a 1960 resurgence. The Rookie of the Year in the American League also played shortstop, 22-year-old Ron Hansen of the Baltimore Orioles. Hansen had 22 home runs, batted .255, and helped bring Baltimore to a second place finish behind New York. In the Senior Circuit, Rookie of the Year honors went to Frank Howard of the L.A. Dodgers. Howard, who primarily played in right field, hit 23 home runs with a .268 batting average. Pitcher Vern Law of the National League champion Pirates captured baseball's Cy Young Award with 20 wins, 9 losses, and a 3.08 earned run average.

The World Series of 1960 featured the New York Yankees, recovered from their third place finish the previous year, against the National League champion Pittsburgh Pirates. The Series was scheduled to begin at Forbes Field, home of the Pirates. Forbes Field had been home to the Pittsburgh Pirates since 1909 and was located on the University of Pittsburgh campus in Pittsburgh's Oakland section adjacent to Schenley Park. Key players for both teams were as follows.

CATCHER - New York, Elston Howard, 31, and Pittsburgh, Smoky Burgess, 33. Howard was in his sixth year with the Yankees and also had played extensively as an outfielder. 1960 was a down year for him. In 107 games Howard batted .245 with 6 home runs. Burgess had started with the Cubs back in 1949. In 110 games for the Pirates he batted .294 with 7 home runs. Position is rated as a toss-up.

FIRST BASE - New York, Bill Skowron, 30, and Pittsburgh, Dick Stuart, 28. After an off year in 1959, Skowron was back to normal. He batted .309 for the year with 26 home runs. Stuart had completed his third year with Pittsburgh. He hit 23 home runs with an average of .260 in 122 games. Rated as a slight advantage to the Yankees. Skowron had good success in both the 1957 and 1958 Series.

SECOND BASE - New York, Bobby Richardson, 25, and Pittsburgh, Bill Mazeroski, 24. Richardson had been with the Yankees since 1955 and was becoming the regular at second base. He batted .252 in 1960 in 150 games and was primarily a contact singles hitter. Mazeroski joined the Pirates in 1956.

His batting average was .273 with 11 home runs in 151 games. Both good defensively. A slight edge to Pittsburgh on the basis of more occasional power.

SHORTSTOP - New York, Tony Kubek, 25, and Pittsburgh, Dick Groat, 30. Kubek had slightly improved power numbers from previous years with 14 home runs and an average of .273. In 1960 Groat was voted the National League's Most Valuable Player. He batted .325 in 138 games for the Pirates with limited power. He had been with the Pirates since 1955 and had a batting average of over .300 in two previous seasons. The advantage must go to Pittsburgh based on the outstanding MVP season by Groat.

THIRD BASE - New York, Gil McDougald, 32, and Pittsburgh, Don Hoak, 32. This was the final year in baseball for McDougald as a player. He was a career .276 hitter; and averaged .258 in 1960 in 119 games. This would be his eighth World Series in a Yankees' uniform. Hoak had been in the big leagues since 1954 and with the Pirates since 1959. In 155 games, he hit 16 home runs with an average of .282. Slight edge to Pittsburgh.

LEFT FIELD - New York, Yogi Berra, 35, and Pittsburgh, Gino Cimoli, 31. The always versatile Berra batted .276 and hit 15 home runs for the Yankees in 1960. He appeared in 120 games in the regular season. In his first year with the Pirates, Cimoli hit .267 in 101 games. 1960 was his fifth Major League campaign. Advantage goes to New York on the basis of Berra's experience in big games.

CENTER FIELD - New York, Mickey Mantle, 29, and Pittsburgh, Bill Virdon, 29. In the peak of his career, Mantle led the Yankees with 40 home runs and a batting average of .275 in 153 games. Virdon broke in with the Cardinals in 1955 and came over to the Pirates in 1956. Virdon acted as the Pittsburgh leadoff hitter and batted .264 with 8 home runs in 120 games for the year. With Mantle on the field, New York should be considered the favorite.

RIGHT FIELD - New York, Roger Maris, 26, and Pittsburgh, Roberto Clemente, 26. Maris was voted the American League Most Valuable Player Award for 1960, his fourth year in the Major Leagues and first with the Yankees. He hit 39 home runs and batted .283 in 136 games. The Yankees trade obtaining Maris from Kansas City was proved to be a resounding success. Clemente had been with the Pirates since 1955. He had his best season to date in 1960 with a .314 batting average and 16 homers in 144 games. Rated even with little advantage to either team.

STARTING PITCHING - For New York: Art Ditmar, 31, won 15, lost 9. Whitey Ford, 32, won 12, lost 9. Bob Turley, 30, won 9, lost 3. For Pittsburgh: Vern Law, 30, won 20, lost 9. Bob Friend, 30, won 18, lost 12. Vinegar Bend Mizell, 30, won 14, lost 8. Both teams had excellent pitching with New York having prior World Series experience. No edge to either team.

MANAGERS - New York, Casey Stengel, 70, and Pittsburgh, Danny Murtaugh, 43. At age 70, this was to be Stengel's last year as manager of the New York Yankees and his last World Series appearance. Murtaugh had assumed the position of manager of the Pirates starting with the last 51 games of the 1957 season. Earlier, the Pittsburgh skipper had a career as a player, mostly with the Phillies and Pirates, from 1941 through 1951, including time away for military service in World War II.

INTERLUDE - CASEY STENGEL

Casey Stengel was one of the most memorable and colorful individuals in the history of baseball. Stengel was born July 30, 1890, in Kansas City, Missouri. He was most known for his years as the manager of the New York Yankees for twelve years from 1949 through 1960, during which the Yankees won ten American League pennants and seven World Series championships. Prior to this, Stengel was also manager of the Brooklyn Dodgers, from 1934 through 1936, and the Boston Braves, from 1938 through 1943. Following his time as Yankees manager, Stengel topped off his managerial career as the legendary and lovable manager of the expansion New York Mets from 1962 through 1965. As a younger man, Stengel had a 14-year playing career from 1912 through 1925 with the Dodgers, Pirates, Phillies, Giants, and Braves. He accumulated 1,219 hits and a career batting average of .284. He appeared in the World Series of 1916 for Brooklyn and those of 1922 and 1923 for the New York Giants. For the three of them combined, Stengel posted a .393 batting average with two home runs. Stengel truly was an eyewitness to twentieth century baseball history from its modest beginnings to its coast-to-coast identity in the fifties and sixties. Stengel passed away in 1975, at the age of 85. His remains were laid to rest at Forest Lawn in Glendale, California.

New York, with 97 wins and 57 losses, won the American League pennant by eight games. After a slow start in April and May, they finished the season strong by going 20-7 in September, plus two more regular season wins in October. The Yankees managed a winning record against all seven other American League teams. In home games the Yankees won 55 and lost 22. In the National League, Pittsburgh won by seven games with a record of 95-59. The Pirates started the season by going 11-3 in April and had a winning record each month thereafter. After July 31, they won 38 and lost 20. They evenly split 22 games each with Los Angeles and St. Louis and had a winning record against the other five clubs in the league.

On Wednesday, October 5, with Casey Stengel in the dugout for New York, the Pittsburgh Pirates made their first World Series appearance since 1927. That World Series also happened to be against the New York Yankees in the Babe Ruth era. After Roger Maris homered for New York in the top of the first inning, the Pirates scored three runs in the bottom of the first to knock Yankees' starter Art Ditmar out of the game and take an early 3 to 1 lead. New York picked up one run in the top of the fourth, but Pittsburgh countered again, scoring on a two-run homer by second baseman Bill Mazeroski. Then the Pirates added one run in the sixth inning for a 6 to 2 lead in the game. In the top of the ninth inning, Yankees' pinch-hitter Elston Howard hit a two-run homer to make the final score Pirates 6 and the Yankees 4. Art Ditmar (0-1) took the loss for New York. The winner was Pirates' ace, Vern Law (1-0), who scattered 10 Yankees' hits for two runs over the first seven innings. Pittsburgh relief pitcher Roy Face worked the last two innings to get credit for a save. There were 36,676 fans at Forbes Field in Pittsburgh to see the Pirates take the first game and gain the Series advantage.

Game two at Pittsburgh and the third game back in New York were dominated by the Yankees. The Bronx Bombers took the second game 16 to 3 and shut out the Pirates 10-0 in the third game. Winning pitchers were Series veterans Bob Turley (1-0) in game two and Whitey Ford (1-0) in game three. Game four would be played Sunday, October 9, at Yankee Stadium with the Pirates' backs against the wall.

The game four pitching matchup was Vern Law for Pittsburgh against Ralph Terry for New York. The Yankees took a 1-0 lead on a solo home run by Bill Skowron in the bottom of the fourth. The Pirates scored three in the fifth with two runs driven in by center fielder Bill Virdon and the other by pitcher Vern Law. The Yankees rallied for a single run in the stretch half of the seventh but fell short losing the game to Pittsburgh 3 to 2. Virdon also came through with an outstanding defensive play on his catch at the wall in right center field off the bat of Yankees' hitter Bob Cerv to help save the day. Vern Law (2-0) was the winner with a save going to Roy Face, who pitched the final two and two-third innings for the Pirates. The loss went to New York starter Ralph Terry (0-1). After four games, the Series was tied at two wins each.

Pittsburgh also won a close victory in the fifth game at New York by a score of 5 to 2. Pitcher Harvey Haddix (1-0) was credited with the win and Roy Face earned his third save. After a travel day, the Series returned to Pittsburgh for the sixth game on Wednesday, October 12. Whitey Ford (2-0) shut out the Pirates 12-0 to tie the Series. The Yankees hit safely seventeen times in the game compared to just seven hits for the Pirates. The stage was set for a seventh game. Pittsburgh had won three close ball games and the Yankees had won three blowouts by a combined score of 38 to 3.

The seventh game, played Thursday, October 13, at Forbes Field, was one of the most tense and dramatic games ever in the annals of baseball history. The Pirates managed a close 10 to 9 victory, which all took place in an amazingly quick 2 hours and 36 minutes. Starting pitchers were Bob Turley for New York and Vern Law for Pittsburgh. The Pirates scored two in the first and two in the second for an early 4-0 lead which lasted through four complete innings. Rocky Nelson, substituting for Dick Stuart at first base, homered in the first inning with one man on for the initial lead. In the fifth, Bill Skowron hit a solo homer to make the score 4 to 1. In the sixth, the Yankees managed four more runs to take a 5 to 4 lead. Three of these runs came on Yogi Berra's three-run home run. The game went into the late innings and no one scored in the seventh, so the score was still 5 to 4 for the Yankees with only the eighth and ninth innings to play.

In the top of the eighth, the Yankees added two more runs to extend their lead to 7 to 4. In the last of the eighth, Gino Cimoli led off the inning with a single for the Pirates. The next batter, Bill Virdon, hit an ideal double-play ground ball to the left side of the infield, which almost unbelievably took a horrific bad hop and ended up hitting Yankees' shortstop Tony Kubek in the throat -- knocking him out of the game. Instead of two out nobody on, there was nobody out with two men on base. The Pirates went on to score two runs to make it 7 to 6, and then, with two out and two on base, catcher Hal Smith banged a three-run homer to send the Pirates into the lead 9 to 7. At this point, they just needed three outs in the top of the ninth to win the Series.

It was not going to be that easy. In the top of the ninth, the Yankees tied the game with runs driven in by Mickey Mantle's single and Yogi Berra's hot smash, fielded by Pittsburgh first baseman Rocky Nelson. The two runs were charged to Pirates' reliever Bob Friend, but Harvey Haddix came in to retire the side with the game knotted at 9 runs each. To start the bottom of the ninth inning, Yankees' pitcher Ralph Terry faced Pirates' second baseman Bill Mazeroski. The first pitch was a ball, and then, Mazeroski slammed Terry's second offering over the Forbes Field left center field wall for a 10 to 9 Pirates win. This gave pitcher Harvey Haddix (2-0) his second win of the Series.

For the entire Series, New York batted .338 and scored 55 runs compared to .256 and 27 runs for the Pirates. Yet, the Pittsburgh Pirates were World Series champions. Whitey Ford was spectacular. He won two games in the Series for New York with complete game shutouts. The normally light hitting New York second baseman Bobby Richardson had 11 base hits and set a new World Series record with 12 runs batted in. For Pittsburgh, both Vern Law and Harvey Haddix pitched well and won two games each. However, the improbable heroic figure for the Pirates and all of baseball was unquestionably Bill Mazeroski. He hit .320 for the Series and homered in both the first and seventh game Pittsburgh triumphs. Over fifty years later, a portion of the left center field wall still remains standing on the University of Pittsburgh campus as a monument to Mazeroski's home run. It has become a tradition in Pittsburgh that every October 13, fans gather at the location to listen to a recording of the NBC radio broadcast of the seventh game.

1960 World Series Summary

Game 1	At Pittsburgh	Pirates 6, Yankees 4
Game 2	At Pittsburgh	Yankees 16, Pirates 3
Game 3	At New York	Yankees 10, Pirates 0
Game 4	At New York	Pirates 3, Yankees 2
Game 5	At New York	Pirates 5, Yankees 2
Game 6	At Pittsburgh	Yankees 12, Pirates 0
Game 7	At Pittsburgh	Pirates 10, Yankees 9

Pittsburgh wins the World Series by 4 games to 3.

Interlude - Bill Mazeroski

Pittsburgh Pirates' second baseman Bill Mazeroski was born September 5, 1936, in Wheeling, West Virginia. Mazeroski broke in with the Pirates in 1956, at the age of 20. He spent his entire playing career in Pittsburgh, and retired at the conclusion of the 1972 season. In seventeen seasons he accumulated 2,016 hits, including 138 home runs, for a career batting average of .260. His highest batting average was .283 in 1957. He exceeded 160 hits in three separate years, 1964, 1966, and 1967. He made spectacular contributions to the Pirates defensively and was selected eight times for the National League Gold Glove Award at second base. In his career, he participated in 1,706 double plays.

In the 1960 World Series overall, Mazeroski had eight hits, including his two home runs, in 25 at bats for an average of .320. When Pittsburgh won the World Series again in 1971, Mazeroski was still a member of the Pirates, but he had a considerably less prominent role. In seven All-Star game appearances, he managed only two hits for an average of .125. Although he is primarily remembered for his seventh game walk-off home run, Mazeroski's defensive accomplishments over his career could also be considered an equally significant achievement. He was finally selected by the Veterans Committee for induction into the Baseball Hall of Fame in 2001.

MARIS AND MANTLE - 61 IN 61

The old Washington Senators relocated to Minneapolis-St. Paul to become the Minnesota Twins for the 1961 season. The Twins first game was a 6-0 opening day victory over the New York Yankees on Tuesday, April 11, at Yankee Stadium in New York. The winner for the Twins was Pedro Ramos (1-0). Ramos pitched a complete game giving up only three hits to the Yankees and striking out five. The Cuban-born Ramos would go on to finish 1961 for the Twins with 11 wins and 20 losses with a 3.95 earned run average. Opening day home runs for the Twins were hit by right fielder Bob Allison in the seventh and 26-year-old third baseman Reno Bertoia in the eighth. Left-hander Whitey Ford (0-1) of New York pitched six scoreless innings as the starter, but then gave up three earned runs in the seventh to take the loss. The only Yankees' base hits were harmless singles by Yogi Berra, Bill Skowron, and Ford. Mickey Mantle and Roger Maris for New York were a combined no hits in seven at bats for the game.

On April 30, in the National League, the San Francisco Giants, with Willie Mays leading the way, defeated the Milwaukee Braves at County Stadium in Milwaukee 14 to 4 for their 10th win of the season against 6 losses. After giving up three runs in the first inning, 31-year-old Billy Loes (2-1) settled down to pitch the complete game victory for the Giants. The Braves used seven pitchers in the game, with the loss going to starter Lew Burdette (1-1), who lasted the first three innings and gave up five runs, all of them earned. Giants' slugger Willie Mays banged out 4 home runs in the game bringing his season total to 6 and drove in eight runs. Jose Pagan also homered twice for San Francisco, his 1st and 2nd of the year. Orlando Cepeda also homered, his 3rd of the year. For Milwaukee, Henry Aaron hit his 2nd and 3rd homers of the season; but on this occasion the Giants' offense was just way too much for Braves pitching to handle. As April ended, the Giants had a one-half game lead over defending World Series champion Pittsburgh in the National League standings. The accomplishment by Willie Mays of hitting 4 home runs in a single nine inning game had been done only four other times in baseball history since 1900. These were by Lou Gehrig of the Yankees in 1932, Gil Hodges of the Dodgers in 1950, Joe Adcock of the Braves in 1954, and Rocky Colavito of the Cleveland Indians in 1959.

Friday, May 5, 1961, was an important day in U.S. history and in manned space flight. Astronaut Alan B. Shepard became the first American in space when he rode the Mercury spacecraft Freedom 7 on a fifteen minute sub-orbital flight. This was less than one month after the flight of the Soviet Union's Yuri Gagarin, the first man to be launched into Earth orbit. On the day of the historic flight by Shepard, the Braves hosted the Cincinnati Reds in a game at County Stadium in Milwaukee. The Reds prevailed in a 6 to 5 game, which took twelve innings, and 3 hours and 36 minutes to play. The Braves led 4 to 1 going into the top of the ninth inning, behind the pitching of starter Lew Burdette. Pinch-hitter Wally Post hit a three-run homer in the ninth, his 3rd of the season, to put Cincinnati up 5 to 4. Then the Braves tied the game in the last half of the ninth to force extra innings. Cincinnati scored one run in the twelfth inning for the win. A triple by Reds' third baseman Gene Freese was a key hit in extra innings. The Reds outhit the Braves in the ballgame by sixteen to nine, including a four-for-six performance by center fielder Vada Pinson. The winner for the Reds was Jim Brosnan (1-0), who worked three and two-third innings in relief and yielded one run on three hits. The loser for the Braves was right-hander Ron Piche (1-1). Piche was on the mound for the last three innings but gave up the winning run to the Reds. With the win, Cincinnati improved to 11 wins and 10 losses. Milwaukee dropped to 8-8 thus far in the 1961 season.

In the American League on Saturday, May 13, at Yankee Stadium, the Detroit Tigers defeated the Yankees 8 to 3. The win for Detroit in the young season extended their lead over the Yankees and the Baltimore Orioles to four and one-half games. The Tigers were now 20-7. The winning pitcher for Detroit was second year pitcher Phil Regan (3-0). Regan went all the way for the Tigers and gave up three runs on only five Yankees' hits. He would go on to complete the 1961 season for Detroit with 10 wins and 7 losses. Left fielder Rocky Colavito for Detroit hit two home runs, giving him 7 for the year, and had four runs batted in. Catcher Dick Brown also hit his 5th homer with one runner on base in the eighth inning, which broke a three-all tie score in Detroit's favor. The loser for New York was veteran Bob Turley (3-2), who pitched the first eight innings, gave up ten hits, and six earned runs.

Home runs for the Yankees were hit by Johnny Blanchard, his 2nd and Yogi Berra, his 3rd of the season.

Detroit picked up their 30th win against 16 losses with a 2-0 whitewash of the Minnesota Twins on Friday, June 2. The win in Detroit was earned by veteran Jim Bunning (4-4). Bunning pitched all nine innings for a complete game shutout yielding only four hits and one walk. He had six strikeouts in the game. The losing pitcher for Minnesota was starter Jack Kralick (4-3). Kralick would go on to pitch 242 innings for the Twins in 1961, winning 13 games and losing 11. The Tigers' runs both came on solo home runs by Rocky Colavito, his 13th, in the second inning and by Al Kaline, his 4th, in the sixth inning. The game drew a crowd of 22,141 to Tiger Stadium. At this point, Detroit maintained a two game lead over the Cleveland Indians and a four game lead over the New York Yankees. In the National League, the Cincinnati Reds and Los Angeles Dodgers were in a virtual tie for first place with the Giants only one-half game behind.

Detroit won in a slugfest at Tiger Stadium against the Yankees on Saturday, June 17, by a score of 12 to 10 for win number 40 of the season. Yankee outbursts of five runs in the fourth followed by a five run rally in the ninth fell short against Detroit's runs scored in six of the eight innings they were at bat. In a game which lasted 2 hours and 58 minutes, before 51,509 excited fans there were 27 hits, 14 by the Tigers and 13 by New York. The winner for Detroit was Paul Foytack (4-4), who pitched five innings in relief of starter Don Mossi, who lasted only three and two-third innings. Although Detroit led in the game at Mossi's departure, he did not pitch the required five innings by a starting pitcher needed to qualify for the win under baseball scoring rules. The loser for New York was left-hander Bud Daley (4-9). The Yankees used four pitchers in the game with the Tigers scoring runs against every one of them. Home runs in the game included shortstop Chico Fernandez, his 3rd, and Al Kaline, his 7th for Detroit. The Yankees pounded out four in a losing effort. Roger Maris hit his 23rd, Clete Boyer, his 3rd, Mickey Mantle, his 20th, and catcher Elston Howard, his 1st of the season. Al Kaline set the pace for the Tigers' offense with four hits in five at bats resulting in five runs batted in. Detroit was now 40-22 which was one game in front of the Cleveland Indians and two games ahead of the Yankees. One hundred games still remained in the expanded American League ten-team, 162 game schedule. In the National League, the Cincinnati Reds had a one-half game edge over the Dodgers and a full one game lead over the San Francisco Giants. After starting the season with a 6-10 won-lost record, the Reds won 30 of their next 43 games to assume their narrow lead.

In the second game of a July 4 doubleheader at Yankee Stadium, Detroit came away with a 4 to 3 win to bring their record to 50 wins and 28 losses, which allowed them to maintain a slim one game lead over New York in the standings. New York had defeated Detroit in the day's first game 6 to 2. The second game, which took 10 innings, lasted 3 hours and 29 minutes, before a patriotic holiday crowd of 74,246 in New York. The Yankees rallied for two in the eighth and one in the ninth to produce a 3 to 3 tie game after regulation. The two runs in the eighth came on the 31st home run of the year for right fielder Roger Maris. The Tigers managed a single run in the top of the tenth off Yankees' losing pitcher 22-year-old Bill Stafford (6-4). Stafford would go on to achieve a 14-9 record in 1961 with an earned run average of 2.68 runs per game. The win for the Tigers went to Frank Lary (12-4). Lary pitched nine innings giving up three runs and nine hits, before being relieved in the tenth by Detroit pitchers' Hank Aguirre and Terry Fox. Fox, who was credited with his 6th save of the season, had a big league career spanning 1960 through 1966 all in relief and mostly with the Tigers. His career record was 29 wins and 19 losses with a 2.99 earned run average in 397 innings pitched.

One week later on July 11, the year's first of two All-Star games was played at Candlestick Park in San Francisco before 44,115. The contest went into extra innings tied at three runs each. The American League scored a single run in the top on the tenth but ultimately lost the game as the National League scored twice in the home half of the tenth for a 5 to 4 triumph. The Pirates' Roberto Clemente drove in the winning run off Hoyt Wilhelm of the Baltimore Orioles. For the National League team, the winning pitcher was Stu Miller of the San Francisco Giants. There were two home runs hit in the game. Third baseman Harmon Killebrew of the Minnesota Twins hit one in the sixth and outfielder George Altman of the Chicago Cubs in the eighth inning. The line score was 5 runs, 11 hits, 5 errors for the National League. The American League had 4 runs on only 4 hits and 2 errors.

The parade of heavy hitting continued in the American League on July 20, as Detroit defeated Baltimore 15 to 8 for their 60th win against 33 losses and remained one-half game in front of the Yankees. Detroit put the game on ice at Tiger Stadium with eight big runs in the eighth inning. The Orioles managed fifteen hits in the game including home runs by third baseman Brooks Robinson, his 2nd, reserve catcher Hank Foiles, his 3rd, and two by Jim Gentile, numbers 25 and 26 of the season. The Tigers hit safely fourteen times, including home runs by 24-year-old rookie Jake Wood, his 7th, and two by Rocky Colavito, numbers 26 and 27 for the year. The winner in relief for Detroit was Hal Woodeshick (4-3) and the loser for the Orioles was starting pitcher Steve Barber (10-8), who allowed seven runs in four and one-third innings. At 51 wins and 42 losses, the Baltimore Orioles were having a good year but were nine full games back of Detroit in the standings.

The season was interrupted for the second All-Star game which took place on July 31, at the home of the Boston Red Sox, Fenway Park, before 31,851 fans. Unfortunately, the game was called after nine innings because of rain and went into the record books as a 1 to 1 tie game. The American League scored in the first on a home run by Detroit's Rocky Colavito. The National League tied it in the sixth and the rains poured down on Fenway. Starting pitchers were Bob Purkey of the Cincinnati Reds and Jim Bunning of the Detroit Tigers. There was no won or loss decision awarded for the tie.

INTERLUDE - THE *GAME OF THE WEEK* - DIZZY DEAN AND PEE WEE REESE

By the early nineteen-sixties, the magic of television was quickly becoming an important vehicle for watching Major League Baseball. The most prominent national television broadcasting pair of the time were announcers Dizzy Dean and Pee Wee Reese. Dean and Reese were both former ballplayers for the St. Louis Cardinals and Brooklyn Dodgers, respectively. Dean was born in Arkansas and Reese in Kentucky and both were far better known by their well-earned nicknames than by the names on their birth certificates. With Dean doing play-by-play and Reese providing color commentary, the two men together brought to the small screen a unique blend of southern humor, baseball legend, and baseball savvy. In their playing days, Dean had been part of the 1934 St. Louis Cardinals Gashouse Gang and Pee Wee had played shortstop for the Brooklyn Dodgers in the forties and fifties. Reese, as a Southerner from Kentucky, was openly supportive of his teammate Jackie Robinson in 1947, when Robinson became the first African American player in Major League Baseball.

The Yankees swept the Twins in a doubleheader on Sunday, August 6, at Yankee Stadium to go 71-37 on the year. The Yankees won the first game 7 to 6 in fifteen innings. The second game was a 3 to 2 win for New York behind a complete game eight-hit performance by 25-year-old rookie pitcher Rollie Sheldon (8-3). Sheldon would go on to win 11 and lose 5 for the Yankees in 1961. The loser for the Minnesota Twins was Al Schroll (0-1), who pitched eight and two-third innings, gave up seven hits, and struck out five in the loss. Schroll would end the 1961 season, which was his last in the Major Leagues, with 4 wins and 4 losses for the Twins. Yankees' center fielder Mickey Mantle hit his 43rd home run of the year in the second inning. The game was tied at 2 each after eight innings; but New York captured the win with one tally in the last of the ninth. The Yankees had gone 13-5 over their last eighteen games while second place Detroit was 9-7 in their last 16 games up to August 6.

In their 121st game of the season on August 19, the Yankees picked up their 80th win at Cleveland in ten innings by a score of 3 to 2. The only home run in the close contest was in the fifth inning by Indians' Catcher Johnny Romano, his 18th of the year. In his baseball career, Romano, born in Hoboken, New Jersey, would hit 129 total home runs including a stretch of seven years from 1960-1966 of at least 10 each year. For New York, Whitey Ford (21-3) went nine and two-third innings for the win. Reliever Luis Arroyo got the last out of the game for his 24th save of the year. For Cleveland, the losing pitcher was Bobby Locke (4-2), in relief of starter Barry Latman. Locke pitched the final two full innings and surrendered the lead run to the Yankees in the tenth. In the pennant races, Detroit was 77-44 which put them three games behind the Yankees. In the National League, the Cincinnati Reds at 75-46 were three full games in front of the second place Los Angeles Dodgers.

When the season moved into the final month of September, the Yankees swept a three game series over Detroit at home in the Bronx. The game on Sunday, September 3, was Yankees 8, Tigers 5 for New York's 90th win against 45 losses. The lead over Detroit was now four and one-half games. The Yankees assumed a 3 to 1 lead after one inning, only to see the Tigers score two runs in the top of the ninth to take the lead in the game 5 to 4. The game winning hit in the last of the ninth for the Yankees was a three-run homer by pinch-hitter Elston Howard, his 15th of the season. The Yankees also had home runs from Yogi Berra, his 19th, and two from Mickey Mantle, numbers 49 and 50 of the season. His second homer tied the score at four each in the bottom of the ninth. For Detroit, first baseman Norm Cash hit his 33rd homer in the sixth inning. Neither starting pitcher figured in the decision. Despite giving up three runs in his two innings, Luis Arroyo (13-3) was credited with the win for New York. The loss for Detroit was charged to 41-year-old veteran Gerry Staley (2-5), who in 1961 was finishing up a Major League Baseball career that stretched back to 1947.

A few days later on September 12, at Comiskey Park in Chicago, the Yankees improved to 100-45 with a 4 to 3 win in a rain-shortened game over the White Sox. The game was called after five and two-third innings with New York up by one run. The Yankees were in command the whole game after scoring three in the top of the first inning. The winner was Ralph Terry (14-2), who gave up seven hits and just one earned run in the contest. Terry would finish the season 16-3 with an ERA of 3.15. The loser for Chicago was Billy Pierce (9-9), who lasted just the first inning. Shortstop Luis Aparicio homered for Chicago, his 6th of the season. Catcher Elston Howard, who banged his 5th triple of the season in the first inning, drove in three runs to set the pace for the New York offense. The Yankees were 10-0 in their last ten games and were a whopping eleven and one-half games in front of second place Detroit.

As of September 12, Roger Maris had hit 56 home runs. As Maris seriously challenged Babe Ruth's single-season home run record of 60, which had been set in 1927, Commissioner of Baseball Ford Frick announced that if a new record was to be truly established, it would need to be accomplished in 154 games or less. The traditional length of the baseball schedule was 154 games. In order to remain balanced with ten teams facing each other an equal number of times, the American League schedule had been lengthened by eight up to 162 games in 1961. If Maris hit 60 or more home runs in 155 games or more, Ruth's official record would remain intact, and the accomplishment by Maris would bear an asterisk annotation. The memory of Ruth was held so high in baseball legend that there were those who apparently did not want to see his record broken. Other players had approached the record over the years; but all had ultimately failed in the quest. As the season wore into September, the media attention and the pressure on Maris became increasingly difficult for him to handle.

Much attention was devoted in newspapers and other media about the combined Maris and Mantle assault on Ruth's single-season home run record. Especially in the latter half of the season, comparisons were made almost daily to the home run pace set by Ruth back in 1927 and especially to his total of 17 home runs hit in September. Because two popular Yankees were challenging the record, the interest of fans in New York and around the country reached unprecedented levels. For the record, this chart shows the number of home runs by month of Ruth in 1927, plus Maris and Mantle in 1961.

	Ruth-1927	Maris-1961	Mantle-1961
April	4	1	7
May	12	11	7
June	9	15	11
July	9	13	14
August	9	11	9
September	17	9	6
October	0	1	0
Total	60	61	54

The Yankees 154th game was against the Baltimore Orioles on Wednesday, September 20, at Memorial Stadium. Going into the game, Maris had 58 home runs so he needed two to tie Ruth and three to pass him. The Yankees won the game 4 to 2 behind the pitching of Ralph Terry (15-3); but the real story of the game was Maris. In his second time up in the game, in the third inning, Maris hit number 59 off Baltimore pitcher Milt Pappas (12-9). His last chance for his 60th in that game came in the ninth inning facing Orioles reliever Hoyt Wilhelm. Wilhelm retired Maris on a soft ground ball squibber to the right side of the infield. With the win, the Yankees improved their record to 104-50. Eight more games remained on the Yankees schedule. Baltimore, with the loss, dropped to 89 wins and 65 losses for the season thus far. Maris would hit number 60 on September 26, six days later, in another game against Baltimore at Yankee Stadium.

The 1961 regular season came to a close on Sunday, October 1. In terms of the league pennant races, there was no remaining drama. In their 162nd game, the New York Yankees defeated the Boston Red Sox at Yankee Stadium by a score of 1-0. The Yankees final won-lost record was 109-53 which was eight games better than the Detroit Tigers 101-61. Almost unnoticed, the Orioles of Baltimore finished with a very good 95-67. In the National League, the Cincinnati Reds won the pennant with a record of 93-61, four games in front of Los Angeles, at 89-65, and eight games in front of the San Francisco Giants, at 85-69.

The only run scored for the Yankees in the game that final day of the regular season came in the fourth inning on the record breaking 61st home run for Roger Maris. Maris became baseball's reluctant hero. As he did that Sunday, he just wanted to play baseball and help his team win. The home run by Maris was off Boston starting pitcher 24-year-old right-hander Tracy Stallard (2-7). Stallard would go on to play seven years in the Major Leagues. He retired after the 1966 season with a record of 30 wins and 57 losses. The winning pitcher for New York was Bill Stafford (14-9), who gave up three hits and struck out seven in six innings pitched. The record breaking game was played in 1 hour 57 minutes before 23,154 fans in attendance at the House that Ruth Built.

Norm Cash of the Detroit Tigers was the American League batting champion with .361 for the 1961 season. His teammate Al Kaline finished a distant second at .324, followed by Cleveland's Jimmy Piersall at .322, and Mickey Mantle of New York at .317. The M-and-M boys led in home runs with 61 by Maris and 54 by Mantle. In runs batted in, Maris, and Jim Gentile of the Baltimore Orioles topped the list with 141 each. Rocky Colavito of Detroit was only one behind with 140. The Detroit Tigers led the league in team batting average with .266. In power numbers, New York hit the most home runs as a team with 240. The Detroit Tigers, however, actually led in total runs scored with 841.

Two pitchers won over 20 games for the season. The Yankees' Whitey Ford won 25 and Frank Lary of the Detroit Tigers won 23. Dick Donovan of the expansion Washington Senators was the league earned run average leader with 2.40. He was followed by Bill Stafford of the Yankees at 2.68 and Don Mossi of the Tigers at 2.96 runs per game. In strikeouts, the leader board was topped by Camilo Pascual of the Minnesota Twins with 221. Yankees' left-hander Whitey Ford struck out 209 and Jim Bunning of Detroit was third with 194. The improving Baltimore Orioles gained the honors in team ERA with 3.22 and also allowed the fewest base hits with 1,226. The pitchers of the expansion Los Angeles Angels had the most strikeouts with 973.

Roberto Clemente of the Pittsburgh Pirates won the National League batting title with an average of .351. Vada Pinson of league champion Cincinnati was second with .343. Orlando Cepeda and Willie Mays of the San Francisco Giants were the leaders in home runs with 46 for Cepeda and 40 for Mays. Frank Robinson of the Reds finished third with 37. Cepeda led also in runs batted in with 142. Robinson finished with 124, Mays with 123, and Henry Aaron of Milwaukee was next, with 120. In team batting average, the Pittsburgh Pirates led with .273. The Pirates also were tops in base hits with 1,448. In home runs, the team leader was the Milwaukee Braves with 188. The San Francisco Giants led the league with 773 runs scored.

In pitching, Joey Jay of Cincinnati and Braves' veteran Warren Spahn each won 21 games to lead the National League. Spahn had the lowest ERA for the season with 3.02, followed closely by Jim O'Toole of Cincinnati with 3.10, and Curt Simmons of the St. Louis Cardinals with 3.13 runs per game. The Los Angeles Dodgers had the top three pitchers in strikeouts. Sandy Koufax led with 269, Stan Williams had 205, and Don Drysdale was third with 182. The pitching staff of the St. Louis Cardinals finished with the lowest staff ERA of 3.74. National League champion Cincinnati allowed the fewest base hits with 1,300. Team strikeouts were dominated by the Dodgers with 1,105.

Roger Maris of the Yankees was the obvious selection as American League Most Valuable Player. The home run record of 61 achieved by Maris was not just a Yankee Stadium phenomenon. He hit 30 at Yankee Stadium and 31 on the road. His counterpart in the National League was Frank Robinson of the Cincinnati Reds. The 1961 season was the sixth full season for Robinson with the Reds and his statistics in hitting categories had been consistently awesome. National League Rookie of the Year was awarded to Billy Williams of the Chicago Cubs. Williams, primarily playing in left field, hit .278 with 25 home runs for seventh place Chicago. The American League Rookie of the Year was a pitcher, Don Schwall of the Boston Red Sox. At the age of 25, Schwall won 15 and lost 7 for the Red Sox with a 3.22 earned run average. The Cy Young Award was presented to the New York Yankees' ace left-hander Whitey Ford. He finished the season with an .862 winning percentage, the second highest of his career following only his rookie season of 1950.

The World Series for 1961 matched the Cincinnati Reds, National League champions, against the American League pennant winner, the New York Yankees. The powerful Yankees were heavily favored over upstart Cincinnati. Mostly familiar Yankee names would face the young Cincinnati Reds team. This was the first appearance of the Cincinnati Reds in the World Series since 1940.

CATCHER - Cincinnati, Johnny Edwards, 23, and New York, Elston Howard, 32. Edwards was a rookie for the Reds in 1961. In 52 games, he hit for a .186 average with 2 home runs. Howard had an excellent year for the Yankees. He batted .348 with 21 home runs in 129 games. A definite advantage for New York.

FIRST BASE - Cincinnati, Gordy Coleman, 27, and New York, Bill Skowron, 31. Coleman was in his third year in the Major Leagues and second year with the Reds. He was a .287 hitter with 26 home runs in 150 games. Skowron's batting average had fallen off a few points from prior years at .267 but he still hit 28 home runs in 150 games. A slight advantage for New York.

SECOND BASE - Cincinnati, Don Blasingame, 29, and New York, Bobby Richardson, 26. Blasingame was acquired from the Giants in early 1961 and hit .222 in 123 games. This was his seventh year in the Major Leagues. Richardson batted .261 and played in all 162 games during the season for the Yankees. He had batted .367 in the 1960 World Series. The advantage is with New York.

SHORTSTOP - Cincinnati, Eddie Kasko, 29, and New York, Tony Kubek, 26. In his fifth year in the Major Leagues, Kasko hit .271 in 126 games. Now in his fifth season with New York, Kubek batted .276 and hit 8 home runs in a career high 153 games. Narrow edge is with New York.

THIRD BASE - Cincinnati, Gene Freese, 27, and New York, Clete Boyer, 24. Freese had been in the big leagues since 1955, but this was his first season with the Reds. He hit 26 home runs with an average of .277 in 152 games. In 1961, Boyer became the regular third sacker for New York. He batted .224 with 11 homers in 148 games. There seemed to be a slight edge to the Reds.

LEFT FIELD - Cincinnati, Frank Robinson, 26, and New York, Yogi Berra, 36. Robinson broke in with the Reds in 1956. He was voted the National League Most Valuable Player for 1961. He had hit .323 with 37 home runs and 124 runs batted in. Berra had an average of .271 with 22 home runs in 119 games for the Yankees. Robinson was a big asset for the Reds. The advantage is to Cincinnati.

CENTER FIELD - Cincinnati, Vada Pinson, 23, and New York, Mickey Mantle, 30. Pinson led the National League in hits with 208. He had an average of .343 and hit 16 home runs in 154 games. Mantle hit 54 home runs with an average of .317 for the season. Because of injury, it was doubtful how much Mickey Mantle would be able to play in the Series. Therefore, the advantage goes to Cincinnati.

RIGHT FIELD - Cincinnati, Wally Post, 32, and New York, Roger Maris, 27. In just 99 games for Cincinnati, Post hit 20 home runs with a batting average of .294. He had played in the big leagues since 1951, mostly with the Reds. In his legendary 1961 season, Maris was named the American League Most Valuable Player for the second year in succession. He knocked out a record 61 home runs with 141 runs batted in and an average of .269. Advantage to the Yankees.

STARTING PITCHING - For Cincinnati: Jim O'Toole, 24, won 19, lost 9. Joey Jay, 26, won, 21, lost 10. Bob Purkey, 32, won 16, lost 12. For New York: Whitey Ford, 33, won 25, lost 4. Ralph Terry, 25, won 16, lost 3. Bill Stafford, 22, won 14, lost 9. The Ford and Terry combined record for 1961 was 41 wins and 7 losses. Pitching advantage to the Yankees.

MANAGERS - Cincinnati, Fred Hutchinson, 42, and New York, Ralph Houk, 42. Hutchinson became manager of Cincinnati midway through the 1959 season. Under his leadership, the Reds improved from 67 wins in 1960 to 93 wins in 1961. As a player, Hutchinson was a pitcher for the Detroit Tigers from 1939 through 1953. He completely missed five seasons from 1941-1945 for military service. The 1961 season was the first for Ralph Houk as manager of the Yankees. He was chosen to replace the legendary Casey Stengel. As a player, Houk had a relatively minor role for the Yankees as a reserve catcher backing up Yogi Berra during the seasons of 1947 through 1954. In that time span, he appeared in only 91 ball games.

Cincinnati emerged the winner of the National League by four games with 93 wins and 61 losses. The Reds started slowly by going 6-10 in April but had winning months from May through September. In May they won 20 and lost 6. They were 19-3 against Philadelphia but only 10-12 against the Chicago Cubs. They won 34 and lost 14 in games decided by one run. The Yankees were an American League powerhouse winning by eight games at 109-53. They managed a winning record each month of the season and won 65 and lost only 16 at Yankee Stadium. They split eighteen games versus Baltimore but had a winning record in games with the other teams. The Yankees went 14-4 against Cleveland, Kansas City and Minnesota.

The World Series of 1961 opened on Wednesday, October 4, at Yankee Stadium in New York. The Yankees' Whitey Ford (1-0) pitched a complete game shutout of the Reds by a score of 2-0. Ford had six strikeouts while allowing only two hits and one base on balls. The two Cincinnati hits were singles by Eddie Kasko and Wally Post. The two Yankees' runs came on solo home runs by Elston Howard in the fourth and Bill Skowron in the sixth inning. The loser for Cincinnati was Jim O'Toole (0-1), who went seven innings and gave up the two Yankees' homers. The line score read 2 runs, 6 hits, no errors for New York and no runs, 2 hits, no errors for Cincinnati. The time of the game was 2 hours and 11 minutes before a Yankee Stadium crowd of 62,397.

Behind the strong pitching of Joey Jay (1-0), the Reds took the second game the next day by a 6 to 2 margin to even the Series at one game apiece. On Saturday, October 7, the Series resumed in Cincinnati, before a capacity crowd of 32,589, where the Yankees narrowly beat the Reds 3 to 2. Reliever

Luis Arroyo (1-0) received credit for the win. The winning run came on a ninth inning homer courtesy of Roger Maris. The ballpark in Cincinnati, Crosley Field, was located in a mostly industrial area in the West Side of the city. The Reds played baseball at this location for 86 years until 1970. Historic Crosley Field was the host of the first Major League Baseball night game played May 24, 1935. With its location in an older Cincinnati neighborhood, Crosley Field eventually fell victim to the customer's need for a modern downtown stadium that was more freeway accessible. However, in 1961, Cincinnati fans still cheered for the Reds at Crosley.

The Series continued on Sunday, October 8, with the Yankees again riding the strong pitching of Whitey Ford (2-0) to gain a 7-0 win for a three games to one advantage. This time Ford went five innings and gave up four hits with the last four innings hurled by reliever Jim Coates in one-hit fashion. The Yankees had eleven hits in the contest compared to five for the Reds. Cincinnati used three pitchers in the game with the loss going to Jim O'Toole (0-2), who gave up two runs in his five innings pitched. There were no home runs in the game. Bobby Richardson and Bill Skowron each had three hits with Hector Lopez and Clete Boyer each having two runs batted in. The Yankees would have a chance to sweep the three games in Cincinnati the next day and thus end the Series.

In the fifth and final game, the Yankees scored early and often and then coasted to a 13 to 5 win over the Reds at Crosley Field in front of a capacity crowd 32,589 disappointed fans. For New York, right fielder Johnny Blanchard homered in the first inning with one on. Hector Lopez followed with a three-run homer in the fourth. The Yankees scored five runs in the first, one in the second, five in the fourth, and two in the sixth inning. The Reds could counter with only three runs in the third and two more in the fifth inning. These came on a three-run homer by Frank Robinson in the third inning and a two-run shot by Wally Post in the fifth. No runs for either team crossed the plate in the last three innings of the game. For Cincinnati, the loser was Joey Jay (1-1), who lasted only two-third of the first inning. The winning pitcher for New York was left-hander Bud Daley (1-0) in relief of starter Ralph Terry. Daley pitched the final six and two-third innings for New York, surrendered only five hits, and two unearned runs.

Overall the Series seemed to have the expected result. Although Roger Maris hit the winning home run in game three, he and Mickey Mantle didn't really contribute that much from a hitting standpoint. As a team the Yankees hit .255 to the Reds meager .206. The leading hitters for New York were Johnny Blanchard, Bobby Richardson, Bill Skowron, and Hector Lopez. Whitey Ford won two games for New York which had a staff earned run average of 1.60 for the five games of the Series. Jim O'Toole and Bob Purkey pitched well for Cincinnati in losing games one and three. Joey Jay won game two, but then was dispatched quickly by the Yankees in the first inning of the fifth and deciding game.

1961 WORLD SERIES SUMMARY

Game 1	At New York	Yankees 2, Reds 0
Game 2	At New York	Reds 6, Yankees 2
Game 3	At Cincinnati	Yankees 3, Reds 2
Game 4	At Cincinnati	Yankees 7, Reds 0
Game 5	At Cincinnati	Yankees 13, Reds 5

NEW YORK WINS THE WORLD SERIES BY 4 GAMES TO 1.

INTERLUDE - VADA PINSON

The 1961 National League season was vastly overshadowed by the drama of the Mantle and Maris home run chase. With the Reds win in the pennant pursuit, Cincinnati's success was tempered by the decisive World Series loss to the powerful New York Yankees in five games. Since the 1961 Yankees team is generally considered one of the best ever assembled, there can be little regret or shame in that loss. Center fielder Vada Pinson, who led the National League in base hits with 208, was a key player for the Reds in 1961. Pinson was born in Memphis, Tennessee on August 11, 1938. He attended high school in Oakland, California. When he was age 20, he started his career with Cincinnati in 1958. In an eighteen-year Major League playing career through the 1975 season, Pinson accumulated lifetime totals of 2,757 hits, 256 home runs, and a .286 overall batting average. He remained a fixture in Cincinnati through the end of the 1968 season and then played for the Cardinals, Indians, Angels, and Kansas City Royals.

In twelve seasons from 1957 through 1968, Pinson batted .297 with 1,881 hits, 186 home runs, and 221 stolen bases. Win or lose, he was consistently in the everyday lineup for the Reds. In the nine years from 1959 through 1967, Pinson had at least 607 at bats each year and averaged 20 home runs per year, with a high of 23 in 1962 and 1964. In his 1961 World Series appearance for Cincinnati, against strong Yankees pitching, he had only 2 hits in 22 at bats for an .091 batting average. In only two plate appearances in All-Star games, Pinson walked one time and struck out once. He was classically underrated as a player and deserved more recognition than he received. After his playing career ended, Pinson was a Major League coach for four teams, most notably for the Detroit Tigers from 1985 through 1991.

1962 Sᴇᴀsᴏɴ
Yᴀɴᴋᴇᴇs ʙʏ ᴀɴ Iɴᴄʜ

The 1962 season opened in the National League with the Pittsburgh Pirates winning 10 straight games to go 10-0. The tenth win came on April 22 at Pittsburgh in a 4 to 3 decision over the expansion New York Mets. The Pirates' starting lineup was still largely the same as the World Series winner from two years before. The Pirates broke a three-all tie with a run in the last of the eighth, driven in with a triple by their second baseman Bill Mazeroski. Left fielder Bob Skinner had previously homered in the sixth for Pittsburgh, his 2nd of the season. The winning pitcher was starter 27-year-old rookie Bob Veale (1-0). In his first victory in the Major Leagues, Veale pitched all nine innings, struck out six, and allowed only two earned runs. The losing pitcher for the Mets was Sherman Jones (0-3) in relief of starter Roger Craig. The loss dropped the Mets to nine consecutive defeats to start the young season.

On Sunday, May 6, at Wrigley Field in Chicago, the San Francisco Giants won their 20th game, against only 6 losses, by a score of 7 to 3 over the Cubs. The complete-game winner for the Giants was Billy O'Dell (4-0). O'Dell would go on to complete the year with 19 wins, 14 losses, and a 3.53 ERA. In this game he gave up seven hits, two earned runs, and struck out six. The losing pitcher for the Cubs was former Milwaukee Braves' hurler Bob Buhl (1-2). San Francisco scored two runs in the first inning and never trailed in the game. For the Giants, Willie Mays, who went three-for-four, hit his 10th homer of the season in the first and Harvey Kuenn hit his 1st of the year in the third inning. Following this first Sunday in May, the Giants led the second place St. Louis Cardinals by three full games in the standings.

In the American League three days later on Wednesday, May 9, the New York Yankees captured win number 15 for the year 4 to 1 over the Red Sox at Yankee Stadium. There was no score in the game through the first six innings. The Yankees, on an error by Red Sox center fielder Gary Geiger, picked up four unearned runs in the last of the seventh inning for the lead and then limited Boston to a single run in the ninth for the triumph. There were no home runs in the game. Whitey Ford (3-1) was the winner. He scattered seven hits, walked none, and had seven strikeouts. The loser was Red Sox pitcher Bill Monbouquette (2-3), who allowed no earned runs, only three hits, and struck out five. Catcher Elston Howard for New York drove in three runs in the seventh inning with his 4th double of the young season. The only run for Boston was driven in by third baseman Frank Malzone with his 7th double. There were 12,500 fans on hand at Yankee Stadium for this game which took only 1 hour and 41 minutes. The Yankees were now 15-7 for the season. Boston dropped to 11 wins and 12 losses.

INTERLUDE - WHITEY FORD

Edward Charles "Whitey" Ford was born October 21, 1928, in New York City. Whitey broke in with the Yankees in 1950 and played his entire career in New York finally retiring after the 1967 season. He was the ace pitcher on the dominant New York Yankees teams of the fifties and sixties. The left-hander compiled a regular season record of 236 wins and 106 losses (a .690 winning percentage) with an overall earned run average of 2.75 runs per game. From 1953 through 1965, Ford won at least eleven games every year. His two most successful years were 1961 and 1963 when he was 25-4 and 24-7, respectively. As a measure of his consistent performance, the highest earned run average that he ever had in his pitching career was 3.24 in the 1965 season. Even in his last two years of baseball, as his career was winding down, his ERA was 2.47 in 73 innings in 1966 and 1.64 in 44 innings in 1967. Ford was not an overpowering type of pitcher. Instead he was able to use his control, craftiness, and intelligence to keep opposing hitters off stride. The overall success of the New York Yankees teams on which he played was, in no small part, due to his contributions as a pitcher and team leader.

Ford had especially outstanding success in the World Series. He pitched in eleven of them and compiled an overall record of 10 wins and 8 losses. In the 1960 and 1961 Series, he was the winning pitcher twice against Pittsburgh and twice against Cincinnati. Ford gave up no earned runs and 17 hits in a total of 32 innings pitched in those two years combined. He also was the winning pitcher in two games in the 1955 Series against the Brooklyn Dodgers. Ford made appearances in six All-Star games, but did not have nearly the success he had in the World Series. He was the losing pitcher twice for the American League in 1959 and 1960. Overall, in twelve innings pitched, his earned run average was 9.00 runs per game.

In the early season, the Giants maintained a narrow lead in the National League as they defeated the Philadelphia Phillies 10 to 7 on May 25, at Candlestick Park in San Francisco. After six innings of play, the Giants led 10 to 1. Then, they held off a late rally by the Phillies in the eighth and ninth for the win. Four errors in the field hampered the Philadelphia cause. The Giants scored four unearned runs in the sixth inning. Although he gave up seven runs, the winner for San Francisco was Billy Pierce (7-0). Pierce lasted eight and one-third innings with reliever Stu Miller picking up his 4th save of the season. The loser for Philadelphia was 24-year-old rookie pitcher Jack Hamilton (3-4). Hamilton would go on to complete the 1962 season with 9 wins, 12 losses and an ERA of 5.09. There were four home runs in the game. For the Giants, Willie Mays hit his 14th in the third inning and Orlando Cepeda his 14th in the fifth. For the Phillies, Tony Gonzalez notched his 5th in the eighth inning and Johnny Callison hit number 6 in the ninth inning, in the rally which fell three runs short. San Francisco was now 30-14, which was a game and a half in front of the Dodgers.

INTERLUDE - WILLIE MAYS

Willie Mays was born on May 6, 1931, in Westfield, Alabama. He made his Major League debut in 1951 with the New York Giants. He played with the Giants in New York and then moved along with them to the West Coast to San Francisco beginning with the 1958 season. Mays remained with the Giants until the 1972 season. Then he was traded to the New York Mets where he retired from actively playing after the 1973 World Series. In his 22-year baseball career, Mays accumulated 660 home runs, 3,283 hits, 338 stolen bases, and a lifetime batting average of .302. He was selected as National League Rookie of the Year in 1951 and was named the Most Valuable Player in the National League in 1954 and 1965. He was an extremely enthusiastic ballplayer and was an inspiration to many younger players.

During the seasons from 1957 through 1968, Mays hit 435 home runs with a high of 52 in 1965 and a low of 22 in 1967. He exceeded 50 one other time with 51 homers in 1955. Mays was on pennant winning teams that were in four World Series. These were the 1951 New York Giants, 1954 New York Giants, 1962 San Francisco Giants, and 1973 New York Mets. As leader of the Giants, he made many clutch contributions to the San Francisco pennant drive, playoff series, and World Series of 1962. In overall World Series play, Mays had 17 hits in 71 at bats for a .239 average and did not hit a home run. In the 1954 World Series, he made one of the most spectacular defensive plays in baseball history on a running catch of a drive to deep center field in the Polo Grounds in New York. In twenty-four All-Star games, Mays batted .307 and hit a total of three home runs in games of 1956, 1960, and 1965.

On Tuesday, June 5, at Wrigley Field in Chicago, the Giants rolled over the Cubs 11 to 4 for their league leading 40th win against only 15 losses. The win maintained their slim one and one-half game lead in the standings over the Los Angeles Dodgers. Left-hander Billy O'Dell (7-3) went all nine innings to pick up the win for the Giants. O'Dell struck out ten while giving up five hits and three earned runs to Chicago. He would go on to finish the 1962 season with 19 wins and 14 losses. The losing pitcher for the Cubs was starter Bob Buhl (3-4). San Francisco broke open a tight 5 to 4 game with five big runs in the top of the eighth to seal the win. Right fielder Felipe Alou hit his 7th home run of the season in that eighth inning off Buhl. The Giants outhit the Cubs by thirteen base hits to five for the game. Attendance at Wrigley Field was only 6,087.

By June 28, that slim lead of the Giants over the Los Angeles Dodgers was gone as the Dodgers edged the expansion created New York Mets at Dodger Stadium in L.A. by 5 to 4 in thirteen innings. The game lasted 4 hours and 9 minutes before an L.A. crowd of 19,080 fans. Ed Roebuck (5-0), who pitched the last five and one-third innings in scoreless fashion, was the winning pitcher for the Dodgers. Roebuck pitched in 64 games for the Dodgers in 1962 and finished the season with 10 wins and 2 losses. Although Dodgers' starter Johnny Podres struck out ten in seven innings, he came away with a no-decision. Both teams ended up with ten hits in the game; however, there were no home runs. Dodgers' shortstop Maury Wills stole his 41st base of the season and scored two runs. The Mets used two pitchers in the game. The loser was right-hander Ken MacKenzie (2-3), who came on in relief of starter Al Jackson. Jackson worked the first seven innings for New York. The Dodgers were now 50-28 with a one-half game lead over the 49-28 San Francisco Giants.

President John F. Kennedy was on hand to throw out the ceremonial first pitch at the first 1962 All-Star game played at D.C. Stadium in Washington, D.C. before 45,480 fans on Tuesday, July 10. The National League defeated the American League squad 3 to 1 and doubled them down in hits by eight to four. There were no home runs in the game. Juan Marichal of the Giants was the winning pitcher, with the loss going to Camilo Pascual of the Minnesota Twins. Shortstop Maury Wills of the Dodgers scored two runs in the game, including the lead run in the sixth inning after he stole second base. Wills was voted the game's Most Valuable Player.

Three days later on Friday, July 13, the Dodgers picked up win number 60 versus 31 losses over the Mets in New York by a 5 to 4 margin. L.A. broke a four-all tie with a single run in the top of the ninth on a solo home run by Ron Fairly, his 8th of the season. Maury Wills also homered for the Dodgers, his 3rd of the season in the fifth inning. New York third baseman Felix Mantilla had staked the Mets to an early lead with a three-run homer in the first, his 7th of the year. Both teams used their starting pitchers to complete the game. For Los Angeles, Don Drysdale (16-4) struck out nine on his way to the win. Left-hander Al Jackson (4-10) went all nine innings in the loss for New York. At this point just over halfway into the season, the first-year expansion New York Mets were one of the major stories in baseball. They were solidly established in tenth place with 23 wins and 61 losses, 33 and one-half games in back of the first place Los Angeles Dodgers.

Later in the month on Saturday, July 28, it was the Dodgers over the Giants by a score of 8 to 6. After the Giants had taken an early 2-0 lead in the first, the middle innings at Dodger Stadium were big for L.A. The Dodgers picked up three runs in the fourth, four in the fifth, and another single run in the sixth inning. The line score was 8 runs, 16 hits, 2 errors for the Dodgers and 6 runs, 12 hits, no errors for San Francisco. The winner was Ed Roebuck (7-0), who pitched four innings in relief and the loser was 23-year-old Bobby Bolin

(6-1). Bolin would go on to have a thirteen-year big league career through 1973 mostly with the Giants. His lifetime record was 88 wins, 75 losses, and a 3.40 earned run average. The home runs in the game for Los Angeles were by Tommy Davis, his 16th, and Frank Howard, his 19th of the year. San Francisco catcher Tom Haller belted his 10th as the Giants late inning rally fell two runs short. There were 49,228 pleased spectators at Dodger Stadium to see this important win. The Dodgers were now 70-35 which was three games up on the Giants, eight and one-half on Pittsburgh, and nine full games ahead of the Cincinnati Reds.

1962 was the last of the four years in which two All-Star games were played. The second game in 1962 took place on Monday, July 30, before 38,359 fans gathered at the home of the Cubs, Wrigley Field, on the North Side of Chicago. With more offense in the second game, it was the American League 9 runs, 10 hits, no errors and the National League 4 runs, 10 hits and 4 errors. The win went to pitcher Ray Herbert of the White Sox and the loss to the Philadelphia Phillies' Art Mahaffey. American League home runs were hit by Pete Runnels of Boston, Leon Wagner of the Los Angeles Angels, and Rocky Colavito of the Detroit Tigers. Catcher Johnny Roseboro of the Dodgers homered for the National League.

On August 16, the L.A. Dodgers record reached 80-42 with a 7 to 3 victory over the Pittsburgh Pirates at Forbes Field in Pittsburgh. Pittsburgh scored three runs in the first inning off Dodgers' starter Stan Williams but the Pirates were shut out the rest of the way. Williams (12-8) lasted seven and one-third innings for the win. Relief specialist Ron Perranoski recorded the last five outs for his 13th save of the season. For Pittsburgh, the loser was 27-year-old left-hander Joe Gibbon (2-4). For the Dodgers, reserve catcher Doug Camilli hit his 3rd homer of the season in the eighth inning. Shortstop Maury Wills also had two stolen bases in the game, his 61st and 62nd of the year. In second place behind Los Angeles, the Giants were still keeping pace, just two and one-half games out.

Over in the American League, the New York Yankees were on the road in Southern California to face the Los Angeles Angels on Tuesday, August 21. In a game that went into extra innings, the Yankees exploded for seven runs in the visiting half of the tenth inning to defeat the Angels 11 to 4. The line score was 11 runs, 10 hits and no errors for New York versus 4 runs, 13 hits and 1 error for Los Angeles. There were four home runs in the game. For the Yankees, Elston Howard hit his 15th in the sixth inning and Roger Maris cleared the bases with a grand slam home run in the tenth inning, his 29th of the season. The Angels' first baseman Lee Thomas hit two solo home runs, his 18th and 19th of the season. The win for New York was credited to Bud Daley (6-3) with the loss for the Angels charged to Ryne Duren (2-9). This game was timed at 3 hours and 32 minutes and the attendance in Los Angeles was 50,830. New York improved to 75 wins and 49 losses. The Angels dropped to 71-55 for the season thus far.

The season moved into its final month with the Braves in Los Angeles in very early September. On Sunday, September 2, Don Drysdale (23-7), the ace right-hander of the Dodgers staff, threw a five-hit shutout at Milwaukee in an 8-0 win. For L.A. it was win number 90 against 47 losses and placed them three and one-half games in front of the San Francisco Giants at 86-50. Drysdale had five strikeouts in the game and also had two of the Dodgers' thirteen hits. There were no home runs in the game. The game highlights did feature the 6th triple of the season for six feet seven inches tall, 255 pound, Dodgers' right fielder Frank Howard and stolen base numbers 75 and 76 of the season for shortstop Maury Wills. The loss for Milwaukee was charged to starting pitcher right-hander Bob Shaw (15-9). Shaw pitched into the fourth, going three and one-third innings, giving up eight hits and five earned runs. The Dodgers kept their season rolling along but the loss dropped Milwaukee to, a still respectable, 72-66 for the season.

Eight days before the end of the 1962 regular season on Saturday, September 22, the Dodgers were on a road trip in St. Louis where they defeated the Cardinals 4 to 1 for their 100th win of the year. St. Louis, actually outhit Los Angeles in the game by twelve hits to six. The decisive frame turned out to be the fourth inning in which Tommy Davis for Los Angeles connected for a three-run homer, his 26th of the season, off 24-year-old St. Louis starter Ray Washburn (11-9). The lone Cardinals' tally was also in the fourth and was scored by first baseman Bill White, who had three base hits in the game. Veteran left-hander Johnny Podres (14-12) went six and one-third innings to get credit for the win. He was relieved by Larry Sherry who finished the game on the mound and recorded his 10th save of the year for the Dodgers. The win put Los Angeles, 100-55, four full games in front of San Francisco, 96-59.

The next few days would prove to be one of the most dramatic finishes to a league pennant race in baseball history. In the days leading up to Sunday, September 30, Los Angeles lost six of their last seven games. The Dodgers dropped their last game at St. Louis, lost two out of three against Houston at Dodger Stadium, and then were swept by the Cardinals in the last three game series at home. They ended the regular season at 101-61. Meanwhile, the Giants managed to win five of their last seven games to finish the regular season also at 101-61. The Giants won their last road game at Houston and then at Candlestick took two out of three games each from St. Louis and Houston. The Giants won their last regular season game, which tied the race on September 30, in a narrow 2 to 1 decision over Houston. In the fourth inning, catcher Ed Bailey homered for the 17th time in the season to give the Giants a one run lead. After Houston tied it in the sixth, it was center fielder Willie Mays with the game winner in the eighth, his 47th home run of the season. The winner in relief for San Francisco was Stu Miller (5-8). Miller pitched scoreless eighth and ninth innings, following seven strong innings from starting pitcher Billy O'Dell. The losing pitcher for Houston was starter Turk Farrell, who ended the season for the expansion Colt 45s with 10 wins, 20 losses, and a good earned run average of 3.02 in 241 innings pitched. A crowd of 41,327 fans witnessed the Giants spectacular feat of pulling the pennant race into a dead heat on the last day of the season.

This set the stage for a two out of three game playoff for the National League pennant similar to the conclusion of the 1959 season. The opponents this time would be the San Francisco Giants playing the Los Angeles Dodgers for the right to play in the 1962 World Series against the New York Yankees. The first game was played Monday, October 1, at San Francisco and was a one-sided win for the Giants as they shut out the Dodgers by a score of 8-0 behind a three-hitter from pitcher Billy Pierce (16-6). For the second game played the next day, the scene shifted to Los Angeles where the Dodgers tied the playoff series at one game each by virtue of an 8 to 7 victory in a marathon game which lasted 4 hours and 18 minutes. The third and final contest was played Wednesday, October 3, at Dodger Stadium.

The opposing pitchers for the climactic contest were Juan Marichal for San Francisco and Johnny Podres for Los Angeles. The Giants assumed a lead with two runs in the top of the third inning. The Dodgers struck back in the middle innings with one run in the fourth, two in the sixth on a two-run homer by Tommy Davis, his 27th of the season, and one in the last of the seventh. The score stood at 4 to 2 for the Dodgers going into the top of the ninth. Incredibly, the Giants scored four times to take a 6 to 4 lead. Then in the last of the ninth, the Dodgers were set down in order by Billy Pierce to end the series and win the pennant for the Giants. Official totals in the game were 6 runs, 13 hits, 3 errors for San Francisco and 4 runs, 8 hits and 4 big errors for Los Angeles. The winner for the Giants was former Yankee Don Larsen (5-4), who pitched a scoreless eighth inning. The loss for Los Angeles went to Ed Roebuck (10-2), who was on the mound for four hits and three bases on balls to the Giants in their pennant winning ninth inning rally.

The individual leader in batting average in the American League was Pete Runnels of the Boston Red Sox at .326. He was followed by the Yankees' Mickey Mantle at .321. In home runs, Harmon Killebrew of the Minnesota Twins was tops with 47, followed by Detroit teammates Norm Cash with 39 and Rocky Colavito with 37. For the Los Angeles Angels, Leon Wagner also hit 37. In runs batted in, Killebrew was also the leader with 126. Norm Siebern of Kansas City finished second with 117 and Detroit's Colavito was third with 112. In team batting average and total runs scored, the New York Yankees led with .267 and 817, respectively. The Detroit Tigers led the league with 209 home runs.

Ralph Terry of the Yankees led in pitching with 23 wins. Three pitchers won exactly 20 games each. They were Dick Donovan of Cleveland, Ray Herbert of the White Sox, and Camilo Pascual of the Minnesota Twins. Hank Aguirre of the Detroit Tigers wound up with the lowest earned run average of 2.21 runs per game. Veteran pitcher Robin Roberts of Baltimore finished with 2.78 and the Yankees' Whitey Ford was third at 2.90. The only American League pitcher to have more than 200 strikeouts was Camilo Pascual with 206. Jim Bunning of Detroit was runner-up at 184. In team pitching, the staff of the Baltimore Orioles posted the lowest ERA at 3.70 and allowed the fewest base hits at 1,373. The Minnesota Twins' pitchers led the league with 948 strikeouts and also allowed the fewest walks with 493.

In the National League, the most remarkable achievement by an individual player was the record breaking 104 stolen bases by Los Angeles Dodgers' shortstop Maury Wills. The National League batting champion was Tommy Davis of the Dodgers with .346, followed by Frank Robinson of Cincinnati with .342, and Stan Musial of St. Louis with .330. In home runs, San Francisco star Willie Mays led with 49 followed by Henry Aaron of Milwaukee with 45. Frank Robinson hit 39 and Ernie Banks of the Chicago Cubs hit 37. Tommy Davis of Los Angeles won the league RBI title with 153, followed closely by Willie Mays with 141. Team batting statistics were dominated by San Francisco. The Giants were league leaders in batting average, .278, hits 1,552, home runs, 204, and runs scored, with 878 for the year.

Don Drysdale of the Los Angeles Dodgers led National League pitchers in wins with 25, followed by Jack Sanford of the Giants with 24. Cincinnati pitchers Bob Purkey won 23 and Joey Jay won 21 games. Sandy Koufax of the Dodgers finished with the lowest ERA of 2.54. Bob Shaw of the Milwaukee Braves finished second at 2.80 runs per game. Koufax led the National league with 232 strikeouts. His teammate, Drysdale, finished second with 216. Bob Gibson of the St. Louis Cardinals came in third with 208. Team pitching honors for earned run average went to the Pittsburgh Pirates with 3.38. The Los Angeles pitching staff allowed the fewest base hits with 1,386 and had the most strikeouts with 1,104.

For the third consecutive year, a New York Yankees' ballplayer was named American League Most Valuable Player. This season it was Mickey Mantle, for the third time in his career. The Yankees' Tom Tresh was American League Rookie of the Year. Tresh, at 24 years of age, made the powerful Yankees' starting lineup partly because he could be employed both at shortstop and left field. Maury Wills, the Los Angeles Dodgers' crafty and speedy shortstop, won the Most Valuable Player Award in the National League. For most of the season, L.A. seemed very much in command of the pennant race and only lost out to the Giants at the very end of the season. Rookie of the Year honors went to 21-year-old second baseman Ken Hubbs of the Chicago Cubs. He hit .260 with 5 home runs in 160 games for Chicago and was an outstanding defensive player. This was the second year in a row that a Cubs player had won the National League Rookie Award. Hubbs would unfortunately only be able to play one more year in baseball for the Cubs. He tragically died in a plane crash near Provo, Utah in February of 1964. The improvement of the Cubs as a team to an 82-80 record in 1963 was attributed in part to the fine play of Ken Hubbs at second base. Right-hander Don Drysdale was selected for the Cy Young Award as the best pitcher in baseball. In his seventh Major League season, Drysdale finally broke the twenty win barrier with a 25-9 mark for the Dodgers in 1962.

INTERLUDE - BILL SKOWRON

The 1962 season would be the final year of baseball with the New York Yankees for first baseman Bill Skowron. After the 1962 season, he was traded to the Los Angeles Dodgers for pitcher Stan Williams. Also known as Moose, Skowron was born December 18, 1930, in Chicago, Illinois. He was with the Yankees for nine years from 1954 through 1962. Although he did not achieve Hall-of-Fame type numbers in his career, he was a good hitter and important teammate to the other Yankees' players of this era, like Berra, Mantle, Maris, and Ford. He always seemed to be around in the big games making a key contribution towards another Yankees' win. In nine years with New York, Skowron hit 165 home runs and overall batted .294. His peak year for hitting home runs was 1961 with 28.

Later in his career, Skowron played for other teams including the Los Angeles Dodgers in 1963, the Senators in 1964, the White Sox from the second half of 1964 through early 1967, and then the Angels for the remainder of 1967. In his entire career, he homered 211 times while batting .282. Skowron played in seven World Series with the Yankees and the 1963 World Series with the Dodgers. In 39 games, he had an average of .293 with eight home runs. In the 1960 World Series loss against Pittsburgh, he hit two home runs and had a batting average of .375. In five All-Star games, Skowron managed six hits in fourteen at bats for a .429 batting average.

INTERLUDE - MAURY WILLS

Maury Wills was born October 2, 1932, in Washington, D.C. His career in Major League Baseball ran from 1959 through 1972 and was primarily with the Los Angeles Dodgers. Wills was a key member, as shortstop, of the Los Angeles Dodgers World Series championship teams of 1959, 1963, and 1965, as well as the Dodgers National League pennant winning team of 1966. From 1960 through 1965, Wills led the National League in stolen bases. In 1962 he achieved his greatest notoriety as he challenged, and finally broke, the Major League Baseball modern record for stolen bases in a single-season. The record of 96, set in 1915 by Ty Cobb of the Detroit Tigers, was broken by Wills with a total of 104. The art of stealing bases in baseball was popular in the pre-1920 era of Ty Cobb, but then declined with the advent of Ruth and the increasing emphasis on home runs. It was not until the late nineteen-fifties and sixties that the art was brought back to prominence, especially, by Luis Aparicio of the White Sox and by Wills, along with other Dodgers' teammates. The team that by far best exemplified the use of speed and defense to help win ballgames was the Dodgers and Maury Wills led them in this effort.

In his fourteen-year career, Wills, aided by his speed on the bases, maintained a lifetime batting average of .281. He accumulated 2,134 hits, 71 triples, and 586 stolen bases -- an average of 42 per year, with a success ratio of .738. In the years from 1957 through 1968, Wills had 502 stolen bases, which ranks first in baseball for the twelve-year period. His highest total of 104 in 1962 was followed by the 1965 season with 94. In the 1962 season, Wills was caught while stealing only 13 times, for a stolen base success percentage of .889. Wills was selected for the 1962 National League Most Valuable Player Award.

In 21 World Series games, Wills had 19 hits in 78 at bats for an average of .244. In World Series play he stole six bases, including three in the 1965 Series against the Minnesota Twins. In six All-Star game appearances, Wills batted .357 with one stolen base. After retiring from baseball as an active player, Wills was a Major League manager for a brief period and also worked in television and radio broadcasting. His personal life was for a time, unfortunately, influenced by alcohol and drug use; but with the fortitude and tenacity that made him an exceptional athlete, he courageously overcame these problems to become a great example of hope and determination for all.

For the first time in ten years, since 1952, the Yankees would be playing the Giants, winners over the Dodgers in a three-game playoff, in the World Series. This time, however, the Series would open on the West Coast at Candlestick Park in San Francisco. These were the key players in the Series.

CATCHER - New York, Elston Howard, 33, and San Francisco, Ed Bailey, 31. In 1962 Howard had a batting average of .279 with 21 home runs in 136 games. Bailey broke into the Major Leagues in 1953 with Cincinnati and was traded to the Giants in 1961. He had 17 home runs in 96 games and a batting average of .232. Advantage to New York.

FIRST BASE - New York, Bill Skowron, 32, and San Francisco, Orlando Cepeda, 25. Skowron had another consistent year for New York with 23 home runs and an average of .270 in 140 games. It was his third consecutive year with more than 20 home runs. Cepeda was in his fifth year with the Giants. He played in 162 games, hit 35 home runs, and batted .306. He had been an extremely durable player and had an average of over .300 in four of his first five years with San Francisco. Two outstanding veteran players. No advantage for either team.

SECOND BASE - New York, Bobby Richardson, 27, and San Francisco, Chuck Hiller, 28. Richardson improved his average up to .302 and increased his home runs to 8 for the season in 161 games. Hiller was in his second year in the Major Leagues and batted .276 with 3 home runs also in 161 games. A narrow edge goes to the Yankees.

SHORTSTOP - New York, Tony Kubek, 27, and San Francisco, Jose Pagan, 27. Kubek missed the early part of the season but returned to the lineup for the Yankees in August. In 45 games his batting average was .314. Pagan was in his fourth year with the Giants and his second year as a regular. He averaged .259 with 7 home runs for the season. If only based on experience in the World Series, there is a slight edge to New York.

THIRD BASE - New York, Clete Boyer, 25, and San Francisco, Jim Davenport, 29. Boyer, in his fourth year with the Yankees, hit .272 with 18 home runs. These results were up from his previous seasons. Davenport was in his fifth year with San Francisco and also experienced his best year so far. He batted .297 and hit 14 home runs in 144 games. Two players are rated even.

LEFT FIELD - New York, Tom Tresh, 24, and San Francisco, Willie McCovey, 24. Tresh was voted 1962 American League Rookie of the Year.

He finished the year with a .286 batting average and 20 home runs in 157 games. McCovey was in his fourth season. Playing in only 91 games, he belted 20 home runs with a .293 batting average. Advantage goes to New York with the rookie.

CENTER FIELD - New York, Mickey Mantle, 31, and San Francisco, Willie Mays, 31. Mantle hit .321 with 30 home runs in 123 games. Mantle was named 1962 American League MVP. At age 31, Mays was more durable and in 1962 batted for an average of .304 with 49 home runs in 162 games. A very narrow advantage is with San Francisco.

RIGHT FIELD - New York, Roger Maris, 28, and San Francisco, Felipe Alou, 27. Maris followed his 1961 record season with another fine year for the Yankees. He had 33 home runs with an average of .256 in 157 games. Alou was in his fifth year with the Giants. He batted .316 with 25 home runs in 154 games. Both were veteran outfielders who had good years. No advantage for either team.

STARTING PITCHING - For New York: Whitey Ford, 34, won 17, lost 8. Ralph Terry, 26, won 23, lost 12. Bill Stafford, 23, won 14, lost 9. For San Francisco: Jack Sanford, 33, won 24, lost 7. Billy O'Dell, 30, won 19, lost 14. Billy Pierce, 35, won 16, lost 6. Both teams featured experienced starting pitching. Because of Ford's reliability in crucial games, an advantage seemed to be with New York.

MANAGERS - New York, Ralph Houk, 43, and San Francisco, Alvin Dark, 40. Houk was in his second year as manager of the Yankees. Dark became the San Francisco manager at the beginning of 1961. He had a career as a player mostly as a shortstop for the Giants, starting in 1946 through the 1960 season.

New York won 96 and lost 66 to finish first by five games in the American League. The best month for the Yankees was July with a record of 23-8. In August, they slumped to 17-18, but then finished strong in September by going 17-9. Against Baltimore and Cleveland, they won only 7 and lost 11 but had winning results against the other seven clubs in the League, including

15-3 against the Washington Senators. San Francisco (103-62) won the National League in a two out of three playoff series over Los Angeles. The Giants had a winning record each month of the season. Early on in April and May, they had a combined 35 wins and 15 losses. They finished with a winning record against the other National League teams, except for St. Louis. Against the Cardinals, they split 18 games. The Giants won 11 and lost 10 in games against Los Angeles, including the season ending playoff. In their home park, the Giants went 61-21; but they were only 42-41 on the road.

The 1962 World Series began on Thursday, October 4, in San Francisco at Candlestick Park. The Yankees took a one game lead in the Series with a 6 to 2 win over the Giants. Dependable southpaw Whitey Ford (1-0) went all the way for the win giving up two runs on ten hits. The Yankees scored two runs in the first inning off San Francisco starting pitcher Billy O'Dell. Then, the Giants countered quickly with one in the second and one in the third inning off Ford. The score remained tied until the top of the seventh when Yankees' third baseman Clete Boyer hit a solo home run for a 3 to 2 Yankees' lead. New York picked up insurance runs of two in the eighth and one in the ninth inning to put the 6 to 2 victory on ice. O'Dell (0-1) was the loser for the Giants. In seven and one-third innings he yielded five runs on nine base hits. In a losing cause, both Willie Mays and Jose Pagan went three-for-four for the Giants. There were 43,852 fans for the first World Series game ever played in San Francisco at Candlestick Park.

The Giants evened the Series at one game each with a 2-0 shutout win on Friday. The masterful three-hitter was pitched by right-hander Jack Sanford (1-0). After a travel day, the Series resumed on Sunday, October 7, at Yankee Stadium, where New York edged the Giants by a score of 3 to 2 behind the pitching of Bill Stafford (1-0) and with the lead runs in the game driven in by Roger Maris in the seventh inning. New York then led the Series two games to one.

In the fourth game on Monday, October 8, San Francisco won a game at Yankee Stadium to square the Series at two games each. The Giants scored first in the second inning on a two-run homer by catcher Tom Haller. In the last of the sixth, the Yankees picked up two runs to tie the game. The biggest hit of the game came in the seventh inning. San Francisco second baseman Chuck Hiller hit a grand slam home run to put the Giants ahead in the game 6 to 2. Each club scored a single run in the ninth inning to make the final totals 7 runs, 9 hits, 1 error for the Giants and 3 runs, 9 hits and 1 error for the Yankees. The winning pitcher, in relief of starter Juan Marichal, was former Yankee Don Larsen (1-0), who got the last out in the sixth inning. Billy O'Dell, of the Giants, worked the last three innings and received credit for a save. The loser for New York was Jim Coates (0-1), in relief of starter Whitey Ford. The game summary could simply say that, on this one day, the Yankees were done in by Haller and Hiller.

The weather turned uncooperative and the Series was hit with a series of postponements. The two clubs traded victories in the fifth game at New York and the sixth game back in San Francisco. The Yankees won game five on Wednesday, October 10, by 5 to 3, with Ralph Terry (1-1) picking up the win. Game six finally took place on Monday, October 15, with the Giants winning at home 5 to 2 behind the pitching of left-hander Billy Pierce (1-1).

The concluding seventh game was played Tuesday, October 16, at Candlestick. The starting pitchers were Ralph Terry for New York and Jack Sanford for San Francisco. The game was scoreless until the fifth inning when Bill Skowron scored a run on an infield double play with the bases loaded. Ralph Terry kept the Giants shut out into the ninth inning. With two out and Matty Alou on first base, Willie Mays doubled to right. Alou was forced to stop at third base on a fine defensive play by New York right fielder Roger Maris. The game was on the line for the Giants next batter, Willie McCovey. With the count one ball and one strike, McCovey smashed a vicious line drive which second baseman Bobby Richardson was instinctively able to catch for the final out to give the Yankees the World Series title. Unlike two years before, this time the last pitch from Ralph Terry (2-1) resulted in a 1-0 win thanks to the fine play in the field by Richardson. If McCovey had hit the ball literally a few inches higher, there might have been a different result.

It was a Series dominated by pitching. The Yankees as a team batted .199 to the Giants .226. The Giants had a 2.66 earned run average compared to New York's 2.95. The teams simply alternated victories among the rain postponements until it was finally over. For the Yankees, Tom Tresh and

Clete Boyer hit .321 and .318, respectively. Roger Maris had one home run and was outstanding defensively in right field. Jose Pagan hit .368 to lead the Giants in batting average among regulars. Ralph Terry won two games for the Yankees and finished with a 1.80 ERA in 25 innings pitched. To their credit, Jack Sanford and Billy Pierce pitched well for the Giants and won one game each in the Series.

1962 WORLD SERIES SUMMARY

Game 1	At San Francisco	Yankees 6, Giants 2
Game 2	At San Francisco	Giants 2, Yankees 0
Game 3	At New York	Yankees 3, Giants 2
Game 4	At New York	Giants 7, Yankees 3
Game 5	At New York	Yankees 5, Giants 3
Game 6	At San Francisco	Giants 5, Yankees 2
Game 7	At San Francisco	Yankees 1, Giants 0

NEW YORK WINS THE WORLD SERIES BY 4 GAMES TO 3.

Roger Maris at Yankee Stadium. Maris was 1960 and 1961 American League Most Valuable Player and helped the New York Yankees compete in the World Series five times from 1960 through 1964.

THE ART OF THE K

⌒

In an early season game on April 24, which attracted 8,773 fans at Candlestick Park in San Francisco, the St. Louis Cardinals defeated the defending National League champion Giants 4 to 3. Picking up the win for St. Louis was 34-year-old Curt Simmons (3-0). Simmons pitched all nine innings, gave up nine hits, and recorded five strikeouts. The losing pitcher for the Giants was Billy Pierce (1-2). Pierce lasted five and one-third innings and gave up all four runs to the Cardinals in the top half of the sixth inning. There were no home runs in the game. Shortstop Dick Groat had two hits in the game and batted in two of the Cardinals' four runs. Groat, 33-years old, had just come over in the offseason to the Cardinals in a trade with the Pittsburgh Pirates. The Cardinals early season record was 10 wins and 5 losses, which was one game in front of Pittsburgh and San Francisco in the standings. In early season action in the American League, the Kansas City Athletics at 9-5 were one-half game in front of both the White Sox and the Orioles.

On Friday, May 10, Comiskey Park in Chicago was the scene of another early season game as the White Sox hosted the Los Angeles Angels. The game was a pitchers' duel won by the White Sox by a score of 2-0. The winner for Chicago was starter Juan Pizarro (2-0), who gave up only three hits, one base on balls, and struck out six. Pizarro also homered in the third inning to score the first run for the White Sox. It was his first home run of the season. Pizarro, formerly with the Braves, was with the White Sox for six years from 1961-1966. In this six-year time span, he won 75 games and lost only 47. The losing pitcher for the Angels was Ken McBride (2-4). He also worked the complete game and in eight innings allowed two runs on six hits. In the seven Major League seasons through 1965, mostly with the Angels, McBride won 40, lost 50, and finished with a 3.79 earned run average. With the shutout win, the White Sox improved their record to 16-10. The Angels dropped to .500, at 15 wins and 15 losses.

Four days later on May 14, at Candlestick Park, the Giants won their 20th game of the season against 13 losses over Pittsburgh by a score of 3 to 1. There were no home runs in the game and both teams had strong pitching. After the Pirates scored one run in the second, the Giants picked up two runs in the fourth and one run in the eighth for the win. The winner for San Francisco was Jack Sanford (6-2), who went eight and one-third innings, with the save going to Bobby Bolin, his 3rd of the year. Bob Friend (3-3) was the losing pitcher for the Pirates. In a baseball career spanning from 1951 through 1966, almost all with the Pirates, Friend would post a record of 197 wins and 230 losses, with an earned run average of 3.58 runs per game. Willie Mays scored two of the three San Francisco runs in the game, which featured only five hits by the Giants and four by Pittsburgh. At this point, the Giants' lead over the second place St. Louis Cardinals was one and one-half games.

In the American League, the Baltimore Orioles won their ninth game out of their last ten on May 28, at Kansas City by a score of 4 to 2. The Orioles scored all four of their runs in the fifth inning off Athletics' losing pitcher Ted Bowsfield (3-5). Then, they held off Kansas City's late comeback attempt of one run in the eighth and one in the ninth inning. Three of the four tallies for Baltimore came on a fifth inning three-run homer by right fielder Al Smith, his 7th of the season. Smith spent only one season with Baltimore. In a twelve-year big league career, mostly with the Indians and White Sox, which ended in 1964, Smith had 164 home runs and a lifetime average of .272. The veteran Robin Roberts (4-4) was the winning pitcher for Baltimore. He lasted seven and one-third innings and gave up one run. The save for the Orioles went to Stu Miller, his 7th of the year. There were 13,739 fans on hand to see the game at Municipal Stadium in Kansas City. The win brought the Orioles' record to 30 wins and 15 losses and put them three and one-half games in front of the second place New York Yankees.

At Dodger Stadium on Saturday, June 15, Don Drysdale pitched a 4 to 1 complete game victory over the Chicago Cubs for his eighth win against seven losses. He allowed Chicago seven hits and only a single run in the third inning. He struck out six and walked none. The losing pitcher for Chicago was Larry Jackson (7-6). Jackson was pitching in his first year with Chicago after being traded by the St. Louis Cardinals, where he had played since 1955. In this game, in seven innings, he allowed the Dodgers one run in the first inning and three more in the second. He allowed nine hits, no bases on balls, and struck out three. There were no home runs in the game. Center fielder Willie Davis had two hits and drove in two of the four runs for Los Angeles. The only Cubs run was driven in by pitcher Larry Jackson on a sacrifice fly. The win improved the record for the Dodgers to 35 wins and 26 losses. The loss dropped the Cubs to 33-30 for the 1963 season thus far.

After games of Wednesday, June 19, St. Louis, with a record of 40-27, was in first place by one-half game over the Giants at 40-28. It was the Cardinals over the New York Mets 9 to 4 that day at Sportsman's Park in St. Louis. The big inning for the Cardinals came in the fourth when they scored four runs on a grand slam home run by 29-year-old first baseman Bill White, his 12th home run of the season. That blow gave the Cardinals a 6 to 3 lead after the fourth, which they never relinquished. In his career in baseball, Bill White hit 202 home runs. In the six years from 1961 through 1966, White hit at least 20 each year, with a peak total of 27 in 1963. Both teams used four pitchers in the game. The winner was Cuban-born Ed Bauta (3-2). Bauta went four and one-third innings in relief giving up only one Mets' run. Bobby Shantz got the final two outs in the ninth for his 5th save of the season. Starting pitcher Tracy Stallard (2-4) of the Mets was charged with the loss. In three and one-third innings, he walked five and allowed seven hits including, the Bill White grand slam.

It was about this time in July 1963, that the United States Postal Service began the use of a five digit postal code called a ZIP code, to help speed mail delivery. Along with the advent of the ZIP code use, the now familiar two letter standardized state abbreviations were also introduced. On July 7, which was the Sunday prior to the All-Star break, Cleveland hosted the Yankees in a doubleheader. The Indians routed the Yankees 11 to 3 in the first game. Then, in the second game, New York captured win number 50 against 31 losses over the Indians, by 7 to 4. It was a lengthy game of 3 hours and 9 minutes with attendance of 37,220. Since May 28, the Yankees had won 27 and lost 15 to take a lead of five full games in the standings over the White Sox. New York took a 4 to 2 lead into the last half of the ninth, only to have the Indians tie the score at four runs each to force extra innings. In the tenth, the Yankees quickly scored three runs to bring about the win. Each team used four pitchers and the starters did not enter into the decision. The winner for New York was Jim Bouton (11-4), with Whitey Ford working the tenth for his first save of the season. The four pitchers for New York combined for fifteen strikeouts. The loss for Cleveland went to 30-year-old right-hander Ted Abernathy (3-1), who came on to pitch the tenth and gave up the go-ahead Yankee runs. Each team had one home run in the game. For New York left fielder Hector Lopez hit his 8th of the season in the fifth inning and for the Indians 24-year-old right fielder Al Luplow hit his 5th, also in the fifth inning. Meanwhile over in the National League, the Los Angeles Dodgers had come on strong to go 50-33 which gave them a three game lead over the San Francisco Giants who were 48-37.

For the All-Star game in 1963, Major League Baseball returned to a one game only format after four years of holding two separate games a few weeks apart. The 1963 game was played at Municipal Stadium in Cleveland on July 9, before attendance numbering 44,160. Although outhit by the American League squad 11 to 6, the National League came away with the win by a score of 5 to 3. Starting pitchers were Jim O'Toole of the Cincinnati Reds and Ken McBride of the Los Angeles Angels. The National League scored one run in the fifth inning and one in the eighth to pick up the win. The winning pitcher was Larry Jackson of the Chicago Cubs with the loss going to the Detroit Tigers' Jim Bunning. Willie Mays of the San Francisco Giants was voted the MVP of the game by virtue of his two stolen bases, two runs scored, and two runs batted in.

INTERLUDE - TED WILLIAMS AND STAN MUSIAL

Two legends of baseball retired after lengthy and distinguished careers early in the nineteen-sixties. Ted Williams of the Boston Red Sox retired following the 1960 season and Stan Musial of the St. Louis Cardinals retired after the 1963 campaign. Ted Williams was born August 30, 1918, in San Diego, California. Williams' career began in 1939 with the Red Sox, where he played for nineteen seasons. He was away from baseball from 1943-1945 because of his service in World War II and much of the 1952 and 1953 seasons because of service in Korea. Among his many achievements in baseball were a .344 lifetime batting average and 521 home runs. He was twice selected for the American League's Most Valuable Player Award, for 1946 and 1949. In 1941, he completed the season with a .406 average and even in his final season of 1960 he batted .316. In 1957, he nearly batted .400 for a second time but ended the season at .388. He appeared in one World Series, in 1946, which the Red Sox lost to the St. Louis Cardinals. In eighteen All-Star games, Williams hit four home runs and hit for an average of .304 in 46 times at bat.

Stan Musial broke into the Major Leagues in 1941 and played for 22 years. He missed only the 1945 season for Military Service in the Navy. His entire career was with one team, the St. Louis Cardinals. He was born November 21, 1920, in Donora, Pennsylvania. He achieved a lifetime batting average of .331 with 475 home runs. His longevity allowed Musial to accumulate a total of 3,630 hits. Musial was selected for three National League Most Valuable Player Awards, for the seasons of 1943, 1946 and 1948. He hit .256 with one home run in a total of 23 World Series games in 1942, 1943, 1944, and 1946. In twenty-four All-Star games, his average was .317 with six home runs. Williams and Musial were two of the finest baseball players of their era and of the World War II generation spanning the forties, fifties, and early sixties. They were highly intelligent and skilled left-handed batters at the plate. Each played their entire careers with only one team and will be always remembered as sports heroes in the cities of Boston and St. Louis.

After the All-Star break, the Dodgers won ten of their next twelve games to go 60-35 for the year. On July 20, they won number 60 in a narrow 5 to 4 triumph over the Braves at Milwaukee's County Stadium. This extended the L.A. lead over now second place St. Louis to seven and one-half games and the third place Chicago Cubs to eight games. First baseman Gene Oliver of the Braves had four base hits in five at bats including his 10th home run of the season to stake Milwaukee to a 1-0 lead in the fourth. Later, the game winning hit for the Dodgers was an eighth inning solo homer by right fielder Frank Howard, his 16th of the season. Dodgers' starting pitcher Sandy Koufax lasted five and one-third innings, gave up three runs, and had six strikeouts. Koufax also hit a three-run home run in the top of the fifth inning, his first home run of the season. The winning pitcher in relief was Ron Perranoski (10-2), who completed the last three and two-third innings of the game. For the Braves, the loss went to 26-year-old Claude Raymond (4-5), who worked the seventh and eighth innings and gave up the game winning home run.

Over in the American League, the New York Yankees had forged an eight game lead over Chicago as they defeated the Washington Senators 9 to 1 at D.C. Stadium in Washington on August 7. The victory brought their record to 70 wins and 40 losses. The winning pitcher for the Yankees was left-hander Al Downing (8-3). Downing went all the way, gave up only three hits, walked six, and allowed the Senators one unearned run in the fourth inning. Downing would go on to finish the 1963 season with 13 wins and 5 losses with a 2.56 earned run average. For their nine runs, New York scored three in the first, three in the fourth and three in the fifth inning. The Yankees hit two home runs in the game. First baseman Joe Pepitone hit number 20 of the year in the first inning. Catcher Elston Howard hit his 22nd in the fourth. The starter for the cellar-dwelling Senators, 34-year-old Steve Ridzik (2-3), took the loss as the Senators dropped to 41 wins and 71 losses for the season.

On Wednesday, August 21, the Yankees won two close games over Cleveland in a doubleheader at Yankee Stadium by identical scores of 3 to 1. Attendance for the games was 25,983. The second game was New York's win number 80, versus only 44 losses. Over this latest two week span, New York had won 10 of 14 games and extended their lead over the White Sox to ten full games. Although outhit by the Indians in the second game, eight hits to six, New York scored two runs in the first, driven in by Joe Pepitone's 14th double of the season, and then added one more in the sixth inning. There were no home runs in the game. The winning pitcher for New York was Stan Williams (7-3). Williams gave up eight hits and struck out nine in the complete game victory. The loser for Cleveland was 27-year-old starting pitcher Barry Latman (7-9). Meanwhile in the National League, the Los Angeles Dodgers were well established in first place by seven and one-half games over the second place Cardinals of St. Louis.

On August 28, 1963, at Yankee Stadium, New York defeated the Boston Red Sox by a score of 4 to 1. This was the same day as the March on Washington and the "I Have a Dream" speech at the Lincoln Memorial on the National Mall, given by civil rights leader Martin Luther King, Jr. This would eventually become one of the most celebrated events ever in American history. For the Yankees, Whitey Ford pitched the complete game to win his 19th game of the season against 7 losses. He gave up five hits and struck out five. The only tally by the Red Sox was a second inning solo home run by first baseman Dick Stuart, his 34th of the year. The Yankees were without Mantle and Maris for the game, but had six hits to only five hits for Boston. New York third baseman Clete Boyer had two hits and scored two runs in the contest. The loss for Boston went to starting pitcher Earl Wilson (9-15), who allowed all four New York runs in five innings pitched. The win improved the Yankees record to 86-46 and Boston dropped to 62-70 for the season. The time of the game was 2 hours and 9 minutes before a Yankee Stadium crowd of 23,427.

The season moved into its final month, and the Yankees won their 90th game by 5 to 4 over the Detroit Tigers in the first game of a Labor Day doubleheader on Monday, September 2, at Tiger Stadium in Detroit. Yankees' southpaw Whitey Ford won his 20th game of the year. In seven innings, Ford gave up three runs, only one of them earned, and had seven strikeouts. Frank Lary (4-7) went the first seven innings for Detroit and picked up the loss. The big inning for New York was the fifth, during which the Yankees broke a two-all tie game with a three-run home run by Joe Pepitone, his 21st of the season. A Detroit rally in the last of the eighth fell one run short of tying the game. Yankees' relief pitcher Steve Hamilton came on to pitch the last inning and one-third for his 5th save of the season. The line score was 5 runs, 6 hits, 3 errors for New York and 4 runs, 10 hits, 1 error for Detroit. Detroit avoided a sweep by beating the Yankees in game two of the doubleheader by a score of 2 to 1. The Yankees were now 90-48 and twelve solid games ahead of the White Sox in the race with twenty-four games remaining. In the National League, the race had tightened, but the Dodgers were still six games in front of St. Louis.

At Metropolitan Stadium in Minnesota on September 15, New York edged the Twins 2 to 1 for their 100th win against 52 losses. After the loss, the Twins were now 85-67. Whitey Ford (23-7) pitched all nine innings for the Yankees for the complete game win. He gave up only two hits and struck out four. The losing pitcher for Minnesota was Lee Stange (10-5). Stange gave up six hits in eight innings and the two runs the Yankees scored in the second inning. There were only two extra base hits in the game, both doubles by the Yankees. Hector Lopez hit his 13th double of the year and center fielder Phil Linz, his 7th. Both Yankees' runs were driven in by third baseman Clete Boyer. Harmon Killebrew received credit for one RBI for the Twins' only run scored in the fourth. The time of the game was just 1 hour and 55 minutes with 35,010 fans in the stands for the game. The Yankees' lead over the Chicago White Sox, who were 85-65, was fourteen games with only ten games left to play.

As of September 15, the National League race further tightened with the Dodgers just one game ahead of St. Louis. The Dodgers were 91-59 with the Cardinals 91-61. The Cardinals then lost eight of their last ten games of the season, which included being swept by the Dodgers in a three game series in Los Angeles. The Dodgers finished 99-63 compared to 93-69 for St. Louis to win the pennant by a margin of six games. The Dodgers last game of the regular season was a 3 to 1 loss to the Philadelphia Phillies at Dodger Stadium on Sunday, September 29. The Phillies finished a good 1963 season in fourth place with a record of 87 wins and 75 losses. Don Drysdale started the game for the Dodgers and gave up no runs but worked only five innings to pace himself for the World Series later in the week. The loser for the Dodgers in relief was 24-year-old Pete Richert (5-3), who surrendered the go-ahead runs to the Phillies in the seventh. Philadelphia shortstop Bobby Wine hit his 6th homer of the season as part of that game winning rally. In relief for the Phillies, the winner was left-hander Chris Short (9-12), who closed out his 1963 season with a 2.95 ERA in 198 innings pitched.

The leading hitter in the American League was Carl Yastrzemski of the Boston Red Sox with a batting average of .321. He was followed by the Detroit Tigers' Al Kaline with .312 and Rich Rollins of the Minnesota Twins at .307. In home runs, three members of the Minnesota ballclub were among the leaders. Harmon Killebrew led with 45. His teammates Bob Allison and Jimmie Hall had 35 and 33, respectively. Dick Stuart of the Red Sox finished second with 42. Stuart was the clear leader in runs batted in with 118 followed by Al Kaline with 101. The Minnesota Twins were dominant in team batting statistics for the year. The Twins were tops in team batting average with .255, runs scored with 767, and in home runs with 225.

In pitching, Whitey Ford of the Yankees won 24 games to lead the league. His Yankees' teammate Jim Bouton and Camilo Pascual of the Minnesota Twins were next at 21 each. Gary Peters of the Chicago White Sox finished with the lowest earned run average of 2.33 followed closely by his Chicago teammate Juan Pizarro with 2.39. Pascual ended the season with 2.46. Pascual did top the American League with 202 strikeouts followed by Jim Bunning of the Detroit Tigers with 196. In team pitching, the Chicago White Sox had the lowest staff ERA with 2.98 runs per game. The fewest base hits of 1,239 were allowed by New York and Cleveland Indians' pitchers finished with the most strikeouts of 1,019.

Tommy Davis of the Los Angeles Dodgers won the National League batting title with an average of .326. Roberto Clemente of Pittsburgh was second at .320, followed by Henry Aaron of Milwaukee and Dick Groat of St. Louis with .319 each. In home runs, the co-leaders were Aaron and Willie McCovey of San Francisco with 44 each. They were followed by two other San Francisco Giants; Willie Mays had 38 and Orlando Cepeda had 34. Aaron was the runaway leader in runs batted in with 130, followed by Ken Boyer and Bill White both of St. Louis with 111 and 109, respectively. Team batting was paced by the St. Louis Cardinals with a season average of .271 and 747 runs scored. Three of the top four leaders in home runs were with the Giants. As a team, they led the National League with 197 home runs.

In pitching, Sandy Koufax of the Dodgers and Juan Marichal of the Giants led the National League with 25 wins each. Jim Maloney of Cincinnati and Warren Spahn of Milwaukee both had 23. Koufax finished a spectacular season with a 1.88 earned run average. Dick Ellsworth of the Chicago Cubs was second with 2.11. Koufax also was dominant in strikeouts with 306, followed by Maloney with 265 and Don Drysdale of L.A. with 251. Los Angeles Dodgers' pitchers had the lowest staff ERA with 2.86 and the highest strikeouts total with 1,095. Philadelphia Phillies' pitchers allowed the fewest base hits with 1,262.

The 1963 American League Most Valuable Player was another New York Yankee, versatile catcher Elston Howard. The Rookie of the Year Award went to a pitcher, left-hander Gary Peters of the Chicago White Sox. Peters went 19-8 with a 2.33 earned run average. In the National League, the outstanding performance of Sandy Koufax earned him both the League's Most Valuable Player Award and the Cy Young Award which recognized him as the best pitcher in baseball. There was little question about that for 1963. The Rookie of the Year Award for the National League was won by 22-year-old Pete Rose of the Cincinnati Reds. In his rookie season for Cincinnati, Rose produced 170 base hits which gave him a batting average of .273.

In the 1963 World Series the New York Yankees were making their fourth consecutive appearance and were returning as two-time defending World Series winners. The Los Angeles Dodgers, with a team featuring speed, defense, and pitching, were in the Fall Classic for the first time since 1959.

CATCHER - Los Angeles, Johnny Roseboro, 30, and New York, Elston Howard, 34. In his seventh year with the Dodgers, Roseboro hit .236 with 9 home runs in 135 games. Howard, the American League MVP, had been with the Yankees for nine years. In 1963 he had 28 home runs and a batting average of .287 in 135 games. It was the third consecutive year in which he had hit more than 20 home runs. The advantage goes to New York.

FIRST BASE - Los Angeles, Bill Skowron, 33, and New York, Joe Pepitone, 23. Former Yankee Bill Skowron had been traded after the 1962 season to the Dodgers for pitcher Stan Williams. Skowron had batted only .203 with 4 home runs for the Dodgers in 1963. Pepitone, in his second season, hit 27 home runs and batted .271 in 157 games. He had largely replaced Skowron at first Base for the Yankees. Based on the year's performance, the edge goes to New York.

SECOND BASE - Los Angeles, Dick Tracewski, 28, and New York, Bobby Richardson, 28. Tracewski was in his second year with the Dodgers. In 104 games his average was .226. Richardson was now in his fifth season as New York's primary fixture at second. In 151 games he batted .265 with 3 home runs. This was an apparent advantage for New York.

SHORTSTOP - Los Angeles, Maury Wills, 31, and New York, Tony Kubek, 28. Wills was in his fifth year with the Dodgers. In 1963 he hit .302 with 40 stolen bases in 134 games. Kubek batted .257 with 7 home runs for the Yankees in 135 games. This was his lowest batting average in seven years of Major League Baseball. Wills could strike terror to the opponent's defense once he was on base. Advantage goes to Los Angeles.

THIRD BASE - Los Angeles, Jim Gilliam, 35, and New York, Clete Boyer, 26. An eleven-year Dodgers' veteran, Gilliam batted .282 with 6 home runs in 148 games. Boyer had been with the Yankees since 1959. He hit .251 with 12 home runs in 152 games. Both players had consistent seasons in 1963. Rated even.

LEFT FIELD - Los Angeles, Tommy Davis, 24, and New York, Tom Tresh, 25. In his fourth year as a regular with Los Angeles, Davis was the 1963 National League batting champion with an average of .326. He also had 16 home runs in 146 games. Tresh was in his second season as a Yankees regular. He hit 25 home runs with a batting average of .269 in 145 games. Rated as an advantage to Los Angeles.

CENTER FIELD - Los Angeles, Willie Davis, 23, and New York, Mickey Mantle, 32. Davis had been a member of the Dodgers since 1960. He hit .245 with 9 home runs in 156 games. Mantle was plagued by injury for most of the 1963 season. He played in only 65 games, hit 15 homers, and batted .314. The two would be rated even because Mantle was handicapped by his injuries. No advantage for either club.

RIGHT FIELD - Los Angeles, Frank Howard, 27, and New York, Roger Maris, 29. Howard broke in with the Dodgers in 1958. He smashed 28 home runs with a .273 batting average in 123 games. 1963 was his fourth consecutive season with at least 15 home runs. Maris appeared in 90 games for New York and batted .269 with 23 home runs. No apparent advantage to either team.

STARTING PITCHING - For Los Angeles: Sandy Koufax, 28, won 25, lost 5. Johnny Podres, 31, won 14, lost 12. Don Drysdale, 27, won 19, lost 17. For New York: Whitey Ford, 35, won 24, lost 7, Al Downing, 22, won 13, lost 5. Jim Bouton, 24, won 21, lost 7. L.A. appeared to have an edge in experience and in the season's relative performance results.

MANAGERS - Los Angeles, Walter Alston, 52, and New York, Ralph Houk, 44. Alston was by this time an experienced manager, but as a player he had appeared in only one game for the St. Louis Cardinals in 1936. He had exactly one Major League at bat, in which he struck out. Houk had managed the Yankees to the American League pennant for each of his three years as the team's manager and had been successful in the both the 1961 and 1962 World Series.

Los Angeles won the National League pennant by a margin of six games with a record of 99-63. The Dodgers started slowly by going 10-11 for the month of April and then posted five consecutive winning months. They closed out the season in September by winning 19 against only 9 losses.

They feasted against the New York Mets by going 16-2 but were only 8-10 against Milwaukee. They evenly split eighteen games against San Francisco. In 51 games decided by one run, the Dodgers won 33 and lost 18. New York captured the American League by ten and one-half games by winning 104 and losing 57. The Yankees played winning ball each of the six months of the year. Their best months were 22-9 in July and 22-10 in August. Their wins exceeded losses against all the other American League clubs, but they were only 10-8 versus both Chicago and Detroit. In 53 one run games, they won 36 and lost 17.

The opening game took place at Yankee Stadium in New York on Wednesday, October 2. Sandy Koufax (1-0) dominated the Yankees from the Yankee Stadium pitching mound with fifteen strikeouts in nine innings pitched, as the Dodgers won 5 to 2. Koufax struck out the first five Yankees' hitters he faced. His fifteen strikeouts were a new World Series record for one game. The Dodgers scored four runs in the second and one in the third inning to take a five run lead. Three of the runs in the second were on a three-run home run by Dodgers' catcher Johnny Roseboro. The loss for New York went to starter Whitey Ford (0-1), who pitched five innings and gave up all five Dodgers' runs in the game. In the eighth inning, Yankees' left fielder Tom Tresh connected for a two-run homer off Koufax, the only two runs the Dodgers' ace permitted. The line score was 5 runs, 9 hits and no errors for L.A. and 2 runs, 6 hits and no errors for the Yankees.

The next day Los Angeles also took the second game 4 to 1 over the Yankees behind the pitching of Johnny Podres (1-0). In game three in Los Angeles on Saturday, October 5, Don Drysdale (1-0) shut out the Yankees on a three-hitter by a score of 1-0. Drysdale recorded nine strikeouts in the game. Los Angeles led in the Series over New York three games to none.

The Dodgers swept the Series four games to none on Sunday, October 6. The line score was 2 runs, 2 hits, 1 error for Los Angeles and 1 run, 6 hits, 1 error for New York. Sandy Koufax (2-0) went all the way for the win and had eight strikeouts. Right fielder Frank Howard had both hits for Los Angeles. His solo home run in the bottom of the fifth gave the Dodgers a 1-0 lead. In the seventh inning, Mickey Mantle hit a solo home run off Koufax to tie the game. But the Dodgers won the game with a single run in the stretch half of the seventh inning, driven in on a sacrifice fly by center fielder Willie Davis.

Although he surrendered only two hits to the Dodgers, Yankees' left-hander Whitey Ford (0-2) was the losing pitcher, as in the first game.

The Series was a shockingly quick and decisive win for Los Angeles. It was the first time in history that a New York Yankees team had ever been swept in a World Series. The game times of the four games even seemed quick. The times were 2 hours 9 minutes, 2 hours 13 minutes, 2 hours 5 minutes, and 1 hour 50 minutes for the deciding Dodgers win. The Dodgers batted .214 as a team compared to the Yankees .171. Koufax, Podres, and Drysdale were brilliant pitching in Dodger Blue. Former Yankee Bill Skowron, now with the Dodgers, had five hits, including one home run, in thirteen at bats for a .385 average. Tommy Davis had six hits in the Series, including two triples, for a .400 batting average. It was a victory for pitching, speed, and defense over the Yankees' power which was mostly dormant for the four games over five days.

1963 WORLD SERIES SUMMARY

Game 1	At New York	Dodgers 5, Yankees 2
Game 2	At New York	Dodgers 4, Yankees 1
Game 3	At Los Angeles	Dodgers 1, Yankees 0
Game 4	At Los Angeles	Dodgers 2, Yankees 1

LOS ANGELES SWEEPS THE WORLD SERIES 4 GAMES TO NONE.

1964 Season

Redbirds Flying High

⌒

T**he New York Yankees opened their defense of the American
League pennant on Thursday, April 16, at Yankee Stadium facing
the Boston Red Sox.** In eleven innings, the Red Sox came away
with a 4 to 3 victory. The winning pitcher for Boston was 27-year-old Dick
Radatz (1-0), who pitched three and two-third innings in relief of starter
Bill Monbouquette. Radatz was in his third year with Boston and would go
on to complete the 1964 season with 16 wins, 9 losses, and an ERA of 2.29
in a total of 79 relief appearances. Starter Whitey Ford (0-1) took the loss
for the Yankees. Ford worked all eleven innings, gave up thirteen hits, and
the winning Red Sox run in the top of the eleventh inning. There were no
home runs in the game for either team. Boston shortstop Eddie Bressoud
and catcher Bob Tillman each tripled, and combined for seven of the team's
thirteen base hits.

In the Spring of 1964, the United States was still recovering from the shocking
and unexpected loss of President Kennedy to assassination on November 22,
1963. It was a difficult time of sorrow. One of the ways to for the country
to focus again on the coming years was the beginning of the World's Fair,
which opened in Queens, New York on April 22. On that date, the St. Louis
Cardinals defeated the World Series champion Los Angeles Dodgers 7 to 6,
at Sportsman's Park in St. Louis. The Cardinals led 6-0 after three innings
and then managed to hold off a late inning comeback by the Dodgers which
fell short by one run. Both teams had eight hits in the game, which included
two home runs by the Dodgers and three by St. Louis. Sandy Koufax (1-2)
lasted only one inning as starter for the Dodgers and took the loss. Cardinals'
left fielder Charlie James hit his 1st homer in the first inning off Koufax with
two runners on. In the third, right fielder Carl Warwick hit his 1st also with
one on to put St. Louis up by six. Then in the seventh inning, first baseman
Bill White hit a solo home run, his 1st of the year, for the Cardinals' seventh
run. In a losing cause for Los Angeles, Frank Howard hit a two-run homer

in the sixth, his 3rd, and Willie Davis hit a solo shot in the seventh, his 1st of the season. The winner for the Cardinals was southpaw Curt Simmons (2-0). Simmons allowed five runs in six and two-third innings. He was relieved by Roger Craig, who worked the final two and one-third innings, gave up one run, and two hits for the save. The Cardinals improved to 5-3 for the young season, and Los Angeles, at 1-7, had been able to win only one out of their first eight games.

As the 1964 National League season continued, the Philadelphia Phillies set the early pace. On Friday, May 1, at County Stadium in Milwaukee, the Phillies defeated the Braves 5 to 3. The winning pitcher for Philadelphia was right-hander Jim Bunning (3-0). This was the first year in Philadelphia for Bunning after pitching with Detroit since 1955. Bunning recorded eight strikeouts in the game. There was no score after three innings. The Phillies picked up a run in the fourth, three in the sixth inning, and one in the ninth for a 5-0 lead. Milwaukee rallied for three runs in the last of the ninth off Bunning, but Ed Roebuck came on to record the final out for his 2nd save of the season. In sixty games for Philadelphia in 1964, Roebuck would post a 2.21 ERA in 77 innings pitched. The loser for Milwaukee was starter Warren Spahn (1-2). There were two home runs in the game, both coming in the ninth inning. Twenty-two-year-old third baseman Dick Allen of the Phillies, hit his 6th of the year, and Milwaukee's catcher Ed Bailey hit his 3rd. The game attracted a crowd of only 4,727 to County Stadium. The win improved the Phillies record to 10-2, which gave them a two game league lead over the second place San Francisco Giants.

INTERLUDE - JIM BUNNING

Jim Bunning was born in Southgate, Kentucky on October 23, 1931. He was a Major League pitcher for seventeen seasons from 1955 through 1971. He pitched for the Detroit Tigers from 1955 through 1963 and for the Philadelphia Phillies from 1964 through 1967. In his last four years of baseball, Bunning was with the Pirates and Dodgers before ending with two more years at Philadelphia in 1970 and 1971. For his career, he accumulated 224 wins, 184 losses, a 3.27 earned run average, and 2,855 strikeouts. His 224 lifetime wins included 118 in the American League and 106 in the National League.

In the twelve years from 1957 through 1968, Bunning won 188 games. He was so consistent that he finished with at least 11 wins each year from 1957 through 1967, including 20 wins in 1957 and 19 in four other years (1962, 1964, 1965, and 1966). Unfortunately, he was never on a pennant winning team and was never able to participate in the World Series. He was an integral part of some excellent teams, notably the 1961 Tigers which finished 101-61, and the 1964 Phillies which finished the season 92-70. Bunning did appear in eight All-Star games with an ERA of 1.00 over eighteen innings pitched. For the American League, he was the winning pitcher in the 1957 game at St. Louis and the losing pitcher in the 1963 game at Cleveland, even though the run scored against him was not earned.

After retirement from baseball, Bunning returned to his native northern Kentucky and started a political career, which brought him all the way to his election to the United States Senate where he served two six-year terms.

The Giants won twelve of their next nineteen games and reached win number 20 with a 3-0 shutout over the Phillies on May 19, at San Francisco. At this point, the Giants were 20-11 and led Philadelphia at 18-11 by one full game in the standings. The game was well-pitched by the starters for both teams, Jack Sanford for the Giants and 25-year-old southpaw Dennis Bennett for the Phillies. Finally, in the seventh, the Giants scored twice. Then, they added an insurance run in the eighth inning for the 3-0 margin. Sanford (4-3) went all the way for the win, giving up only four hits and two walks. Bennett (4-3) pitched all eight innings for the Phillies and was charged with the loss. The Giants' rookie third baseman, Jim Ray Hart, had four hits in four at bats including his third double of the season. Hart would go on to finish the 1964 season with 31 home runs and a batting average of .286. The attendance at Candlestick Park in San Francisco was 16,936.

By early June the leader in the American League race was the Baltimore Orioles. On Wednesday, June 3, the Orioles defeated the Athletics at Kansas City to improve their record to 30-15, which was one and one-half games ahead of the Chicago White Sox at 25-13. The game was tight through six innings with the Orioles ahead 1-0 by virtue of a solo home run in the top of the fourth by shortstop Luis Aparicio, his 3rd of the season. The Orioles then scored two in the seventh, two in the ninth, and eventually prevailed 5 to 1. Baltimore's Boog Powell homered in the seventh and the ninth to give him 11 home runs for the season. Center fielder Willie Kirkland hit his first of the season, also for Baltimore, in the ninth inning. Thirty-eight-year-old Robin Roberts (4-2) was the complete game winner. Roberts was in his third year at Baltimore, following many outstanding years with the Phillies. The loser for Kansas City was their starter Diego Segui (3-5), who had nine strikeouts in eight innings pitched. The Cuban-born Segui would go on to complete the 1964 season with 8 wins, 17 losses, and a 4.56 earned run average.

In the middle of June, the Yankees came on strong by winning 16 of 22 games to challenge Baltimore for first place in the American League. In a game played at Memorial Stadium in Baltimore on June 23, the Orioles defeated the Yankees 9 to 8 to maintain a slim one-half game edge in the pennant pursuit. There were 31,860 fans in attendance to witness a line score of 9 runs, 14 hits, no errors for Baltimore and 8 runs, 12 hits and no errors for New York. After seven innings, the Yankees seemed in command with a 7 to 2 lead behind their starter Rollie Sheldon. Then, the Orioles rallied with seven runs in the eighth inning to lead 9 to 7. A ninth inning home run by Roger Maris, his 12th, made the final score 9 to 8 Orioles. Other home runs for New York were by Elston Howard, his 7th, and by Mickey Mantle, his 14th of the season. Boog Powell banged two home runs for Baltimore, bringing his season total up to 15. Baltimore used four pitchers in the game with the win credited to 26-year-old right-hander Chuck Estrada (3-1). Estrada was in his fifth, and final year, of pitching for Baltimore. He would be finished as a player by the end of the 1967 season. New York employed three pitchers with the loss going to Pete Mikkelsen (4-2), who came on in relief of Sheldon in the eighth inning. Even though there were 17 runs and 26 hits, the game was played in a rather speedy 2 hours and 23 minutes. The pitchers combined for only four bases on balls in the game.

In celebration of Independence Day, the Houston Colt 45s were at home against the Pittsburgh Pirates on Saturday, July 4. In the second inning, Houston took a 1-0 lead on a solo home run by right fielder Joe Gaines, his 4th of the season. Houston added two runs in the fourth and the Pirates remained scoreless until the top of the eighth, when they managed one run driven in by shortstop Gene Alley. The final totals were 3 runs, 7 hits, no errors for Houston and 1 run, 4 hits and 1 error for Pittsburgh. Going all the way for the win, was Houston right-hander Bob Bruce (9-4). Bruce was on his way to complete the year with 15 wins, 9 losses, and a 2.76 earned run average. Veteran Pirates' hurler Bob Friend (6-8) took the loss. Friend allowed three runs and five hits in five innings pitched. There were 13,692 fans in the stands to see the holiday affair at Houston. With the season nearly half complete and with the All-Star break approaching, Houston improved to a record of 37 wins and 42 losses. Pittsburgh fell to 39-35.

The 36th All-Star game took place on Tuesday, July 7, at Shea Stadium, home of the National League New York Mets, before a crowd numbering 50,850. Starting pitchers were Dean Chance of the Los Angeles Angels and Don Drysdale of the Los Angeles Dodgers. After the American League scored one run in the first inning, the National League established a 2 to 1 lead, thanks to home runs by Billy Williams of the Chicago Cubs and Ken Boyer of the St. Louis Cardinals. Two runs in the sixth and a single run in the seventh gave the American League a 4 to 3 lead going into the last of the ninth. Boston Red Sox closer Dick Radatz was on the mound, when the Giants' Willie Mays walked, stole second, and then scored on a single to tie the game. Following another walk and with two men out, Philadelphia Phillies' outfielder Johnny Callison slammed a three-run homer to right field to win it for the National League 7 to 4. Juan Marichal of the San Francisco Giants was credited with the win and the loss was charged to Radatz, who had surrendered the winning home run.

As the season continued in early July, Baltimore had won 10 of 13 games to extend its lead over the second place Yankees to three and one-half games. The Orioles win number 50 against 28 losses came on Thursday, July 9, over the Indians in game two of a doubleheader at Cleveland by a 2 to 1 margin. Baltimore also claimed the victory in the first game in a close 4 to 3 contest. In American League standings, the Yankees trailed with a record of 46-31 with the White Sox one game further behind at 44-31. Starters Milt Pappas for Baltimore and Sam McDowell for Cleveland were locked in a scoreless tie through six innings of the day's second game. In the seventh, the Indians picked up a run driven in by their 24-year-old rookie second baseman Chico Salmon. The Orioles tied the game in the eighth, and then won it in the top of the ninth inning on a solo homer by right fielder Sam Bowens, his 7th of the season, off losing pitcher Sam McDowell (3-3). Bowens would go on to finish the 1964 season with 22 home runs along with an average of .263. The winning pitcher for the Orioles was Harvey Haddix (3-2), who gave up no hits and recorded four strikeouts over the last two innings, in relief of Pappas. Haddix was a veteran National Leaguer at age 39, and was in his first year with Baltimore. He posted a record of 5 wins and 5 losses for the 1964 season, with an ERA of 2.31 runs per game in 49 relief appearances. Meanwhile over in the National League, the Philadelphia Phillies with a record of 48-28 maintained a lead of one and one-half games over the second place San Francisco Giants, with Pittsburgh and Cincinnati each seven and one-half games back.

On Wednesday, July 25, the Orioles narrowly edged the Washington Senators 5 to 4 at Memorial Stadium in Baltimore. The Orioles had to come from behind to score four runs in the bottom of the eighth inning for the win. Journeyman catcher Don Leppert had hit a two-run homer, his 3rd of the season, for Washington in the fourth inning to give the Senators a 4 to 1 lead. Relief pitchers were involved in the decision for both clubs. The winner for Baltimore was 37-year-old Stu Miller (5-5). Miller worked an inning and two-third, giving up only three Washington hits. Thirty-two-year-old right-hander Ron Kline (5-6) gave up the lead run in the eighth and took the loss for the Senators. After this win, the Orioles had won 60 and lost 37, which gave them a one game lead over the Yankees and a two game margin over the Chicago White Sox. Washington was in tenth place with 37 wins and 65 losses.

At Memorial Stadium on Tuesday, August 11, Baltimore managed a one run victory over the Boston Red Sox by a score of 8 to 7. The win moved the Orioles to 70-43, which was one game ahead of Chicago at 69-44 and three and one-half games in front of the third place Yankees. The winner for Baltimore in relief was veteran Dick Hall (8-1). Hall would complete the season with 9 wins, 1 loss, and an ERA of 1.85 in 45 games. Hall allowed one Red Sox run in three innings pitched. The loser for Boston was their relief workhorse Dick Radatz (10-7), who surrendered two runs in two and one-third innings pitched. In the game the Red Sox outhit Baltimore by fourteen to eight. Helping to propel the Orioles to the win, were three big home runs. In the fourth inning Sam Bowens hit his 14th homer of the year with one on base, third baseman Brooks Robinson hit his 16th with one runner on in the sixth, and in the seventh Boog Powell slammed his 30th with one on and two out. Powell's blast made the score 8 to 6 in favor of the Orioles. In the eighth inning, Boston did pick up one run to pull within 8 to 7, but that was the final score. In a losing effort for Boston, Dick Stuart had four hits in four at bats and two runs batted in.

Chicago and Baltimore ended the month on Sunday, August 30, with a White Sox 3-0 shutout at Memorial Stadium in Baltimore before a crowd of 22,339. The line score was 3 runs, 7 hits, 3 errors for Chicago and no runs, 5 hits and no errors for the Orioles. Joel Horlen (10-8) of Chicago was the winner. He pitched the first seven innings of the game with nine strikeouts. Horlen pitched in the Major Leagues for twelve years beginning in 1961. He retired at age 35 with a total of 116 wins, 117 losses, and an ERA of 3.11 runs per game. Hoyt Wilhem worked the last one and one-third innings for his 20th save of the season. The loser for Baltimore was Robin Roberts (11-6). There was one home run in the game by White Sox first baseman Bill Skowron, his 15th of the season. Skowron had been traded to Chicago from the Washington Senators the previous month, on July 13. Following this contest, Baltimore at 79-52 led Chicago at 80-54 by one-half game. The Yankees trailed by three games at 75-54. In the National League, Philadelphia enjoyed a five and one-half game lead over Cincinnati, six and one-half games over the Giants, and a seven full game advantage over the St. Louis Cardinals.

On Wednesday, September 16, in New York, the Yankees won their 85th game with a win over the Los Angeles Angels. The line score read 9 runs, 9 hits, 1 error for the Yankees and 4 runs, 8 hits and 2 errors for the Angels. After a scoreless first three innings, New York struck first with three runs in the bottom of the fourth inning, which the Angels quickly matched with three runs in the top of the fifth. This included a two-run home run by Angels' fifth inning pinch-hitter Tom Satriano, his 1st of the year. In a ten-year baseball career mostly with the Angels, Satriano had an average of .225 with 25 home runs. With the score tied at three each, the winning runs were produced by Roger Maris in the sixth inning, with his two-run homer, number 22 of the 1964 season. The Yankees then led 5 to 3 and went on for the 9 to 4 victory. The winner for New York was Jim Bouton (16-13). He worked six and one-third innings. In relief, Pedro Ramos earned his 2nd save of the season with two and two-third innings of no-hit ball. The loss for Los Angeles was charged to 26-year-old middle reliever Aubrey Gatewood, who pitched three innings and surrendered the Maris home run. The win improved the Yankees' record to 85 wins and 59 losses. This was the first of eleven consecutive wins for New York. The loss dropped the Angels to 76-73 for the season.

In the National League at Dodger Stadium on Sunday, September 20, Philadelphia won their 90th game against 60 losses by a score of 3 to 2 over Los Angeles. This put them six and one-half games ahead of both Cincinnati and St. Louis with twelve games left to play. Jim Bunning (18-5) of the Phillies, went all nine innings for the win. Bunning allowed five hits and had six strikeouts. Both of the Dodgers' runs came in the last of the ninth inning and were unearned. The losing pitcher for L.A. was starter Jim Brewer (2-3), who gave up two runs in the first inning and one run in the fourth. The only extra base hit in the game was a double by Philadelphia second baseman Tony Taylor, his 11th double of the season. Dodgers' shortstop Maury Wills had two hits and also his 49th stolen base of the year. The line score read 3 runs, 8 hits, 2 errors for Philadelphia and 2 runs, 5 hits and 4 errors for Los Angeles.

After September 20, for some unknown reason, the Phillies season just fell apart and they went into a swoon from which there was no recovery. They lost their next ten games in a row, before winning their final two ballgames at Cincinnati. The streak included being swept by St. Louis in a three game series at St. Louis on September 28-30. On the other hand, after September 20, the Cardinals won ten out of their last thirteen games including the three game sweep over Philadelphia. On the last day of the season, Sunday, October 4, the Cardinals' 11 to 5 win over the New York Mets at St. Louis clinched the pennant by only one game over both Philadelphia and Cincinnati. The Cardinals scored runs in five out of the eight innings in which they came to bat. There were Cardinals' home runs by Bill White, his 21st, in the sixth inning, and by center fielder Curt Flood, his 5th, in the eighth inning. Also 23-year-old catcher Tim McCarver for St. Louis had three hits in four at bats and three runs batted in. For the Mets, third baseman Charley Smith hit his 20th home run of the year in the fourth inning. The winning pitcher in middle relief for the Cardinals was right-hander Bob Gibson (19-12), who pitched four innings and gave up two runs in the game. The loser was starter Galen Cisco (6-19), who gave up five runs in four innings pitched for the Mets. St. Louis ended the 1964 season at 93-69. Philadelphia and Cincinnati both ended 92-70 in a tie for second place honors.

For some perspective on the long season, St. Louis played their 81st game on July 10. At that point in the season, the Cardinals had 40 wins and 41 losses. In the second half of the season, they dramatically improved to 53 and 28. By contrast, Philadelphia over the first half of the season managed to go 49-32 and then over the last half tailed off to 43-38. Over the same periods, the Cincinnati Reds were 43-37 in the first half and 49-33 in the second half of the season. So the Cardinals staged an amazing comeback over the last two and one-half months. They were helped along, not only by the unexpected Philadelphia ten game losing streak, but also by the Phillies' wins over the Reds in the last two games of the season.

In the American League, the race in 1964 also went down to the wire with the relentless New York Yankees prevailing once again. At the end of August, Baltimore led the White Sox by one-half game and New York by three full games. For the rest of the season beginning on September 1, New York went 24-9, Chicago went 18-10, and Baltimore went 18-13. When the dust finally settled, New York finished 99-63, Chicago was 98-64, and Baltimore ended 97-65. No team had really collapsed. None of the three played badly; but the Yankees had just enough momentum to finish on top for the fifth year in a row. The matchup for the World Series was set. It would be the New York Yankees versus the St. Louis Cardinals.

The American League batting title was won by rookie Tony Oliva of the Minnesota Twins with an average of .323. He was followed by Brooks Robinson of Baltimore at .317 and Elston Howard of the Yankees at .313. The Twins' Harmon Killebrew hit the most home runs with 49. Boog Powell of the Orioles had 39 and New York's Mickey Mantle had 35. The league leader in runs batted in was Brooks Robinson with 118. He was closely followed by Dick Stuart of Boston with 114. Killebrew and Mantle finished the season tied for third with 111 each. In team batting average, the leader was the Boston Red Sox with .258. In power numbers, the Minnesota Twins topped the league with 221 home runs and the Twins also scored the most runs with 737 for the season.

Two pitchers in the American League, Dean Chance of the Los Angeles Angels and Gary Peters of the Chicago White Sox, won exactly 20 games. Dean Chance had the lowest earned run average with 1.65, followed by Joel Horlen of the White Sox at 1.88, and the Yankees' Whitey Ford with

2.13 runs per game. Four pitchers struck out more than 200 hitters for the year. These were Al Downing of the Yankees with 217, Camilo Pascual of Minnesota with 213, Chance with 207, and Peters with 205. The Chicago White Sox pitching staff finished with the lowest ERA of 2.73 runs per game. Cleveland Indians' pitchers led with 1,162 strikeouts. The Chicago pitchers allowed the least number of hits at 1,216.

The National League batting champion was Roberto Clemente of the Pittsburgh Pirates with an average of .339. Three teammates from the Milwaukee Braves were next. These were Rico Carty with .330, Henry Aaron with .328, and Joe Torre with .321. Willie Mays of San Francisco was the leader in home runs with 49, followed by Billy Williams of the Chicago Cubs with 33. In runs batted in, the league leader was Ken Boyer of the Cardinals at 119. He was followed by Ron Santo of the Cubs with 114 and Willie Mays at 111. The Milwaukee Braves were first among National League teams in batting average with .272 and in total runs scored for the season with 803. The San Francisco Giants hit the most home runs with 165.

In pitching, right-hander Larry Jackson of the Chicago Cubs led the National League with 24 wins. Juan Marichal of San Francisco won 21 and Ray Sadecki of St. Louis won 20. Left-hander Sandy Koufax of the Los Angeles Dodgers had the lowest earned run average by a wide margin, with 1.74. His teammate Don Drysdale was second with 2.18, followed closely at 2.20 by Chris Short of the Philadelphia Phillies. Bob Veale of the Pittsburgh Pirates had the most strikeouts with 250. He was followed by Bob Gibson of St. Louis with 245, and Drysdale at 237 for the year. The best team earned run average was by the Dodgers at 2.96. The Dodgers' pitchers also allowed the fewest base hits over the season with 1,289. In strikeouts, the pitching staff of the Cincinnati Reds led the league with 1,122.

The 1964 Most Valuable Player designation in the American League was awarded to Brooks Robinson, third baseman of the Baltimore Orioles. The 1964 Orioles finished in third place, only two games behind the Yankees. Robinson, who cleaned up nearly everything hit his way at third base, had the best season in his career so far with 28 home runs and an average of .317. The Rookie of the Year was 26-year-old Cuban-born Tony Oliva from the Minnesota Twins. Third baseman Ken Boyer of the National League champion St. Louis Cardinals was chosen as National League MVP. Boyer appeared in all 162 Cardinals games during 1964. Dick Allen, age 22, of the Philadelphia Phillies was National League Rookie of the Year. He also appeared in all 162 games of the Phillies season and batted .318 with 29 home runs. The Cy Young Award as baseball's best pitcher went to 23-year-old Dean Chance of the Los Angeles Angels. Chance won 20 games and lost only 9 for a winning percentage of .690. The Award remained in Los Angeles for the third straight year following two years of Dodgers' pitching success.

The 1964 baseball season was the last of a period of five consecutive years, from 1960 through 1964, in which the New York Yankees were the dominant American League team. The Yankees won the American League pennant each of those years and had two seasons, 1961 and 1963, with more than 100 wins. As illustrated in Figure 2, over the five years New York won 63.0% of its games followed in order by the Chicago White Sox with 56.1%, the Baltimore Orioles with 55.4%, the Detroit Tigers with 52.6%, and the Minnesota Twins with 51.3%. The teams winning less than half their games were the Cleveland Indians with 48.9%, the Los Angeles Angels with 47.7%, the Boston Red Sox with 45.7%, the Kansas City Athletics with 40.1%, and the Washington Senators with 39.0%. By 1964 Yankees' star players Mickey Mantle and Roger Maris were being slowed down by nagging injuries and other key players like Yogi Berra, Bill Skowron, Hank Bauer, Tony Kubek, Elston Howard, and Whitey Ford were either on the verge of retiring or had moved on to other teams. Improved competition from other contenders made it difficult for the Yankees to sustain their customary high level of play over the next few years.

If the American League was dominated by one franchise over these five years, then the situation in the National League was exactly the opposite. In each of the five years a different team won the National League pennant. As shown in Figure 2, on an overall basis Los Angeles had the best results. The Dodgers won 56.7% of its games, followed by the San Francisco Giants with 55.8%, the Cincinnati Reds and the St. Louis Cardinals both with 54.9%, the Milwaukee Braves with 54.0%, and the Pittsburgh Pirates with 52.6%. Among the four other teams, the Philadelphia Phillies won 46.2%, followed by the Chicago Cubs with 42.9%, the Houston Colt 45s with 40.5%, and lagging much further behind, the New York Mets with 29.8%. Houston and New York were the National League expansion teams that began play in 1962. The Mets had lost 120 games in 1962, 111 games in 1963, and 109 games in 1964, an improvement each year. A one hundred win season in the National League had been achieved only in 1962 by San Francisco and Los Angeles. This was the year the National League pennant was decided in the dramatic three game playoff series won by the Giants.

The 1964 World Series would open in the home of the National League winner, the St. Louis Cardinals. The Cardinals were making their first appearance in the Series since 1946. The veteran Yankees were in the Series for the fifth consecutive year and for the ninth time in the last ten years. A comparison of the two teams' major players is as follows.

CATCHER - New York, Elston Howard, 35, and St. Louis, Tim McCarver, 23. Howard, in his tenth year with the Yankees, batted .313 with 15 home runs. McCarver had first been with St. Louis at the age of 18, but this was his second season as the Redbirds' regular catcher. In 143 games he averaged .288 with 9 home runs. The advantage goes to New York.

FIRST BASE - New York, Joe Pepitone, 24, and St. Louis, Bill White, 30. In his third year with New York, Pepitone batted only .251 but hit 28 home runs and drove in 100 runs. White had been with the Cardinals since 1959. In 160 games, he hit 21 home runs and had a .303 batting average. This was the fourth consecutive year for St. Louis in which White hit 20 or more homers. Advantage leans to St. Louis.

SECOND BASE - New York, Bobby Richardson, 29, and St. Louis, Dal Maxvill, 25. 1964 was the sixth year for Richardson as the Yankees' regular at second base. His batting average was .267 in 159 games. Maxvill was the replacement for the injured Cardinals' second baseman, Julian Javier. Maxvill had batted .231 in only 26 times at bat in the regular season. Edge is with the Yankees on the basis of experience.

SHORTSTOP - New York, Phil Linz, 25, and St. Louis, Dick Groat, 34. Linz, in his third season with New York, batted .250 with 5 home runs in 112 games. Groat had been the shortstop for the 1960 World Series winner Pittsburgh Pirates and the 1960 National League MVP. This was his second year with the Cardinals. He batted .292 in 161 games during the 1964 regular season. The Cardinals have the advantage.

THIRD BASE - New York, Clete Boyer, 27, and St. Louis, Ken Boyer, 33. These two individuals were brothers. Clete was in his sixth year with the Yankees and suffered a decline in his offensive production. In 147 games, he batted .218 and had 8 home runs. His older brother, Ken, had been with the Cardinals since 1955. He hit 24 home runs with a batting average of .295 and appeared in all 162 games. This was the seventh year in a row that he had hit at least 23 home runs. Ken Boyer was a clubhouse leader for St. Louis and could also be an impact player. Advantage to St. Louis.

LEFT FIELD - New York, Tom Tresh, 26, and St. Louis, Lou Brock, 25. Tresh, in his third full year with New York, had 16 home runs and a batting average of .246 in 153 games. These statistics were down, compared to his first two years. In 1964, Brock came over to the Cardinals in a trade from the Chicago Cubs in time to play in 103 games for St. Louis. Brock batted .348 and had 33 stolen bases. He was a key player in the Cardinals' pennant drive in the second half of the season. Advantage to St. Louis.

CENTER FIELD - New York, Roger Maris, 30, and St. Louis, Curt Flood, 26. Maris was healthy enough to be able to play a more complete season than in the previous year. He finished with a batting average of .281 and 26 home runs in 141 games. Flood had been a member of the Cardinals since 1958. He played in all 162 games and batted .311. In three of the last four seasons, his batting average had exceeded the magic .300 level. The two are rated even.

RIGHT FIELD - New York, Mickey Mantle, 33, and St. Louis, Mike Shannon, 25. Mantle and Maris switched outfield positions for the World Series. Mantle was also able to play a more complete season for the Yankees in 1964. He batted .303, hit 35 home runs, and had 111 runs batted in over 143 games. Shannon, in 88 games for St. Louis, hit .261 with 9 home runs. The advantage is with New York.

STARTING PITCHING - For New York: Whitey Ford, 36, won 17, lost 6. Mel Stottlemyre, 23, won 9, lost 3. Jim Bouton, 25, won 18, lost 13. For St. Louis: Bob Gibson, 29, won 19, lost 12. Curt Simmons, 35, won 18, lost 9. Ray Sadecki, 24, won 20, lost 11. It appeared that both teams had solid pitching. Rated even.

MANAGERS - New York, Yogi Berra, 39, and St. Louis, Johnny Keane, 53. Berra had just retired as an active player with the New York Yankees at the end of the 1963 season. This was his first year as the team's manager. Keane never actually played in Major League Baseball. After several years of coaching and managing in the minor leagues, he became manager of the St. Louis Cardinals midway through the 1961 season.

INTERLUDE - YOGI BERRA

Yogi Berra was born May 12, 1925, in an Italian section of St. Louis, Missouri called "the Hill." His career in baseball with the New York Yankees spanned the years from 1946 through 1963. His peak playing years were prior to the 1957 season. He was the American League Most Valuable Player for 1951, 1954, and 1955. Berra possessed a remarkable ability to hit pitches that were out of the strike zone. At the plate, he did not strike out very much. Five times in his career in the years of 1950, 1951, 1952, 1955, and 1956, he had more home runs than strikeouts. In his career, he hit 358 home runs and struck out 414 times. His real name is Lawrence Peter Berra, but he is far better known as "Yogi" which became the inspiration for the cartoon character Yogi Bear. Berra is probably one of the most quoted individuals in history in any vocation. His most well-known quote is probably, "it ain't over, 'til it's over."

From 1947 through 1963, Berra appeared in fourteen World Series. He totaled 71 hits, including 12 home runs, in 259 times at bat for a batting average of .274. After his playing career, Berra was a Major League manager and coach. He managed the Yankees during the 1964 season. He also was the manager of the New York Mets from 1972-1975, and led them to the World Series in 1973. Later, he was manager of the Yankees again for 1984 and the early portion of 1985.

With a record of 99-63, New York prevailed in the American League race by one game over Chicago and by two games over Baltimore. The Yankees best month of the season was September at 22-6. At their best, they were

15-3 against Cleveland, but lost the season series to Baltimore 10 games to 8. St. Louis finished 93-69 in the National League to win the pennant by one game over Philadelphia and Cincinnati. The Cardinals played better as the season wore on. In August, they were 18-10 and then 21-8 in September. The Cardinals won 13 and lost 5 against Philadelphia, but they were only 8-10 in games against both Cincinnati and Los Angeles.

Game one of the 1964 World Series took place on Wednesday, October 7, at Sportsman's Park in St. Louis with Yogi Berra as Yankees' manager. After five innings, the Yankees led the game by 4 to 2 behind the pitching of left-hander Whitey Ford, and aided by a second inning two-run homer hit by left fielder Tom Tresh. The Cardinals rallied in the last of the sixth inning by scoring four runs to take a 6 to 4 lead, with the major blow coming on a two-run home run off Ford by right fielder Mike Shannon. In the eighth inning, the Yankees added one more run, but the Cardinals scored three unearned runs to go on for a 9 to 5 victory. The winning pitcher for St. Louis was starter Ray Sadecki (1-0), who went six innings and held New York to four runs on eight hits and five bases on balls. Reliever Barney Schultz came on to finish the last three innings for the Cardinals and gave up one run on four hits to earn the save. The loss for New York was charged to Ford (0-1), who surrendered the lead run in the decisive sixth inning. Because of an arm injury, Ford's game one effort turned out to be his only appearance in the 1964 Series. The line score read 9 runs, 12 hits and no errors for St. Louis and 5 runs, 12 hits and 2 errors for New York.

The next day Thursday, October 8, the Yankees evened the Series at one game each with an 8 to 3 win behind the pitching of rookie Mel Stottlemyre (1-0). Game three, at Yankee Stadium on Saturday, October 10, resulted in a close one run victory for New York by a score of 2 to 1. Mickey Mantle slammed a dramatic home run in the last of the ninth, off Cardinals' reliever Barney Schultz (0-1) to break a 1 to 1 deadlock for the win. The winning pitcher was right-hander Jim Bouton (1-0). After three games, the Yankees led the Series two games to one.

The fourth game on Sunday, October 11, was a pivotal contest in the Series. At Yankee Stadium, the Yankees opened the scoring by picking up three runs off St. Louis starter Ray Sadecki in the bottom of the first inning. Sadecki was relieved by veteran pitcher Roger Craig after only one third of an inning.

The Yankees still led 3-0 after five innings, behind the pitching of southpaw Al Downing. Then, in the top of the sixth, the Cardinals exploded by scoring four runs to take the lead on a clutch grand slam home run by their third baseman, Ken Boyer. That was all the scoring there was in the ballgame and the Series stood all tied up at two wins apiece. For St. Louis, relievers Roger Craig and Ron Taylor combined to shut out the Yankees over the final eight and two-third innings, giving up only two hits and recording ten strikeouts. Craig (1-0) received credit for the win with the loss charged to Downing (0-1). Both teams had six hits in the game which was played in 2 hours and 18 minutes.

It took ten innings for the Cardinals to win the fifth game at Yankee Stadium on October 12, by a score of 5 to 2. Bob Gibson (1-1) worked all ten innings for the win. The winning runs came home in the top half of the extra frame on a three-run homer by catcher Tim McCarver. After a day off for travel, the Series resumed in St. Louis on Wednesday, October 14. New York squared the Series with an 8 to 3 victory, highlighted by home runs hit by Mantle, Maris, and Pepitone. Jim Bouton (2-0) picked up his second win of the Series for New York. This made a seventh game necessary, to be played the next day.

In game seven, on October 15, the final score was St. Louis 7 and New York 5. The St. Louis Cardinals were 1964 World Series champions. After three scoreless innings at the start of the game, the Cardinals took a 6-0 lead, with three runs in the fourth and three in the fifth. Left fielder Lou Brock homered for one of the Cardinals' runs in the fifth. In the sixth, the Yankees cut the deficit in half on a three-run home run by Mickey Mantle off seventh game starter Bob Gibson. After six innings, the Cardinals led 6 to 3. In the seventh, Ken Boyer, the fourth game hero, made it 7 to 3 with a solo home run. In the ninth inning, the Yankees tried to rally with two solo home runs by Clete Boyer and Phil Linz. But Cardinals' pitcher Bob Gibson (2-1) held on for the 7 to 5 complete game win. New York used five pitchers in the game with the loss being charged to starter Mel Stottlemyre (1-1).

It was a World Series that featured both good pitching and good hitting. Two of the seven ballgames were decided by only one run, and none of the others were blowouts. The Cardinals won two of three in New York and the teams split the four games in St. Louis. It seemed like it could have gone either way.

The Cardinals hit .254 as a team compared to .251 for the Yankees. The Cardinals' Tim McCarver hit .478 for the Series and Lou Brock, hit .300. Ken Boyer batted only .222 in the Series but his grand slam produced the winning runs in game four, and he also hit a timely home run in game seven. The Yankees out-homered the Cardinals in the Series by 10 to 5, including 3 home runs by Mickey Mantle in what would be his last World Series. Mantle's ninth inning blast won game three for New York. Yankees' second baseman Bobby Richardson turned in another fine Series performance with a .406 batting average. St. Louis pitcher Bob Gibson won 2 games (games five and seven), lost 1, and recorded 31 strikeouts in 27 innings pitched. His earned run average was exactly 3.00 runs per game. The other St. Louis wins were by Ray Sadecki in game one, and by Roger Craig in a key relief appearance in the fourth game. New York's Jim Bouton pitched well and was the winner in 2 games with an overall earned run average of 1.56. The Yankees' other win was by rookie Mel Stottlemyre, who had an earned run average of 3.15 for the Series.

1964 WORLD SERIES SUMMARY

Game 1	At St. Louis	Cardinals 9, Yankees 5
Game 2	At St. Louis	Yankees 8, Cardinals 3
Game 3	At New York	Yankees 2, Cardinals 1
Game 4	At New York	Cardinals 4, Yankees 3
Game 5	At New York	Cardinals 5, Yankees 2
Game 6	At St. Louis	Yankees 8, Cardinals 3
Game 7	At St. Louis	Cardinals 7, Yankees 5

ST. LOUIS WINS THE WORLD SERIES BY 4 GAMES TO 3.

Given the success of both the Cardinals and the Yankees in the 1964 season, a surprising development occurred the day after the World Series was over. This was the resignation of Johnny Keane from his position as manager of the Cardinals, along with the simultaneous firing of Yogi Berra as manager of the New York Yankees. There had been evident dissatisfaction with Keane and Berra among the St. Louis and New York front offices, as the 1964 season had progressed. Then, a few days later on October 20, the announcement was made that Keane had accepted the position as Yankees manager for the 1965 season. Berra, for his part, moved over to the New York Mets to coach under his old mentor, Mets manager Casey Stengel.

INTERLUDE - KEN BOYER

Ken Boyer was a long-time leader for the St. Louis Cardinals on and off the field. Boyer was with the Cardinals, primarily at third base, from his rookie year in 1955 through the 1965 season. He completed his playing career from 1966 through 1969 with the Mets, White Sox, and Dodgers. Boyer was born on May 20, 1931, in Liberty, Missouri. His younger brother, Clete Boyer, who was also a third baseman played for the New York Yankees and Atlanta Braves. In his fifteen-year career, Ken Boyer had 2,143 hits, 282 home runs, and retired with a lifetime average of .287.

In the twelve seasons spanning 1957 through 1968, Boyer accumulated 1,814 hits, 238 home runs, and batted .288. He was very consistent in his play and had a batting average of over .300 for four consecutive years, from 1958 through 1961, with a peak of .329 for 1961. In 1964 with the Cardinals' pennant winning and World Series success, Boyer won the National League Most Valuable Player Award with 24 home runs, a .295 batting average, and a league leading 119 runs batted in. Boyer averaged only .222 against the Yankees in the 1964 World Series, but it was his fourth game grand slam home run at Yankee Stadium that helped turn the Series around in favor of St. Louis. In ten career All-Star games Boyer hit .348 and hit two home runs in 1960 and 1964.

Dodger Blue Seems Routine

T he first meeting of the 1965 season between the Houston Astros (formerly the Colt 45s) and the New York Mets took place at Shea Stadium in New York on Wednesday, April 14. It was the second game of the new season for both teams which began together as the National League expansion clubs for 1962. Starting pitchers were Turk Farrell for Houston and the veteran Warren Spahn for the Mets. Spahn had been released by the Milwaukee Braves in the offseason and this would be his last season as an active player. After the regulation nine innings, the game was tied at three runs each. In the eleventh inning, Houston scored four runs, only to have the Mets come close to tying the game with three runs of their own. The final score was in the books as Astros 7, Mets 6. Farrell (1-0) lasted ten and one-third innings to get credit for the win. He gave up four runs on seven hits and struck out eight. Spahn did not figure in the decision. He worked eight innings and allowed three runs on seven hits. The loss for the Mets went to Larry Bearnarth (0-1), who walked three and gave up four unearned runs in the top of the eleventh inning. There were three home runs in the game by the Mets. They were all the player's first homer of the year. These were by Ed Kranepool in the fourth inning, Joe Christopher in the ninth, and Ron Swoboda in the eleventh inning. Houston catcher Ron Brand had two hits in five at bats with three runs batted in. Houston evened their record at 1-1, and the Mets lost their second straight game to go 0-2.

The Los Angeles Dodgers began the season by winning ten out of their first fifteen games. The Dodgers' tenth win came on April 30, at Dodger Stadium in a 6 to 3 decision over San Francisco. The Dodgers, uncharacteristically, made five errors in the game, but the errors resulted in only one unearned run off starter Sandy Koufax. Koufax worked the first five innings, struck out seven, and gave up three runs, two of which were earned. After six innings, the game was tied at three runs each, but L.A. scored two in the seventh and one in the eighth inning for the winning margin. Each team had one home run in the game. For Los Angeles, center fielder Willie Davis hit his 2nd of the season in the eighth and Giants' reserve catcher, Jack Hiatt, hit his 1st and only homer of the 1965 season in the second inning. The winning pitcher in relief for Los Angeles was right-hander Bob Miller (1-0). Miller pitched the last four innings and gave up no runs and only two Giants' base hits. The loser for the Giants in relief was Bobby Bolin (0-3). Bolin would go on to finish the season with 14 wins, 6 losses, and an earned run average of 2.76 runs per game. The Dodgers maintained an early season one-half game lead in the standings over both Cincinnati and Houston, with the win. The early season attendance at Dodger Stadium was 48,586.

INTERLUDE - WILLIE DAVIS AND TOMMY DAVIS

Los Angeles Dodgers' center fielder Willie Davis played an important part in the World Series winning Dodgers teams of 1963 and 1965. Davis was born April 15, 1940, in Mineral Springs, Arkansas but grew up in Los Angeles, California. He broke in with the Dodgers in 1960, and remained with them through the season of 1973. He finished his career in stints with the Expos, Rangers, Cardinals, Padres, and Angels, finally retiring after the 1979 season. Overall he accumulated 2,561 hits, 182 home runs, 398 stolen bases, and finished with a .279 lifetime batting average.

In the period from 1960 through 1968, Willie Davis batted .266 with a low of .238 in 1965 and a high of .318 in his rookie year of 1960. He managed 216 stolen bases in this period with a peak in 1964 of 42. In three World Series with Los Angeles in 1963, 1965, and 1966, Davis had 9 hits in 54 at bats for an average of .167. He stole three bases in the 1965 Series against the Minnesota Twins. In the second game of the 1966 Series, he, unfortunately, committed three costly errors in center field against the Orioles. Later in his career, Davis appeared in the All-Star games of 1971 and 1973 and was a perfect three hits in three times at bat, including one home run in the 1973 Summer Classic.

Tommy Davis was also an important part of those Los Angeles Dodgers ball clubs of the nineteen-sixties. Many fans thought that Willie and Tommy Davis were brothers, but they were not related. Tommy Davis was born on March 21, 1939, in Brooklyn, New York. He appeared in one game with the

Dodgers in 1959 and then was with them from 1960 through 1966, primarily playing in left field. He spent 1967 with the New York Mets and 1968 with the Chicago White Sox. Overall, in the seasons from 1959 through 1968, he had a batting average of .300 and in the process accumulated 1,208 hits and 110 home runs. In three of his years with L.A. he batted over .300. For two seasons, in 1962 and 1963, he was the National League batting champion, with .346 and .326, respectively. Then in 1966, he hit .313. In 1963 and 1966 World Series play with the Dodgers he had an average of .348 in eight games. In 1965 he was sidelined for the majority of the season due to injury and was unable to play in the Series. In the All-Star games of 1962 and 1963, he managed one hit in eight times at bat for a .125 batting average. For the remainder of his baseball career, from 1969 through 1976, Davis spent time with seven other Major League teams, most notably the Baltimore Orioles, for the three complete seasons of 1973 through 1975. His lifetime total hits increased to 2,121 for an average of .294.

On May 15, at Dodger Stadium, Los Angeles picked up win number 20, against only 9 losses, with an improbable win over the Chicago Cubs by a score of 3 to 1. The Cubs took a 1-0 lead in the fourth inning with a run driven in by third baseman Ron Santo. The score remained 1-0 until the last of the eighth. The pitcher for the Cubs was left-hander Dick Ellsworth, who had a no-hitter going against L.A. through seven complete innings. In the eighth, following an error by third baseman Santo and a walk, Dodgers' pinch-hitter Al Ferrara hit a three-run homer to win the game. It would be his only home run of the season. Ellsworth (3-3), who allowed only the one Dodgers' hit, took the loss for the Cubs. All three runs against him were unearned. The starter for the Dodgers, Claude Osteen, went seven and two-third innings and allowed just one run. Bob Miller (3-1) received credit for the win by getting the last out of the top of the eighth in relief of Osteen. After this win, L.A. was in first place with a two and one-half game lead over the Cincinnati Reds at 17-11. Meanwhile over in the American League, early season results had the Chicago White Sox at 19-8 leading the second place Minnesota Twins by one-half game.

In the game played at St. Louis on Wednesday, June 2, the Dodgers defeated the Cardinals 4 to 1. The win extended the Dodgers record to 30 wins and 17 losses, which was four games in front of both the Cincinnati Reds and the San Francisco Giants in the standings. Don Drysdale (9-3) worked the first six innings and gave up one run on five hits for the win. Ron Perranoski pitched the final three innings for his first save of the season. For Los Angeles, catcher Johnny Roseboro hit his 1st home run of the year in the fifth inning and right fielder Wally Moon followed with his 1st homer in the ninth. The Dodgers scored single runs in the first, fifth, seventh, and ninth innings to outpace the Cardinals single run in the third. Dodgers' shortstop Maury Wills stole two bases, his 31st and 32nd of the season. The losing pitcher for St. Louis was right-hander Ray Washburn (3-3). Washburn yielded three runs and five hits over six and one-third innings pitched. Washburn would go on to pitch in the Major Leagues for a total of ten years, all but his last year with St. Louis. He compiled a record of 72 wins and 64 losses. In a losing cause, the Cardinals outhit the Dodgers in the game nine to eight, with 35-year-old Cardinals' shortstop Dick Groat having three hits in four at bats. The loss dropped the defending World Series champion Cardinals to 24-22, in fifth place in the Senior circuit.

Los Angeles continued to set the pace in the National League through the middle of June. On Thursday, June 17, the Dodgers shut out the Giants 3-0 for their 40th win against 23 losses. The game was witnessed by a Dodger Stadium crowd of 40,707. Dodgers' pitcher Claude Osteen (6-6) went all nine innings, and allowed only one San Francisco hit by catcher Jack Hiatt to record the win. There were no home runs in the game. L.A. scored two runs in the first inning, added one more in the third, and had seven hits. The only player with two hits was catcher Johnny Roseboro, who went two-for-four and drove in the first two Dodgers' runs. The losing pitcher for San Francisco was right-hander Gaylord Perry (6-6), who worked the first six innings of the contest. In the pennant race, the Milwaukee Braves had now risen into second place by going 11-4 over their last fifteen games. The Dodgers' lead was three and one-half games.

As the season moved toward the annual All-Star game, the Minnesota Twins won 14 of 21 games to move one and one-half games in front of second place Cleveland. On Wednesday, July 7, at Metropolitan Stadium, the Twins defeated the Boston Red Sox 5 to 2 to bring their record to 50 wins and 28 losses. The line score was 5 runs, 11 hits, no errors for the Twins and 2 runs, 5 hits and 4 errors for the Red Sox. The winning pitcher for the Twins was left-hander Jim Kaat (7-7), who lasted five and one-third innings and gave up both Boston runs. Kaat would go on to finish the 1965 season with 18 wins, 11 losses, and an earned run average of 2.83 runs per game. After Kaat left the ballgame with the score 4 to 2, relievers Johnny Klippstein and Al Worthington shut down the Boston hitters on no hits the rest of the way. The Boston loss was charged to their rookie starter Jim Lonborg (5-9). Lonborg went five innings, yielding 7 hits and 4 runs, only two of which were earned. There were no home runs in the game. Both right fielder Tony Oliva and catcher Earl Battey, of the Twins, had three hits in four at bats. The defending American League champion New York Yankees at this point were in sixth place with 40 wins and 42 losses. This record trailed the Minnesota Twins by twelve games in the pennant pursuit.

Metropolitan Stadium in Minnesota was also the home of the 1965 All-Star Classic, which took place on Tuesday, July 13. The National League came away with a one run victory by a score of 6 to 5. Starting pitchers were Juan Marichal of the San Francisco Giants and Milt Pappas of the Baltimore Orioles. The game produced five home runs. The National League had three home runs in the early innings by Willie Mays of the Giants and Joe Torre of the Braves in the first inning, and Willie Stargell of the Pirates in the second inning. There were two homers for the American League in the fifth inning, by Dick McAuliffe of the Tigers and by Harmon Killebrew of the Twins. Willie Mays walked and then scored the sixth and winning run in the top of the seventh inning for the National League. The win was credited to Sandy Koufax of the Los Angeles Dodgers with the loss charged to the Cleveland Indians' Sam McDowell. Attendance at Minnesota was 46,706. By virtue of the win, the National League took the lead in the All-Star game series with 18 wins to 17 for the American League.

INTERLUDE - JUAN MARICHAL

Juan Marichal was born in the Dominican Republic on October 20, 1937. Marichal was a right-handed pitcher. He played mostly with the San Francisco Giants, for whom he first pitched at the age of 23 in 1960. On the mound he was especially known for his trademark majestic high leg kick delivery to the plate. His combination of speed and accurate control enabled him to compile a career record of 243 wins, 142 losses, and an ERA of 2.89 runs per game. In his career, he was a twenty game winner six times, including four consecutive years from 1963 through 1966. His record during those four years was 93 wins and 35 losses. He often was overshadowed by fellow National League pitchers Sandy Koufax and Bob Gibson for postseason awards, but Marichal was every bit as effective in his own right.

In the years from 1957 through 1968, Marichal won 170 games and lost only 77. In the Giants 1962 World Series against the New York Yankees, Marichal appeared in just one game. He was the starting pitcher in the fourth game, which was a no-decision for him, eventually won by the Giants by a score of 7 to 3. The Yankees ended up winning the Series by four games to three. In All-Star game competition, Marichal pitched eighteen innings in eight appearances with an ERA of 0.50 runs per game. He was credited with being the winning pitcher in two of the games, in 1962 and 1964. In a well-publicized incident, which took place during the 1965 season, in the heat of the pennant race between the Giants and Dodgers, Marichal struck Dodgers' catcher Johnny Roseboro over the head with his bat. Fortunately, Roseboro was not seriously injured, but because of his actions, Marichal was suspended. Many years later, Roseboro advocated on behalf of Marichal in favor of his induction into the Baseball Hall of Fame.

By late July, Minnesota had increased its league lead to three and one-half games over the Orioles and four and one-half games over the Indians. On Sunday, July 25, at Memorial Stadium in Baltimore, it was the Twins over the Orioles by a score of 8 to 5. It was win number 60 for the Twins against 36 losses. The Orioles jumped on Minnesota starter Jim Kaat, for five hits and four runs in the first two innings. All of the runs were unearned. In the fourth inning, Minnesota center fielder Jimmie Hall hit his 17th home run of the year and made it a 4 to 1 game. Then the Orioles added another run in the fifth on a solo home run by third baseman Brooks Robinson, his 7th of the season. After seven complete innings, the Orioles led 5 to 1. Baltimore starting pitcher John Miller worked the first seven innings, but failed to retire even one hitter in the eighth, as the Twins scored four runs to even the score at five runs each. The big hit was a home run with two men on base by Tony Oliva, his 15th. Then in the ninth, the Twins won the game with three more runs off Baltimore veteran relief pitcher Harvey Haddix (3-1). The key hit in the ninth for Minnesota was a triple by shortstop Zoilo Versalles, his 7th of the season. Versalles would finish the 1965 season with 12 triples, which tied for the most in the American League . The Twins used five pitchers in the game, with the win credited to 36-year-old Al Worthington (7-5), who worked the eighth inning giving up only two bases on balls.

On Friday, July 30, President Lyndon Johnson signed the Medicare Act into law. The law provided federal medical and hospital insurance benefits for people over the age of 65 under the Social Security system. The program was scheduled to become effective in 1966. At County Stadium in Milwaukee that same day, the San Francisco Giants defeated the Braves 9 to 2. The Giants had 9 runs, 13 hits and 3 errors compared to 2 runs, 7 hits and no errors for the Braves. Bob Shaw (11-6) was on the mound to pick up the win for the Giants. In the complete game, Shaw gave up seven hits and struck out four. The 32-year-old right-hander would go on to complete the season with 16 wins, 9 losses, and an ERA of 2.64 runs per game. Milwaukee used five pitchers in the game, with the loss going to starter Hank Fischer (4-5). The Giants' power asserted itself with home runs from Willie McCovey, his 23rd, Tom Haller, his 8th, and Willie Mays, his 24th of the season. Attendance at County Stadium was only 6,787 and was symptomatic of the Braves planned move South to Atlanta for the next season. World Series heroes Henry Aaron and Eddie Mathews were still with the Braves, and each had one hit in four at bats in the loss. Aaron was now 31 and Mathews was 34-years old. After this win, the Giants record was 54-43 and Milwaukee's record fell to 54 wins and 44 losses.

Minnesota defeated the Boston Red Sox 9 to 3 in a game on Friday, August 6, played at Metropolitan Stadium before a somewhat larger crowd of 25,082. Rookie pitcher Jim Merritt (1-0) was the winner for the Twins. Merritt, only in his second Major League appearance, went the first six innings and gave up four hits and two runs. The game was tied at two runs each going into the last of the sixth inning. In the sixth, six big runs crossed the plate for the Twins and they were able to coast the rest of the game for the win. Starter Bill Monbouquette (8-12), who gave up five runs on ten hits in five innings pitched, absorbed the loss for the Red Sox. Second baseman Felix Mantilla homered for the Red Sox in the fourth inning, his 14th of the season. Minnesota home runs were hit by Bob Allison, number 18 in the sixth inning, and shortstop Zoilo Versalles, his 14th also in the Twins' big sixth inning. Minnesota used three pitchers in the game with southpaw Bill Pleis getting credit for his 3rd save of the year. Pleis would go on to pitch six years for the Twins and retire from baseball with 21 wins, 16 losses, and an ERA of 4.07 runs per game. The Twins were 70-38 with this win. Their lead over the second place Baltimore Orioles had expanded to six and one-half games. Meanwhile in the National League, a tighter race was taking shape for the last two months of the season. Los Angeles, at 64-47, led San Francisco and Cincinnati by only two games each and the Milwaukee Braves by just two and one-half games. Both league champions from 1964, the Yankees and the Cardinals, were well out of contention for the pennant.

On Monday, August 23, in a game which lasted ten innings at Metropolitan Stadium, it was the Twins over the New York Yankees 4 to 3. Mudcat Grant was the starter for the Twins. Grant went eight innings, gave up three runs, and did not figure in the decision. The Twins scored the winning run in the last of the tenth. The win was credited to Al Worthington (10-5), who pitched the top of the tenth, giving up two walks and one hit, but no runs. The Yankees used five pitchers in the game. Whitey Ford worked eight and one-third innings as the starter, surrendered three runs on ten hits, and struck out six. Ford would go on to finish the 1965 season with 16 wins, 13 losses, and an earned run average of 3.24. He was still quite effective at the age of 37. The winning run was scored against Jim Bouton (4-13), who took the loss for New York. There were two home runs in the game. Minnesota shortstop Zoilo Versalles, as part of a three-for-five game, hit a solo shot in the third inning, his 16th. In the seventh inning for New York, third baseman Clete Boyer hit his 14th of the year with one runner on base, which gave the Yankees a 3 to 2 lead, before the Twins tied it in the ninth to force extra innings. Attendance at this ballgame, for the first place Twins, was 37,787. For Minnesota this was win number 80 against 46 losses. Their lead over second place Chicago stood at seven and one-half games.

Over in the National League, the pennant race was considerably more clogged. On Saturday, August 28, Los Angeles doubled-up the Philadelphia Phillies 8 to 4 at Connie Mack Stadium, to raise their record to 75-56 and maintain a lead of one and one-half games over the Cincinnati Reds. In the top of the first inning, the Dodgers greeted Philadelphia starting pitcher Chris Short (14-9) by scoring seven runs. Short was removed after one-third of an inning. The Phillies were able to counter with two runs in the third and two more in the fourth inning and held off L.A. until the ninth when they added one more run. The Dodgers' Jim Brewer (3-2) picked up the win in middle relief by hurling five innings, allowing only one hit, and striking out seven. In a rare relief appearance, Sandy Koufax pitched the ninth inning. Koufax gave up just one hit and had two strikeouts. There were two home runs in the game for Philadelphia. Right fielder Johnny Callison hit his 28th in the third inning and left fielder Tony Gonzalez his 13th in the fourth inning. For the Dodgers, shortstop Maury Wills had three hits in five at bats and had two stolen bases, which brought his total for the season up to 82.

As the season continued into September, Minnesota maintained its decisive lead over the rest of the American League. At Fenway Park in Boston on Friday, September 10, the Twins defeated the Red Sox 8 to 5. This was win number 90 for the Twins, against 54 losses. After the third inning, the Twins led 5 to 2. Then each team scored three runs in the sixth for the final 8 to 5 result. The winner for Minnesota was Jim Perry (10-6). Perry worked five and one-third innings and gave up five runs, three of which were earned. Rookie Jim Merritt pitched three and two-third innings in relief, gave up only one hit, and struck out eight. The loser for Boston was 23-year-old starting pitcher Dave Morehead (9-16). The only home run in the game was by Boston right fielder Tony Conigliaro in the sixth inning, his 28th. Five of the ten Minnesota hits were doubles, including the 40th double of the season by shortstop Zoilo Versalles.

INTERLUDE - HARMON KILLEBREW

Harmon Killebrew was born in Payette, Idaho on June 29, 1936. Killebrew first played in the Major Leagues in 1954 at the age of 18 for the Washington Senators. He played in Washington for parts of eight seasons, and then in 1961 the Senators relocated to become the Minnesota Twins. Killebrew was with the Twins through the 1974 season. He spent 1975 with the Kansas City Royals before retiring as a player. He was a powerful right-handed home run hitter and the most popular of all the Minnesota Twins' players of the nineteen-sixties. In his first years in Washington through 1958, he was a part-time player, appeared in only 113 games, and hit a total of 11 home runs. He became a full-time regular in the lineup nearly every day beginning with the 1959 season. From 1959 through 1972, Killebrew was in double figures in home runs every year. His peak home run years were 1964 and 1969, with 49 each year. In 1969 he was selected as American League Most Valuable Player. In eight individual years, Killebrew hit more than 40 home runs. His home run total reached 573 for his Major League career.

Killebrew hit 388 home runs for the twelve years from 1957 through 1968. In his first four years with the Twins, he had at least 45 home runs each year. In the Twins' pennant winning year of 1965, he was injured for part of the season and his total dropped to 25. He was described as a dead pull hitter who was not particularly fast. His lifetime batting average was .256. His peak year for batting average was in 1961, his first year in Minnesota, at .288. Killebrew batted .286 with one home run in the 1965 World Series for Minnesota. In All-Star competition, Killebrew appeared in eleven games, batted .308, and homered three times in 1961, 1965, and 1971. In the field he played 969 games at first base, 791 games at third base, and 470 games in left field. He had good hands, if not good speed.

After his retirement from baseball as a player, Killebrew worked for a time in television and radio for the Minnesota Twins. Harmon Killebrew passed away from cancer in 2011 at the age of 74. His many achievements as a home run hitter in baseball were legendary, but perhaps more importantly, he was simply known as one of the kindest, humblest, soft-spoken, and most highly respected individuals, not only in baseball, but in the entire world of sports.

On Wednesday, September 29, at Baltimore, the Twins edged the Orioles 3 to 2 to go 100-59 with three games to go in the 1965 schedule. By this time, the Twins had already clinched the American League pennant and earned a place in the World Series, which would begin in Minnesota the following week. The game was played in a fast 2 hours and 7 minutes before a disappointing Baltimore crowd of only 6,928. The winning pitcher for the Twins was Mudcat Grant (21-6), who pitched eight innings and gave up two runs on eight hits. The loss for Baltimore went to starter Steve Barber

(14-10). Barber hurled all nine innings for the Orioles, surrendered eight hits, and had seven strikeouts. The 27-year-old Barber would end a fine season for Baltimore with 15 wins, 10 losses, and an ERA of 2.69 runs per game. The game winning hit came in the eighth inning on a two-run homer by left fielder Bob Allison, his 22nd home run of the season. Baltimore dropped to 92-65 for the season with the one run loss, seven full games behind the Twins.

INTERLUDE - CAMILO PASCUAL

Pitcher Camilo Pascual was born on January 20, 1934, in Havana, Cuba. His career in Major League Baseball spanned the years from 1954 through 1971 primarily with the old Washington Senators, that became the Minnesota Twins beginning with the 1961 season. In his Major League career, Pascual won 174 games, lost 170, and had a 3.63 earned run average. His most productive years were the six years from 1959 through 1964, during which he had 100 wins and 66 losses. He was a 20 game winner twice. He won 20 games in 1962 and 21 in 1963. In each year from 1961 through 1964, he had more than 200 strikeouts. He was known for throwing a sharp-breaking, overhand curve ball, reminiscent of one thrown by Sandy Koufax, but delivered right-handed. In twelve seasons from 1957 through 1968, Pascual won 158 games.

Pascual started 27 games and had a record of 9 wins, 3 losses, and an ERA of 3.35 during the Minnesota Twins pennant winning year of 1965. However, because of an injury, he won only one game that year after the month of June. In the World Series, he started the third game and took the loss after giving up three runs in his five innings pitched. Pascual appeared in three All-Star games and pitched a total of eight innings with a 3.38 earned run average. He was the losing pitcher in the 1962 game played at D.C. Stadium in Washington. Pascual worked as a baseball talent scout in the Caribbean area for three Major League clubs after his retirement as a player.

The Twins played their final game of the regular season on Sunday, October 3, at Metropolitan Stadium, where they defeated the Los Angeles Angels 3 to 2. They wound up the season with 102 wins and 60 losses. They finished in first place by seven games over the Chicago White Sox and by eight games over the Baltimore Orioles. The defending league champion Yankees finished 25 games behind at 77-85. In an effort to prepare for the World Series, Twins' pitchers Jim Kaat, Dave Boswell, Al Worthington, and Jim Perry each pitched two innings, and Johnny Klippstein worked the ninth inning against the Angels. Jim Perry (12-7) was credited with the win. Harmon Killebrew hit his 25th home run of the year with one runner on base to give the Twins a 2-0 lead in the first inning. Each team picked up a single run in the third and the Angels ended the scoring with one run in the top of the fifth inning. The losing pitcher for the Angels was 22-year-old rookie Jim McGlothlin (0-3), who worked the first five innings, gave up five hits, and all three Minnesota runs scored. First baseman Don Mincher for the Twins had two hits in four at bats and drove in the Twins' final run in the third inning. Mincher hit 22 home runs for the Twins in 1965 with a batting average of .251. His baseball career ran from 1960 through 1972, during which he had a total of 200 home runs. In the nine-year span from 1963 through 1971, he hit at least 12 home runs each year, with at least 20 in five of those years.

INTERLUDE - TONY OLIVA

Minnesota Twins' right fielder Tony Oliva was born in Pinar del Rio, Cuba on July 20, 1938. He was named American League Rookie of the Year in 1964, his first full season. He was a versatile left-handed hitter, who could hit for both power and average. He was the winner of three American League batting titles in 1964, 1965, and 1971. In a fifteen-year career all with the Twins, which spanned the years from 1962 through 1976, Oliva accumulated 1,917 hits, including 220 home runs, and an overall batting average of .304. In his rookie year of 1964, Oliva produced his highest numbers for hits with 217 and home runs with 32. In later years, he was seriously hampered by knee injuries which limited his speed and mobility.

In the 1965 World Series, Oliva recorded 5 hits in 26 at bats for a .192 average with one home run. He was selected for six All-Star games, in which he had five hits, including three doubles for a batting average of .263.

In the National League, the season ended with the Los Angeles Dodgers winning the pennant by two games over the San Francisco Giants. On September 10, the Giants had a one-half game lead over the Dodgers. In the remaining games of the season Los Angeles won 16 and lost 4, whereas, the Giants won 15 and lost 8. Thus the final standings were L.A. 97-65 and 95-67 for San Francisco. The 1964 winning St. Louis Cardinals finished far back with 80 wins and 81 losses.

The American League batting champion for the second consecutive year was Tony Oliva of the Minnesota Twins with .321. In second place was the Boston Red Sox Carl Yastrzemski at .312. Vic Davalillo of the Cleveland Indians finished third with .301. Tony Conigliaro of the Red Sox had 32 home runs to lead the league. He was followed closely by Detroit Tigers' teammates Norm Cash and Willie Horton, with 30 and 29, respectively. Two American League players had more than 100 runs batted in. Rocky Colavito of Cleveland was the leader with 108, followed by Horton at 104. Oliva finished in third place with 98. As a team, the Minnesota Twins led the league in batting average with .254 and total runs scored with 774. Power honors went to the Boston Red Sox with 165 home runs for the season.

In individual pitching, Mudcat Grant of the Minnesota Twins led the American League with 21 wins, followed by Mel Stottlemyre of the New York Yankees with 20. Jim Kaat of the Twins was next with 18. Sam McDowell of Cleveland had the lowest earned run average with 2.18. Eddie Fisher of the White Sox was next with 2.40, and Sonny Siebert of Cleveland finished third at 2.43 runs per game. McDowell was also tops in strikeouts by a large margin with 325. Mickey Lolich of the Detroit Tigers struck out 226. The Baltimore Orioles had the lowest staff ERA in the league with 2.98. The Cleveland Indians' pitchers led both in fewest hits allowed with 1,254, and in most strikeouts with 1,156.

Three veteran National Leaguers finished on top of the 1965 batting race. Roberto Clemente of Pittsburgh won with .329, followed by Henry Aaron of Milwaukee with .318, and Willie Mays of the Giants at .317. Mays topped the list in home runs with 52. His Giants' teammate Willie McCovey was next with 39 and Billy Williams of the Chicago Cubs was third with 34 for the season. Two members of the Cincinnati Reds led the league in runs batted in. Deron Johnson led with 130, and Frank Robinson finished with 113, which was just one ahead of Mays at 112 for San Francisco. The Cincinnati Reds had the highest team batting average in the league with .273, and scored the most runs with 825. The Milwaukee Braves hit 196 home runs to lead the league. The only category of offense in which pennant winner Los Angeles led the league was stolen bases. Maury Wills was the individual leader with 94 and the Dodgers had the most as a team with 172.

However, In pitching categories the Los Angeles Dodgers were extremely dominant. Dodgers' ace Sandy Koufax led the league with 26 wins, followed by Tony Cloninger of the Milwaukee Braves with 24, and Don Drysdale of the Dodgers with 23. Koufax also ended the season with the best ERA of 2.04 runs per game. He was followed closely by Juan Marichal of the Giants and Vern Law of the Pittsburgh Pirates, with 2.13 and 2.15, respectively. In an outstanding year, Koufax also led in strikeouts with 382. This was well above Bob Veale of Pittsburgh with 276, and Bob Gibson of the St. Louis Cardinals at 270. In team pitching, Los Angeles completed the season with the lowest ERA at 2.81 and allowed the fewest hits at 1,223. In strikeouts, however, the staff of the Cincinnati Reds led the National League with 1,113.

The American League Most Valuable Player Award went to shortstop Zoilo Versalles of the Minnesota Twins. Versalles hit .273 in 1965, led the American League in runs with 126, and tied for the lead in doubles with 45, and triples with 12. American League Rookie of the Year was 22-year-old Curt Blefary of the Baltimore Orioles. In 144 games, Blefary hit 22 home runs with an average of .260. Willie Mays of the San Francisco Giants was the MVP in the National League for the second time. Mays also was MVP with the Giants in New York in 1954. Second baseman Jim Lefebvre was voted National League Rookie of the Year. Lefebvre played in 157 games, nearly all at second base, for the pennant winning L.A. Dodgers. The Cy Young Award, for baseball's finest pitcher, was won by the Dodgers' Sandy Koufax for the second time in his career.

The World Series of 1965 featured the National League winning Los Angeles Dodgers against the American League champion Minnesota Twins. The Dodgers team featured pitching, speed, and defense in the National League style of play. The Twins had been built on the foundation of key players retained from the last Washington Senators club in 1960, and then had gradually improved until they claimed the Yankees, at least temporarily abdicated title, as the American League's best team. The key players at each position were expected to be as follows.

CATCHER - Los Angeles, Johnny Roseboro, 32, and Minnesota, Earl Battey, 30. Roseboro had been with the Dodgers since 1957. In 136 games he batted .233 with 8 home runs. Battey broke in with the White Sox in 1955 and had been with the Senators and then Twins starting in 1960. In 131 games he had a .297 batting average and hit 6 home runs in the 1965 season. Both extremely capable behind the plate. No advantage to either team.

FIRST BASE - Los Angeles, Wes Parker, 26, and Minnesota, Don Mincher, 27. Parker, in his second season with Los Angeles, had 8 home runs and a batting average of .238 in 154 games. Mincher was a rookie with the Senators in 1960, before the team moved to Minnesota. In 128 games for the Twins, he batted .251 and hit 22 home runs. The edge goes to the Twins.

SECOND BASE - Los Angeles, Jim Lefebvre, 23, and Minnesota, Frank Quilici, 26. Lefebvre batted .250 in 157 games, with 12 home runs, and was 1965 National League Rookie of the Year. Quilici was also in his rookie year and was largely a utility infielder. He hit for an average of .208 in 56 games. The advantage goes to Los Angeles.

SHORTSTOP - Los Angeles, Maury Wills, 33, and Minnesota, Zoilo Versalles, 26. By this time, Wills was the undisputed king of stolen bases. In 1965 he stole 94 which was ten short of his peak number in 1962. Wills had a batting average of .286 in 158 games. Versalles had been the Twins full-time shortstop since 1961. This season had been his best year and he was voted American League Most Valuable Player. In 160 games, Versalles batted .273, stole 27 bases, hit 19 home runs, 45 doubles, and 12 triples. No advantage to either team. Both players are immensely important for the Series.

THIRD BASE - Los Angeles, Jim Gilliam, 37, and Minnesota, Harmon Killebrew, 29. Gilliam was in his thirteenth year with the Dodgers. His first year was 1953. He hit .280 with 4 home runs in 111 games. In 1965 Killebrew's playing time had been shortened due to injury. In 113 games he still hit 25 home runs with a batting average of .269. The advantage goes to Minnesota.

LEFT FIELD - Los Angeles, Lou Johnson, 31, and Minnesota, Bob Allison, 31. Johnson was in his fourth Major League season and his first with the Dodgers. In 131 games he batted .259 with 12 home runs. Allison started his career with the Senators organization in 1958. His 1965 offensive numbers had declined from his previous four years in Minnesota. He had a batting average of .233 with 23 home runs in 135 games. The two players are rated even.

CENTER FIELD - Los Angeles, Willie Davis, 25, and Minnesota, Jimmie Hall, 27. Davis broke in with the Dodgers in 1960. In 142 games he had a batting average of .248 with 10 home runs and 25 stolen bases. His average was down from prior years. Hall hit 20 home runs and averaged .285 in 148 games, in his third season with the Twins. These two are also rated even.

RIGHT FIELD - Los Angeles, Ron Fairly, 27, and Minnesota, Tony Oliva, 27. Fairly, in his eighth year with the Dodgers, had a .274 average with 9 home runs in 158 games. Oliva was in his second full season with the Twins. He was the American League batting champion with a .321 average and hit 16 home runs in 149 games. Advantage is with Minnesota.

STARTING PITCHING - For Los Angeles: Sandy Koufax, 30, won 26, lost 8. Don Drysdale, 29, won 23, lost 12. Claude Osteen, 26, won 15, lost 15. For Minnesota: Mudcat Grant, 30, won 21, lost 7. Jim Kaat, 27, won 18, lost 11. Camilo Pascual, 31, won 9, lost 3. The advantage is with Los Angeles with the Dodgers' pitching experience from prior years.

MANAGERS - Los Angeles, Walter Alston, 54, and Minnesota, Sam Mele, 43. Alston had the Dodgers returning to the World Series after only a one year absence. Mele had been the manager of the Minnesota Twins since midway through the 1961 season. He was a Major League player from 1947 through 1956 for primarily the Red Sox, Senators, and White Sox.

Los Angeles won 97 and lost 65 to win the National League by a margin of two games. The Dodgers posted a winning record for each month of the season. They won 22 and lost 8 starting on September 1, for a strong finish.

They had a winning record against the other National League clubs, except for going 9-9 against both Philadelphia and Pittsburgh. Minnesota was the winner in the American League by seven games with a record of 102-60. In 162 games the Twins were shut out only three times. The Twins got off to a good start by going 8-3 in April, and had a winning record every month. They won 22 and lost 9 in July. They were 17-1 against Boston, but only 7-11 against Cleveland. The Twins home and away records were an identical 51-30.

The 1965 World Series opened with the first game on Wednesday, October 6, at the home of the Minnesota Twins, Metropolitan Stadium, before a crowd of 47,797. Opposing pitchers were Don Drysdale for Los Angeles and Mudcat Grant for Minnesota. Dodgers' ace Sandy Koufax could not pitch because the opening game fell on Yom Kippur, a Jewish religious holiday. Each team scored a single run in the second inning, with solo home runs by Ron Fairly of the Dodgers and Don Mincher of the Twins. Then, in the third inning, the Twins erupted for six runs off Drysdale to take a lead of 7 to 1. Shortstop Zoilo Versalles homered with two runners on base to produce three of the third inning runs. Minnesota added one more run in the sixth, and the Dodgers scored a single run in the ninth to make the final score Twins 8 and the Dodgers 2. Both teams finished with ten hits for the game. Minnesota starter Mudcat Grant (1-0) went all nine innings for the win. He allowed ten hits, one walk, and had five strikeouts. The loss was charged to Drysdale (0-1), who lasted two and two-third innings and allowed seven hits and seven runs, with only three of them earned.

The next day, the Twins won their second game in the Series with a 5 to 1 victory, led by the seven-hit pitching of left-hander Jim Kaat (1-0). Sandy Koufax (0-1) was the loser for the Dodgers. In the first two games in Minnesota, the Twins had decidedly beaten both Drysdale and Koufax. However, back in Los Angeles on Saturday, October 9, the Dodgers prevailed in game three in a 4-0 shutout in which the Twins managed only five hits against pitcher Claude Osteen (1-0). This reduced the Twins edge in the Series to two games to one. The time of the game was only 2 hours and 6 minutes in front of a Dodger Stadium crowd of 55,934 fans.

Don Drysdale took the mound again on Sunday, October 10, and the result was an L.A. win by 7 to 2. The Series was squared at two games each. In nine complete innings, Drysdale (1-1) allowed two runs, only five hits, and struck out eleven. Mudcat Grant (1-1) took the loss for Minnesota. He pitched five innings and gave up one run in the first inning, one in the second, one in the fourth, and two of three Dodgers' runs in the sixth inning. Minnesota's two runs in the game came on solo home runs by Harmon Killebrew in the fourth and right fielder Tony Oliva in the sixth. Two of the Dodgers' ten hits in the game were solo home runs by Wes Parker in the fourth and Lou Johnson in the eighth inning. A single by Ron Fairly drove in the three sixth inning runs for the Dodgers. The Dodgers speed on the bases also aided their cause, with stolen bases by Maury Wills and Wes Parker. Ace left-hander Sandy Koufax was scheduled to pitch the next day, and it appeared the tide was switching in favor of L.A.

The fifth game on October 11, at Dodger Stadium was a one-sided win for Los Angeles. Koufax (1-1) pitched a 7-0 four-hit shutout over the Twins. After a day off for travel to Minnesota, game number six was back at Minnesota's Metropolitan Stadium on Wednesday, October 13. With their backs against the wall, the Twins responded with a 5 to 1 win to even the Series. Mudcat Grant (2-1) was not only the winning pitcher for the Twins, but he also hit a three-run home run in the sixth inning. So far the home team had been victorious in each game of the Series. Game seven would be the next day on Thursday, October 14.

The game seven pitching matchup would be a repeat of the fifth game, Sandy Koufax of the Dodgers versus Jim Kaat of Minnesota. Both pitchers were working on only two days of rest. The game was scoreless through three innings. Then in the fourth inning, the Dodgers scored twice to take a 2-0 lead. Dodgers' left fielder Lou Johnson hit a solo home run for one of the runs with the other driven in on a single by Wes Parker. That was the extent of scoring in the game. Koufax (2-1) went the distance for the decisive win. He allowed only three hits by Zoilo Versalles, Harmon Killebrew, and Frank Quilici. Koufax struck out ten. Kaat (1-2) allowed both Dodgers' runs and took the loss for the Twins. The Twins best scoring threat in the game came in the bottom of the fifth inning when Quilici doubled, but was then forced at third by an outstanding defensive play by 37-year-old Dodgers' third baseman Jim Gilliam.

The Los Angeles Dodgers prevailed in the Fall Classic for the second time in three years mostly because of their superior pitching, especially that of

Sandy Koufax. The first six games of the Series were all well-pitched games by the winning team, three by the Dodgers and three by the Twins. The only really tense game that went right down to the wire was game seven, and unfortunately, for the Twins and their fans, Los Angeles had Sandy Koufax on their side. The Dodgers hit .274 for the Series compared to .195 for Minnesota. Four Los Angeles position players hit better than .300. Jim Lefebvre hit .400, Ron Fairly, .379, Maury Wills, .367, and Wes Parker, .304. For Minnesota both Harmon Killebrew and Zoilo Versalles batted .286, but American League batting champion Tony Oliva slumped to .192. Los Angeles managed 64 hits in the seven games compared to only 42 for the Twins. Pitching for the Twins, Mudcat Grant was 2-1 with a 2.74 ERA and Jim Kaat was 1-2 with a 3.77 ERA. Sandy Koufax was 2-1 for the Dodgers and had an outstanding 0.38 ERA in 24 innings pitched, along with 29 strikeouts. Don Drysdale and Claude Osteen both won one game and lost one for L.A.

1965 WORLD SERIES SUMMARY

Game 1	At Minnesota	Twins 8, Dodgers 2
Game 2	At Minnesota	Twins 5, Dodgers 1
Game 3	At Los Angeles	Dodgers 4, Twins 0
Game 4	At Los Angeles	Dodgers 7, Twins 2
Game 5	At Los Angeles	Dodgers 7, Twins 0
Game 6	At Minnesota	Twins 5, Dodgers 1
Game 7	At Minnesota	Dodgers 2, Twins 0

LOS ANGELES WINS THE WORLD SERIES BY 4 GAMES TO 3.

ORIOLES SHOCK L.A. BLUE

L os Angeles Dodgers' pitchers Sandy Koufax and Don Drysdale engaged jointly in a salary dispute with the team's front office before the 1966 season started. Consequently, the pair missed most of the preseason. After some delay, the dispute was settled and the two pitchers joined the team in the last week of spring training. This was the era before the advent of free agency. Major League players would sometimes holdout if they were unhappy with their contract offer, but it was highly unusual for two extremely important players to do this together and at the same time.

The opening game for the Los Angeles Dodgers, in defense of their National League pennant and World Series title was on Tuesday, April 12, at Dodger Stadium against the visiting Houston Astros. The starting pitchers were 40-year-old Robin Roberts for Houston and Claude Osteen for the Dodgers. There were no home runs in the game. The Dodgers picked up one run in the first, but Houston tied the game with one in the third inning. Then L.A. took the lead with one run in the sixth and one in the eighth. A ninth inning rally by the Astros fell short and the final line score read 3 runs, 10 hits, 2 errors for L.A. and 2 runs, 6 hits and no errors for Houston. Osteen (1-0) struck out five in the game and went all the way for the opening day win. The loss was charged to Roberts (0-1). In seven innings, Roberts allowed eight hits and one walk, which resulted in two runs, one unearned. Shortstop Maury Wills had two hits and scored two of the Dodgers' three runs. All three runs were driven in by right fielder Ron Fairly. The Dodgers started the new year with their typical well-pitched, low scoring win. The game drew an opening day crowd of 34,520 to Dodger Stadium.

INTERLUDE - JIM MALONEY AND SAM MCDOWELL

Two pitchers arrived on the scene in the early nineteen-sixties -- in the National League, right-hander Jim Maloney and in the American League, left-hander Sam McDowell. Although neither was on a World Series winning team during the period, both were noted strikeout artists. Maloney was born June 2, 1940, in Fresno, California. He was with the Cincinnati Reds for eleven years from 1960 through 1970 and then finished his career in 1971 with the Angels. Maloney won 134 games, lost 84, and compiled an earned run average of 3.19 during his career. In the years through 1968, he won 122 games and was eighth overall in strikeouts with 1,483 for the period. He won twenty or more games twice, with 23 in 1963 and 20 in 1965. Sam McDowell was born in Pittsburgh, Pennsylvania, on September 21, 1942. He broke in with the Cleveland Indians in 1961 and remained with them through the 1971 season. After brief stints with the Giants, Yankees, and Pirates, his career ended after the 1975 season. In his career, McDowell won 141 games and lost 134 with a 3.17 ERA. In the period through 1968, McDowell had 71 wins, ranked tied for ninth in baseball with 1,384 strikeouts, and posted an ERA of 2.96 runs per game. He pitched in four All-Star games in which his ERA was 1.13 in eight innings pitched.

At the start of the 1966 season, the Cleveland Indians unexpectedly won their first ten games in a row. The tenth win came on Thursday, April 28, as the Indians defeated the California Angels 2 to 1. The line score was 2 runs, 12 hits, no errors for the Indians and 1 run, 5 hits and 1 error for the Angels. The winning pitcher for Cleveland was right-hander Sonny Siebert (1-0), who struck out seven in eight and one-third innings pitched. Siebert would go on to complete 1966 with 16 wins, 8 losses, and a 2.80 earned run average. Reliever Bob Allen recorded the final two outs in the top of the ninth for his first save of the season. The only run for the Angels was in the eighth inning on a home run by left fielder Rick Reichardt, his 4th of the year. The Indians scored single runs in the first and the eighth innings, driven in by right fielder Rocky Colavito and pinch-hitter Leon Wagner. The loss for California went to right-handed relief pitcher Bob Lee (0-1), who worked the last inning and two-third and gave up the winning run to Cleveland. A sparse crowd of only

5,057 were in attendance at Cleveland to see the contest. In the early season, the Indians were one game ahead of the Baltimore Orioles who were 9-1. Over in the National League, Pittsburgh started the season 10-4, one game in front of the Dodgers and Giants who were each 10-6.

In the National League, the San Francisco Giants then strung together ten consecutive wins and moved, with 20 wins and 7 losses, four games ahead of the second place Houston Astros. Win number 20 was May 11, at Forbes Field in Pittsburgh in a 6 to 1 victory over the Pirates before a small crowd of 4,373. The winner for the Giants was Gaylord Perry (5-0). Perry completed all nine innings, gave up six hits, and had eight strikeouts. Perry also had two hits in the game and drove in one run for the Giants. San Francisco scored two runs in the first, two in the sixth, and then two runs in the ninth inning on a two-run homer by Willie Mays, his 9th of the season. For Pittsburgh, starter Don Schwall (1-1) took the loss. Schwall lasted four and one-third innings, gave up five hits, and walked four. Schwall pitched in the Major Leagues for seven years from 1961 through 1967. His overall record was 49 wins and 48 losses, with an earned run average of 3.72 runs per game.

On Sunday, May 22, the Giants won game number 25 in the first game of a doubleheader played at Candlestick Park over the New York Mets by a score of 5-0. Giants' ace Juan Marichal won his 8th game of the season without a loss in a three-hit shutout, in which he struck out five and issued only one walk. There was one home run in the game hit by Giants' third baseman Jim Ray Hart. It was in the bottom of the third inning with one on base, his 10th of the season. Hart drove in three of the five runs scored by San Francisco in the game. The loss for the Mets went to starting pitcher Larry Bearnarth (1-1), who lasted only two and one-third innings and gave up four runs on five hits. In four years with the Mets from 1963 through 1966, Bearnarth won 13 and lost 21, with a 4.13 earned run average. The Giants lost the second game of the twin bill to the Mets 7 to 2 which brought their record to 25-13 for the season. At this point, San Francisco was three games ahead of the Houston Astros at 21-15.

The San Francisco Giants continued to lead the National League through the end of May. On Tuesday, May 31, they won their 30th game over the Cincinnati Reds 5 to 3 at Crosley Field. The Giants provided their starter, Juan Marichal, with three runs in the fifth inning and then scored a run in the seventh thanks to a solo home run by third baseman Jim Ray Hart, his 13th of the year. Hart would finish the 1966 season with 33 home runs for San Francisco. Marichal (10-0) went all nine innings for the complete game win, gave up seven hits, and had nine strikeouts. In a losing cause, shortstop Leo Cardenas hit two home runs, in the seventh and ninth innings, to drive in the Reds' three runs. These were home run numbers 3 and 4 of the season for the Cuban-born Cardenas. The loss for Cincinnati went to starter Sammy Ellis (2-7), who allowed four runs in his seven innings pitched. In a seven-year Major League career, mostly with the Reds, Ellis was 63-58 with a 4.15 earned run average. At the end of May, the Giants were 30-16 which was two and one-half games ahead of Los Angeles at 27-18.

On Monday, June 13, the Supreme Court of the United States announced its ruling by a vote of 5 to 4 that, in general, police may not interrogate an individual unless he has been informed of his constitutional rights to an attorney and to remain silent. These rights have been generally referred to as an individual's "Miranda Rights." That day in baseball at Forbes Field in Pittsburgh, the Pirates edged out the Cincinnati Reds by a 5 to 4 margin. The Reds outhit the Pirates in the game by twelve to eight. Pittsburgh started with an early lead by scoring one run in the second and one in the third inning. In the top of the fourth inning, Reds center fielder Vada Pinson hit a three-run home run, his 5th of the season, to give Cincinnati a 3 to 2 lead. The Reds added one run in the fifth, but Pittsburgh rallied for the 5 to 4 win, with three runs in the last of the eighth on a Roberto Clemente three-run home run, his 9th of the year. The Pirates used three pitchers in the game with the win going to reliever Pete Mikkelsen (5-2), who completed the eighth and ninth innings and allowed only two hits. Mikkelsen went on to finish the year with 9 wins, 8 losses, and an ERA of 3.07. The loss was charged to Billy McCool (2-3) of the Reds, who in one inning pitched, gave up the Clemente home run. With this win, Pittsburgh improved its 1966 record to 33-23. Cincinnati fell to 23 wins and 31 losses.

INTERLUDE - ROBERTO CLEMENTE

Roberto Clemente of the Pittsburgh Pirates was a somewhat overlooked and underappreciated player at this time. Clemente was born in Puerto Rico on August 18, 1934. He played his entire career from 1955 through 1972 with

Pittsburgh. Among his achievements in baseball were four National League batting titles and the 1966 National League Most Valuable Player Award. Clemente finished his eighteen-year baseball career with exactly 3,000 hits, which resulted in a lifetime batting average of .317. In the process, the aggressive swinger at bat accumulated 440 doubles, 166 triples, and 240 home runs. Clemente tragically died in a plane crash on December 31, 1972, while on a humanitarian mission to bring relief supplies to victims of an earthquake in Nicaragua. He was only 38-years old.

In the twelve years from 1957 through 1968, Clemente hit safely 2,094 times for a batting average of .316. His batting average exceeded .300 each year from 1960 through 1967, with peaks of .351 in 1961 and .357 in 1967. In the 1960 World Series, Clemente played in all seven games in the win against the New York Yankees. He went 9 for 29, a .310 batting average. His outstanding season in 1960, in which he batted .314, tended to be overshadowed by the MVP season of teammate Dick Groat and the heroic game seven winning home run hit by Bill Mazeroski. Clemente was also in the 1971 World Series with Pittsburgh during which he batted .414 with two home runs. In fourteen All-Star game appearances, Clemente had 10 hits in 31 times at bat for an average of .323.

The season continued further into the summer, and the Baltimore Orioles took over first place in the American League. On Friday, June 17, the Orioles defeated the Boston Red Sox 5 to 3 at Fenway Park for their 40th win of the season against 21 losses. Both teams had only six hits in the game, but each team had two home runs. Boston scored one run in the first inning, but in the third Orioles' right fielder Frank Robinson hit his 17th home run of the season to give Baltimore a 2 to 1 lead. In the fourth, Red Sox center fielder Don Demeter tied the score at two apiece with his 6th home run. In the top of the fifth, third baseman Brooks Robinson delivered the game winning blow, a three-run homer, his 11th, to make the score 5 to 2. Carl Yastrzemski ended the scoring with his 7th home run in the bottom of the fifth for Boston. Baltimore's Steve Barber (6-2) was the starter and picked up the win. Barber pitched seven innings, surrendered five hits, and struck out eight. Stu Miller pitched the last two innings for the Orioles in relief to get credit for his 10th save of the season. The losing pitcher for the Red Sox was starter Jim Lonborg (3-5), who went seven innings, struck out ten, and gave up all five Baltimore runs. At this stage, the Cleveland Indians were in second place two games behind the Orioles.

INTERLUDE - BROOKS ROBINSON

A trade on December 9, 1965, in time for the 1966 season, brought outfielder Frank Robinson of the Cincinnati Reds to the Baltimore Orioles in exchange for pitcher Milt Pappas and two other players. Before this trade, third baseman Brooks Robinson had been the key player for the Orioles since 1955. Brooks Robinson was born in Little Rock, Arkansas on May 18, 1937. In 23 years with the Orioles, ending in 1977, Robinson accumulated 2,848 hits including, 482 doubles, 268 home runs, and finished with a .267 batting average. Perhaps, of almost greater importance to the Orioles was his defensive ability on the left side of the infield at third base, where he could make spectacular plays look almost routine. In his career Robinson won sixteen Gold Glove Awards at third base.

In the twelve seasons from 1957 through 1968, Brooks Robinson hit safely 1,779 times which produced an average of .278. Twice he batted over .300 with .303 in 1962 and .317 in 1964. In the twelve-year period he hit 172 home runs with a peak of 28 in 1964. For his efforts in the 1964 season, Robinson was named American League Most Valuable Player. He made four World Series appearances with Baltimore in 1966, 1969, 1970, and 1971. During these appearances, Robinson hit .263 in 21 games with three home runs. Over the years, Robinson played in eighteen All-Star games for the American League in which he batted .289, with one home run in the 1967 game at Anaheim Stadium in California. After he retired from his playing career, Robinson worked as color commentator for television and radio broadcasts of Orioles baseball and has greatly contributed his time and talents to many charitable organizations in the Baltimore area.

INTERLUDE - FRANK ROBINSON

Frank Robinson had two almost equally successful careers in baseball. The first was with the Cincinnati Reds from 1956 through 1965 and the second was with the Baltimore Orioles from 1966 through 1971. Even though he is remembered mostly for his years with the Orioles, his achievements with Cincinnati were substantial. Robinson was born in Beaumont, Texas on August 31, 1935, and attended high school in Oakland, California. He was a powerful right-handed hitter with an aggressive batting stance. His style of crowding the plate resulted in him often being hit by the pitch. He began his career with Cincinnati in 1956 and played there through the 1965 season. In those ten years with the Reds, Robinson hit 324 home runs. In his six years with Baltimore, Robinson added another 179 homers. In his last six years, Robinson spent one season with the Dodgers, two with the Angels, and three with the Indians. In those six years, ending in 1976, he added 83 more home runs. Thus his career home run total was 586. In the twelve seasons from 1957 through 1968, he hit 380 home runs. In his career, Robinson amassed 2,943 hits for an overall batting average of .294.

Frank Robinson was named 1956 National League Rookie of the Year. He is the only player ever to be named the Most Valuable Player in both leagues -- in 1961 in the National League, and 1966 in the American League. In the 1961 World Series, which Cincinnati lost to the New York Yankees in five games, Robinson batted .200 and hit one home run in the fifth game of the Series at Crosley Field. In the 1966 World Series, Baltimore swept the Los Angeles Dodgers in four consecutive games. In this Series, Robinson batted .286 with two home runs. He homered once in the first game and again in the deciding fourth game at Memorial Stadium in Baltimore, which the Orioles won by a score of 1-0. Robinson also participated with Baltimore in the 1969, 1970, and 1971 World Series. The Orioles won only the Series in 1970 over Robinson's former team, the Cincinnati Reds. Robinson made appearances in eleven All-Star games in his career, six for the National League and five for the American League. In All-Star competition he had a .250 batting average and hit two home runs, in 1959 and 1971.

On Friday, June 30, Baltimore overcame the Kansas City Athletics 11 to 3 for win number 50, as they pounded out nineteen hits in the game compared to eight for the Athletics. Although they hit no home runs in the game, the Baltimore batters produced seven doubles. After five innings of play, the Orioles led 6 to 3 and then scored five more times in the top of the eighth to close out the win. In a losing cause, Kansas City third baseman Ed Charles hit his 4th home run of the season in the fourth inning. Twenty-three-year-old second baseman Davey Johnson had four hits, including his 9th double of the season, and drove in two runs for the Orioles. Neither starting pitcher lasted very far into the game. Baltimore's Gene Brabender (2-1) picked up the win in relief. The rookie Brabender worked five and two-third innings and scattered two hits and four walks to finish the game. The loss went to the starter for Kansas City, Ralph Terry (1-5), who allowed five runs on ten hits in his three and one-third innings pitched. Terry, the former New York Yankee, would spend just a partial season with Kansas City, and then retire at the beginning of the 1967 season. The win put the Orioles at 50 wins and 25 losses at the end of June. Their lead over Detroit was four games, and over Cleveland was five and one-half games. In the National League, the Giants lead over second place Pittsburgh was three games. The Los Angeles Dodgers were five and one-half games off the pace.

Baseball celebrated the annual 1966 All-Star game at Busch Stadium in St. Louis on Tuesday, July 12. The game was played in 105 degree afternoon heat before a crowd of 49,936. The game itself was dominated by the pitchers on both teams. Each team could only manage six hits and no home runs. The game was tied at one run each after the regulation nine innings. Then the National League eked out an extra inning victory by a score of 2 to 1. Maury Wills of the Dodgers drove in the winning run in the tenth with a single to score St. Louis Cardinals' catcher Tim McCarver. The winning pitcher was Gaylord Perry of the San Francisco Giants, with the loss charged to Pete Richert of the Washington Senators. Despite the loss, Brooks Robinson of the Baltimore Orioles was voted the game's Most Valuable Player. In the second inning, Robinson tripled and scored the only run of the game for the American League team.

Through Sunday, July 17, Baltimore had won ten of its last seventeen games to go to 60-32 for the season. Win number 60 came in a 3 to 2 victory over the Chicago White Sox in the second game of a doubleheader at Comiskey

Park. Chicago won the first game by 5 to 1. The winning pitcher in the second game was 21-year-old right-hander Jim Palmer (10-4). Palmer went six and two-third innings, gave up one run, five hits, and recorded six strikeouts. Stu Miller wrapped up the game in the ninth for his 14th save of the season. The loss for the White Sox went to Jack Lamabe (4-6), who pitched only one inning before giving up the winning run to the Orioles in the top of the second inning. There were no home runs in the game. Third baseman Brooks Robinson went three-for-four. Two of his hits were doubles which brought his season total up to 23. The game was played before a Comiskey Park crowd of 27,789. The win increased the Orioles' lead over the second place Detroit Tigers, at 50-38, to eight games.

By early August, the Baltimore lead over the Tigers was up to thirteen games. On Tuesday, August 2, the Orioles (70-35) defeated the Indians at Cleveland 8 to 6. The Orioles took a 5-0 lead in the third, only to have the Indians claw their way back to a five-all tie after six innings. Then Baltimore scored three runs in the top of the seventh and held off an abortive rally by Cleveland in the ninth. Each team had one home run in the game. For Baltimore second baseman Davey Johnson hit his 6th of the year in the seventh inning with two men on base. The Indians' right fielder Rocky Colavito belted his 24th in the ninth inning for their final tally of the game. In relief, Dick Hall (4-2) was the winner for the Orioles. Hall worked the last three and two-third innings, giving up only the ninth inning home run by Colavito. Cleveland used five pitchers in the game with the loss going to 22-year-old right-hander Tom Kelley (3-6). Kelley pitched only the seventh inning and gave up five hits including the game winning three-run homer by Davey Johnson. The game lasted a lengthy 3 hours and 8 minutes before 17,936 fans. If the pennant race in the American League was nearly over, the one in the National League was just getting started. The San Francisco Giants had 63 wins and 44 losses, which was one game ahead in the standings over both the Dodgers and the Pittsburgh Pirates.

The Baltimore Orioles improved their record to 80 wins and 42 losses with an 8 to 3 victory over Detroit on Saturday, August 20, at Tiger Stadium before 21,235. The winning pitcher for Baltimore was Dave McNally (12-3), who pitched eight innings with seven strikeouts. McNally allowed six hits and three runs in the last of the eighth on a homer by Detroit's Willie Horton, his 18th of the season. The losing pitcher for Detroit was 22-year-old starter

Denny McLain (14-11). He worked four innings and allowed five hits and seven runs, six of which were earned. McLain would go on to complete the 1966 season with 20 wins, 14 losses, and an ERA of 3.92 runs per game. In the second inning, the Orioles had two solo home runs, by first baseman Boog Powell, his 32nd, and left fielder Curt Blefary, his 17th of the season. The Orioles went on to break the game open with five runs in the top half of the fifth inning. Orioles' center fielder Russ Snyder, who batted .306 for the season, hit his 4th triple of the year and drove in three of the runs in the fifth. The line score was 8 runs, 8 hits, no errors for Baltimore and 3 runs, 6 hits and 1 error for Detroit. The loss left the Tigers trailing Baltimore by thirteen and one-half games with a record of 66-55.

At Candlestick Park in San Francisco on Tuesday, August 23, the Giants won their 75th game of the season against 51 losses in a 7 to 3 decision over the slumping Cincinnati Reds. This was the ninth loss in their last ten ballgames for the 60-65 Reds. After four innings, the Giants led 6 to 3 and rode the complete game pitching of Juan Marichal (18-5) for the win. Marichal gave up three runs on eight hits and struck out six. The loss for Cincinnati went to starter Milt Pappas (9-9). Pappas lasted four and one-third innings and allowed six runs on six base hits by the Giants. Both teams had eight hits in the game and both teams also hit two home runs. First baseman Deron Johnson hit his 16th home run in the second for the Reds, and shortstop Leo Cardenas hit his 15th, in the fourth inning. San Francisco homers were by first baseman Willie McCovey, his 26th, in the first inning, and 22-year-old center fielder Ollie Brown, his 6th of the year, in the fourth. This victory put the Giants one game ahead of the Pittsburgh Pirates and three games up on the Dodgers in the pennant pursuit.

Halfway through September, as the season was winding down, the American League margin that Baltimore enjoyed had been reduced slightly to a still large nine and one-half game lead over the Detroit Tigers. On Thursday, September 15, in the first game of a doubleheader, the Orioles record improved to 90-55 with a 2-0 win over the California Angels. The time of the game, played at Memorial Stadium in Baltimore, was 2 hours and 12 minutes. The winning pitcher for the Orioles was Tom Phoebus (1-0). Phoebus, at 24, was making his first Major League appearance. In his debut, he pitched the complete nine innings, allowed only four hits and two walks, and struck out eight. In a seven-year Major League career, Phoebus won 56 games, lost 52, and posted an earned run average of 3.33 runs per game. The loser for the Angels was Dean Chance (10-16). Chance pitched well in the loss. He allowed two runs in seven innings and also had eight strikeouts. Both of the Baltimore runs were on solo home runs in the sixth inning. Third baseman Brooks Robinson hit his 23rd, and left fielder Curt Blefary notched his 21st home run of the season. In the second game of the twin bill, Baltimore defeated California by a score of 4 to 3.

The 1966 regular season for the Orioles came to a conclusion on Sunday, October 2, at home at Memorial Stadium in a doubleheader against the Minnesota Twins. Both games had no meaning for the standings. The Orioles defeated the Twins 6 to 2 in the first game. In the second game, the Twins shut out Baltimore 1-0. Each team managed only four hits and there were no home runs in the game. The winner for Minnesota was Jim Perry (11-7). Perry worked seven and two-third innings, gave up four hits, and had seven strikeouts. Al Worthington completed the last inning and one-third for his 15th save. The loss was charged to rookie reliever Eddie Watt (9-7), who gave up the game's only run in the eighth inning. Watt worked three innings in relief of starter Wally Bunker. Center fielder Ted Uhlaender of the Twins had two hits in the game and scored the winning run, which was driven in by pitcher Jim Perry. Baltimore ended the season with 97 wins and 63 losses. Minnesota finished as runner-up eight games behind with 89 wins and 73 losses. Because of two postponements, the Orioles played only 160 games of the normal 162 game schedule.

The Los Angeles Dodgers ended up narrowly winning the National League pennant by a game and one-half over San Francisco and by three games over Pittsburgh. As of August 20, the Dodgers trailed both San Francisco and Pittsburgh by three games. For the rest of the season, L.A. went 27-14, compared to 21-17 for the Giants, and 21-20 for the Pirates. The 1966 World Series would begin in the National League city with the Los Angeles Dodgers hosting the Baltimore Orioles.

In the American League, Frank Robinson of the Baltimore Orioles won the triple crown by leading the League in the three statistical categories of batting average, home runs, and runs batted in. In batting, Robinson led with .316, followed by Tony Oliva of the Minnesota Twins with .307. Robinson hit 49 home runs, which was far ahead of Harmon Killebrew of the Twins at

39, and Boog Powell of the Orioles at 34. The same three players were also atop the leader board in runs batted in with Robinson, 122, Killebrew, 110, and Boog Powell at 109. The Baltimore Orioles led the league with a team batting average of .258 and with 755 runs scored for the season. The Detroit Tigers' hitters showed the most power with a league leading 179 home runs.

In individual pitching, southpaw Jim Kaat of the Minnesota Twins won 25 games. He was followed by Denny McLain of Detroit with 20. Gary Peters and Joel Horlen both of the Chicago White Sox had the lowest earned run average of 1.98 and 2.43, respectively. Steve Hargan of the Cleveland Indians was third with 2.48. Sam McDowell of the Indians was the leader in strikeouts with 225, followed by Kaat who had 205. In team pitching, the White Sox finished the season with the lowest ERA of 2.69 and also allowed the fewest hits with 1,229. The pitching staff of the Indians had the most strikeouts during the season with 1,111.

The 1966 National League batting title went to Matty Alou of the Pittsburgh Pirates with an average of .342. His brother, Felipe Alou, from the Atlanta Braves finished second with .327, just ahead of Braves' teammate Rico Carty with .326. Henry Aaron of Atlanta led the league with 44 home runs, followed by Dick Allen of the Philadelphia Phillies with 40, and Willie Mays of the Giants with 37. Aaron also had the most runs batted in with 127. Roberto Clemente of the Pittsburgh Pirates was second with 119 and Dick Allen was third at 110. In team batting, the leader was the Pittsburgh Pirates with .279. The Atlanta Braves hit the most home runs with 207, and they led the league in runs scored with 782.

Sandy Koufax of the National League champion Dodgers led National League pitchers with 27 wins, followed by the Giants' Juan Marichal with 25. The Cardinals' Bob Gibson and Gaylord Perry of San Francisco each won 21. Koufax had the lowest ERA at 1.73 runs per game. Mike Cuellar of Houston at 2.22 and Marichal at 2.23 finished a distant second and third. Koufax was also the dominant leader in strikeouts with 317, followed by Jim Bunning of the Philadelphia Phillies with 252. The major categories of team pitching were all led by Los Angeles with an ERA of 2.63, fewest hits allowed of 1,287, and total strikeouts of 1,084.

The Cy Young Award was won by Sandy Koufax of the Los Angeles Dodgers for the third and last time. He retired after the 1966 season and his period of domination as baseball's best pitcher came to an end. The American League Most Valuable Player was Frank Robinson of the Baltimore Orioles. Twenty-four-year-old Tommie Agee of the Chicago White Sox was voted American League Rookie of the Year. He helped the White Sox to a fourth place finish with 22 home runs and a .273 batting average. In the National League, the MVP was Roberto Clemente of the Pittsburgh Pirates. Clemente batted .317 with 29 home runs for Pittsburgh. The National League Rookie of the Year Award belonged to the Cincinnati Reds' Tommy Helms. Helms, at 25 years of age, played mostly at third base in 1966 and batted .284 in 138 games.

The Baltimore Orioles had walked away with the American League pennant. But for the Los Angeles Dodgers, the National League pennant pursuit had been more closely contested. Media analysis focused on the following participants as the Series was getting underway at Dodger Stadium.

CATCHER - Baltimore, Andy Etchebarren, 23, and Los Angeles, Johnny Roseboro, 33. Etchebarren was in his first full year with the Orioles. In 121 games he hit .221 and had 11 home runs. Roseboro was a veteran of three prior Dodgers World Series winning teams. He batted .276 with 9 home runs in 142 games. The advantage is with Los Angeles.

FIRST BASE - Baltimore, Boog Powell, 25, and Los Angeles, Wes Parker, 27. Powell was in his fifth year as a regular at first base with Baltimore. The powerful left-hander hit 34 home runs and batted .287 in 140 games. Parker had an average of .253 and 12 home runs in 156 games. This was his third season in baseball for the Dodgers. Advantage to the Orioles based on Powell's power potential.

SECOND BASE - Baltimore, Davey Johnson, 23, and Los Angeles, Jim Lefebvre, 24. Johnson was in his first full year with Baltimore. In 131 games he hit .257 with 7 home runs. Lefebvre, in his second season, increased his offensive output from the prior year by hitting .274 with 24 home runs, which was twice his total from 1965. Advantage seems to be with Los Angeles.

SHORTSTOP - Baltimore, Luis Aparicio, 32, and Los Angeles, Maury Wills, 34. Aparicio had experience from the 1959 World Series with the Chicago White Sox. This was his fourth season with Baltimore. He hit .276 and had 25 stolen bases in 151 games. Wills was in his eighth year with Los Angeles. In 1966 he batted .273 with 38 stolen bases in 143 games. Aparicio and Wills were the two most preeminent and consistent producers of stolen bases in the Major Leagues at this time. Rated even.

THIRD BASE - Baltimore, Brooks Robinson, 29, and Los Angeles, John Kennedy, 25. Brooks Robinson was an outstanding defensive third baseman who could make a spectacular play in nearly every game. At the plate he batted .269 with 23 home runs in 157 games. His baseball career began with Baltimore in 1955. Kennedy had started in the Major Leagues in 1962. This was his second season with the Dodgers. In 125 games he had a batting average of .201. The overall excellence of Robinson gives a clear advantage to the Orioles.

LEFT FIELD - Baltimore, Curt Blefary, 23, and Los Angeles, Lou Johnson, 32. Blefary was in his second year with the Orioles. He hit 23 home runs and batted .255 in 131 games. In his first two Major League seasons, he had totaled 45 homers. Johnson, in his second season with the Dodgers, had a .272 batting average with 17 home runs in 152 games. The two are rated even.

CENTER FIELD - Baltimore, Paul Blair, 22, and Los Angeles, Willie Davis, 26. Blair was in his second season with Baltimore. He finished the year with an average of .277 with 6 home runs in 133 games. Willie Davis hit for a .284 average and had 11 home runs in 153 games. His average had improved from .238 in the prior year. These two are also rated equal.

RIGHT FIELD - Baltimore, Frank Robinson, 31, and Los Angeles, Ron Fairly, 28. When Frank Robinson came over to the Orioles from Cincinnati, the fortune of the Baltimore franchise was changed for the better. In 1966 Robinson hit 49 home runs, batted .316, and drove in 122 runs. Fairly hit .288 with 14 home runs in 117 games for Los Angeles. It was a career year for Robinson to the advantage of the Orioles.

STARTING PITCHING - For Baltimore: Dave McNally, 24, won 13, lost 6. Jim Palmer, 21, won 15, lost 10. Wally Bunker, 21, won 10, lost 6. For Los

Angeles: Sandy Koufax, 31, won 27, lost 9. Don Drysdale, 30, won 13, lost 16. Claude Osteen, 27, won 17, lost 14. Baltimore had dominated the American League in 1966, but it seemed that the Dodgers' greater experience would give them a pitching advantage.

MANAGERS - Baltimore, Hank Bauer, 44, and Los Angeles, Walter Alston, 55. Bauer became manager of the Baltimore Orioles in 1964. He had a Major League playing career from 1948 through 1961 mostly with the New York Yankees. The Dodgers had won the World Series in 1955, 1959, 1963, and 1965 under Alston's direction.

Baltimore captured the American League pennant by nine games with a record of 97-63. The Orioles had two excellent months, in April (11-1) and June (25-8). They were 15-3 against the Yankees, but only 8-10 against Cleveland. Los Angeles won the National League by just one and one-half games with 95 wins and 67 losses. The Dodgers best months were July (18-10) and September (20-9). They managed a winning record against the other National League teams, except for Pittsburgh and San Francisco. They won 9 and lost 9 against both. The Dodgers recorded 20 shutouts and were 34-19 in games decided by only one run.

The 1966 World Series opened at Dodger Stadium in Los Angeles on Wednesday, October 5. Because the Dodgers used their ace Sandy Koufax in the last game of the regular season to clinch the pennant, Don Drysdale was their starting pitcher for the opener. Right away, In the top of the first inning, the Orioles scored three runs on a two-run homer by Frank Robinson followed immediately by a home run by Brooks Robinson. Then each team picked up a single run in the second inning to make the score Orioles 4 and Dodgers 1. Second baseman Jim Lefebvre homered for the Dodgers second inning tally. Baltimore starter Dave McNally walked three men to load the bases in the third inning and was replaced by 31-year-old relief pitcher Moe Drabowsky. He successfully retired the side with only one run in the inning, and then finished the game by giving up only one base hit and two walks the rest of the way. In six and two-third innings pitched, Drabowsky (1-0) struck out eleven and received credit for the win. With Baltimore scoring another run in the fourth, the line score read 5 runs, 9 hits, no errors for the Orioles and 2 runs, 3 hits and no errors for Los Angeles. Baltimore led the Series one game to none.

The second game played October 6, at Los Angeles and the third game on Saturday, October 8, at Baltimore's Memorial Stadium both turned out to be shutout wins for the Orioles by scores of 6-0 on Thursday and 1-0 on Saturday. Pitchers Jim Palmer (1-0) and Wally Bunker (1-0) were the winners in games two and three, respectively. The Orioles outhit the Dodgers eight to four in game two. The Dodgers also committed six costly errors in the field which hurt their cause. In the third game, the Orioles only had three hits, but one of them was a home run by center fielder Paul Blair in the fifth inning for the game's only run.

Game four was played Sunday, October 9, at Baltimore with the starting pitchers being a repeat of the first game, Dave McNally for the Orioles, and Don Drysdale for the Dodgers. Both pitchers worked the entire game and gave up only four hits. One of the hits that Drysdale allowed was a fourth inning solo home run to Baltimore right fielder Frank Robinson, his 2nd homer of the Series. The sweep was complete. Baltimore had defeated the Dodgers by four games to none. The time of the game was an incredibly fast 1 hour and 45 minutes before a Memorial Stadium crowd numbering 54,458. The Series seemed like it all was over just barely after it had started.

The reality began to sink in that the Baltimore Orioles were World Series champions. Three years prior in 1963, the Dodgers sweep over the Yankees had seemed an enormous shock because the Yankees as a team were loaded with powerful baseball superstars who were so used to being regularly on the national stage. While the 1966 sweep by the Orioles was unexpected, it seemed more commonplace because the Dodgers' lineup was not as fully loaded with the kind of heavy hitting offensive threats of the Yankees. For the Series the earned run average of the Baltimore pitching staff was 0.50 compared to 2.65 for the Dodgers. Moe Drabowsky, Jim Palmer, Wally Bunker, and Dave McNally each won a game for the Orioles. For Los Angeles, Don Drysdale lost two games and Sandy Koufax and Claude Osteen lost one each. Koufax and Osteen had good earned run averages of 1.50 and 1.29, respectively.

Baltimore pitchers held the Dodgers without a run for 33 consecutive innings. In the four games the Dodgers managed only 17 hits. Left fielder Lou Johnson was their leading hitter with a batting average of .267. As a team, Baltimore at least had 24 hits and batted .200 compared to the Dodgers futile average of .142. Boog Powell led the Orioles with an average of .357. Paul Blair and

Frank Robinson each hit solo home runs for the winning margins in games three and four, respectively. In the first game, the two Robinsons, Frank and Brooks, homered in the very first inning and from then on things did not improve for Los Angeles.

1966 WORLD SERIES SUMMARY

Game 1	At Los Angeles	Orioles 5, Dodgers 2
Game 2	At Los Angeles	Orioles 6, Dodgers 0
Game 3	At Baltimore	Orioles 1, Dodgers 0
Game 4	At Baltimore	Orioles 1, Dodgers 0

BALTIMORE SWEEPS THE WORLD SERIES 4 GAMES TO NONE.

INTERLUDE - WALTER ALSTON

Walter Alston was born December 1, 1911, in Venice, Ohio. He became manager of the Dodgers starting with the 1954 season and remained with the Dodgers, first in Brooklyn and then in Los Angeles, as manager through the 1976 season. He spent a total of 23 years at the helm of one of baseball's most successful and iconic franchises. Alston was a four-time World Series champion as manager in 1955, 1959, 1963, and 1965. His overall regular season record as Dodgers' manager was 2,040 wins and 1,613 losses. Alston was noted for his calm demeanor and studious businesslike approach to the game. He respected the game. In his career, he was employed by the Dodgers in a series of 23 one-year contracts. He never requested a multi-year contract. Alston passed away in 1984 at the age of 72.

INTERLUDE - SANDY KOUFAX

Sandy Koufax was born on December 30, 1935, in Brooklyn, New York. Koufax pitched for twelve years for the Dodgers, in Brooklyn and Los Angeles from 1955 through 1966. His overall record was 165 wins, 87 losses, and an earned run average of 2.76 runs per game. In the last five years of his career from 1962 through 1966, he won 111 games and lost only 34.

For many years, Koufax combined with his teammate Don Drysdale to give the Dodgers the best one-two punch on the mound in the Major Leagues. Koufax was a strong left-hander with an overhand motion and delivery which helped produce an almost unhittable fast ball and deadly curve. He actually finished his career with more strikeouts, 2,396, than innings pitched, 2,324. At the end of the 1966 season, he was forced to end his career due mostly to arthritis in his left elbow. He was only 31-years old. It was extremely disappointing for all of baseball to see his career come to an end at such a young age.

In the years of 1957 through 1968, Koufax won 161 games. Koufax appeared in four World Series with the Dodgers in 1959, 1963, 1965, and 1966. He won four games, lost three, and posted an ERA of 0.95 in 57 World Series innings. He won two games each in the Series of 1963, against the Yankees, and in 1965, against the Minnesota Twins. Koufax appeared in four All-Star games and was the winning pitcher for the National League in the 1965 contest. His career included four no-hitters, including a perfect game on September 9, 1965, against the Chicago Cubs. Although his baseball career was not a long one, he was the most dominant and successful pitcher in baseball during his last five years as an active player.

INTERLUDE - DON DRYSDALE

Along with the left-hander Koufax, the Los Angeles Dodgers also featured the outstanding right-hander, Don Drysdale. Born July 23, 1936, in Van Nuys, California, Drysdale was with the Dodgers for fourteen years from 1956 through 1969. In his career he accumulated 209 wins, 166 losses, and an earned run average of 2.95 runs per game. In 3,432 innings pitched, he struck out 2,486 opposing batters. He was an extremely strong and competitive figure on the pitching mounds of the National League. Although his best performances may not have been quite as spectacular as those of Koufax, he was able, through his relative longevity, to accumulate the 209 wins compared to the 165 wins achieved by Koufax. In his fourteen seasons, Drysdale twice was a twenty-game winner with 25 in 1962, and 23 in 1965.

From 1957 through 1968, Drysdale had 199 wins, 157 losses, and averaged 272 innings pitched per season. In World Series play, Drysdale won three games and lost three, with one victory each in the Dodgers' championship years of 1959, 1963, and 1965. In 39 and two-third World Series innings pitched, he struck out 36 and posted an ERA of 2.95 runs per game, which exactly equals his regular season career number. Drysdale appeared in eight All-Star games, winning two and losing one with a 1.40 earned run average in nineteen and one-third innings. He was the winning pitcher in the All-Star games of 1967 and 1968.

After his retirement from baseball, Drysdale was well known for his work as a television and radio broadcaster, both nationally and for individual teams. He conducted many informative interviews of past Major League players. Along with long-time Dodgers' broadcaster Vin Scully, he covered the team from 1988 until his sudden death from a heart attack at the age of 56 in 1993.

REDBIRDS FACE WHO?

In 1965 and 1966 the New York Yankees had a two-season record of 147 wins and 174 losses and Roger Maris, while plagued with nagging injuries, hit a two-year total of only 21 home runs in 165 games. After a World Series win in 1964, the Cardinals had slipped to 80 wins in 1965 and 83 wins in 1966. In the off-season, on December 8, 1966, Maris was traded to the St. Louis Cardinals. 1967 would be the first full season of Cardinals' baseball in the new Busch Stadium located on the downtown Mississippi River frontage near the newly constructed St. Louis Gateway Arch. Following ten seasons in the American League, Maris was ready to begin a new National League career, at the age of 33.

The 1967 season began on a high note for the Cincinnati Reds as they started with 10 wins and 3 losses. On April 24, the Reds won for the 10th time 3 to 1 over Houston at the Astrodome. All three Cincinnati runs were scored in the fourth inning, courtesy of a three-run homer by first baseman Tony Perez, his 2nd of the season. Perez would go on to hit 26 home runs in 1967 with a batting average of .290. Reds' left fielder Pete Rose was two-for-two in the game including his 1st triple of the season. The winning pitcher for Cincinnati was Sammy Ellis (1-2). Ellis pitched seven and one-third innings and scattered ten Houston hits, which resulted in one Astros' run in the sixth inning. Astros' center fielder Jimmy Wynn had four hits in four at bats and scored the Astros' only run. The loser for Houston was right-hander Dave Giusti (0-3). He was credited with three innings pitched, and surrendered the winning hit by Tony Perez in the top of the fourth. After this ballgame, the Reds were in first place by one and one-half games over both the Philadelphia Phillies and St. Louis.

On Sunday, May 14, Cincinnati narrowly defeated the Phillies by a 2 to 1 score at Crosley Field for their 20th win against 10 losses. This was the first game of a doubleheader. There was a combined total of just twelve hits and one walk in a game which took only 2 hours and 7 minutes to play. The Phillies scored their run in the first inning, but the Reds won it with single runs in the fifth and eighth innings. Cincinnati's two runs came on solo homers by shortstop Leo Cardenas, his 1st, and center fielder Vada Pinson, his 3rd of the season. The winner for Cincinnati was right-hander Jim Maloney (2-2), who went eight and one-third innings, gave up one run, four hits, and struck out five. Reliever Ted Abernathy recorded the last two outs of the ballgame for his 11th save of the year. The loser for Philadelphia was 36-year-old veteran Larry Jackson (2-3). Jackson pitched well, but allowed the two solo home runs which won the game for the Reds. In the second game of the day, the Reds shut out the Phillies 1-0. Attendance at Crosley Field for the two ballgames was only 12,381. Over in the American League, only the Chicago White Sox (18-7) and the Detroit Tigers (17-9) had cumulative records over the .500 mark. The White Sox led by one and one-half games.

INTERLUDE - LARRY JACKSON

The baseball career of right-handed pitcher Larry Jackson began in 1955 and continued through the 1968 season. Jackson was born in the state of Idaho on June 2, 1931. He pitched for the St. Louis Cardinals from 1955 through 1962 and for the Chicago Cubs from 1963 through 1965. On April 21, 1966, he was traded to the Philadelphia Phillies where he played through the end of the 1968 season. Throughout his career, Jackson was a model of consistent play. In the twelve years of 1957 through 1968, Jackson won a minimum of thirteen games every year and averaged 250 innings pitched. In the eight years he spent with the Cardinals, his most successful year was 1960, during which he managed 18 wins against 13 losses, with a 3.48 ERA. His overall peak year was in 1964 when he won 24 and lost 11 for the Cubs with a 3.14 earned run average. His career statistics included 194 wins, 183 losses, 37 shutouts, 149 complete games, and an earned run average of 3.40 runs per game. Although Jackson was never with a pennant-winning team and was never able to participate in the World Series, he did pitch in four All-Star games and was the winning pitcher for the National League in the 1963 game at Cleveland. After his retirement from baseball, Jackson returned to his native Idaho where he was elected four times to the state legislature.

In another well-pitched game for Cincinnati by Jim Maloney, the Reds, with only three hits in the game, beat the St. Louis Cardinals 2 to 1 on Tuesday, May 30, at Crosley Field. This brought the Reds to a record of 30 wins and 17 losses which was two and one-half games ahead of the Cardinals at 24-16. Maloney (4-2) pitched eight innings, and gave up one run on seven hits and four walks. He had five strikeouts. Reliever Don Nottebart worked the ninth inning for the Reds to earn his 1st save of the year. In the third inning, a solo home run by St. Louis center fielder Bobby Tolan, his 1st, gave the Cardinals a one run lead. Then the Reds rallied for two runs in the last of the eighth, which gave them the win. The Cincinnati runs in the eighth were driven in by Vada Pinson with his 7th double of the season and shortstop Leo Cardenas. Twenty-nine-year-old pitcher Dick Hughes (2-2) took the loss for St. Louis. In the American League, Detroit at 26-14 was now the leader by one and one-half games over the White Sox.

As the 1967 season moved into the summer, Cincinnati stayed in front by winning 10 of their next 16 games. They moved to 40-23 with a 3 to 2 win over the Dodgers at Dodger Stadium on Friday, June 16. The loss dropped Los Angeles to 23-36, a full fifteen games out of first place. There was superior pitching by both teams, with each offense producing only four hits in the game. The score was tied at two runs each after six innings. The game winning hit came on a home run by Reds' first baseman Lee May with the bases empty, his 4th of the season. May would go on to have a productive Major League career with four different teams, which would last through the 1982 season. In his career, May would hit 354 home runs and have an overall batting average of .267. For Cincinnati the complete game winner was Mel Queen (8-1), who surrendered two runs on four hits by the Dodgers. Queen would go on to finish the 1967 season with 14 wins, 8 losses, and an ERA of 2.76 runs per game. For the Dodgers the loss was charged to starter Bill Singer (1-3), who allowed three runs on three hits in his seven innings. As of June 16, the Reds were one and one-half games ahead of the St. Louis Cardinals in the pennant race. Meanwhile in the American League, the race was still seesawing back and forth with Chicago now a game and one-half in front of Detroit. Also the Minnesota Twins and the Boston Red Sox were lurking four and one-half and five games behind, respectively.

As the month of June came to an end on Friday, June 30, the Red Sox defeated the Athletics 5 to 3 at Municipal Stadium in Kansas City. Although Kansas City outhit the Red Sox seven to five, the Red Sox had two home runs in the game. First baseman George Scott hit his 10th of the year in the fifth inning and right fielder Tony Conigliaro notched his 10th in the sixth inning, with two runners on base. For Boston the winning pitcher was Gary Bell (6-6), who pitched seven and two-third innings and allowed three runs on seven hits. Relief pitcher John Wyatt worked the last inning and one-third to earn his 9th save of the season. The loser for the Athletics was 22-year-old Jim Nash. He went the first six innings of the game, surrendered four runs on four hits, and struck out five. For the Athletics, second year player Rick Monday had two hits in four at bats and two runs batted in during the game. Monday would go on to have a 19-year Major League career with the Athletics, Cubs, and Dodgers ending after the 1984 season. In his career, he batted .264 and hit 241 home runs. With the win, Boston improved to 37-34 for the season and Kansas City fell to 34-41.

The 1967 All-Star game was a lengthy affair which took fifteen innings to decide and was played on Tuesday, July 11, at Anaheim Stadium, the home of the California Angels. Attendance was 46,309. The National League came out on top over the American League 2 to 1 with all three runs resulting from solo home runs. In the second inning the Philadelphia Phillies' Dick Allen homered for the National League. In the sixth Baltimore's Brooks Robinson homered to tie the game at one run each. Finally in the top of the fifteenth inning, Tony Perez of the Cincinnati Reds hit the deciding homer and he was named the game's MVP. Don Drysdale of the Los Angeles Dodgers was the winning pitcher, with the loss being charged to Catfish Hunter of the Kansas City Athletics. There was a total of thirty strikeouts in the game, which was a new All-Star game record, and it was the very first All-Star game in which all of the runs scored resulted from home runs.

Early in July, St. Louis surpassed the Cincinnati Reds in the standings. On July 12, the day after the All-Star game, the Cardinals edged Pittsburgh 4 to 3 at Busch Stadium, for their 50th win against 32 losses. The Cardinals scored two runs in the sixth inning and still led 2-0 after seven innings of play. In the top of the eighth, the Pirates picked up three runs to take the lead. Two of the runs came on a homer by Pittsburgh shortstop Gene Alley, his 5th of the season. Then in the last of the eighth, the Cardinals won it on a two-run home run by third baseman Mike Shannon, his 6th of the year. Relief pitchers figured in the decision for both teams. The winner for the Cardinals was left-hander Al Jackson (6-4), who worked the last inning and two-third and yielded only one base hit. For the Pirates, the loss was charged to former Yankee Pete Mikkelsen (1-2). Mikkelsen pitched two-third of an inning and gave up the game winning hit by Shannon. Since June 16, the Cardinals had gone 15-11 compared to Cincinnati's record of 6 wins and 16 losses. The Cardinals were now four games ahead of the Chicago Cubs, and five and one-half games up on both San Francisco and Cincinnati.

In the American League on Sunday, July 16, at Fenway Park, the Boston Red Sox got the better of the Detroit Tigers by a score of 9 to 5. After the first four innings, the Red Sox led the game 8 to 2 by scoring five runs in the third inning, and three in the fourth. Detroit's effort to come back later in the contest fell four runs short. The winner for Boston was 27-year-old starter Bucky Brandon (3-7), who pitched the first five and one-third innings. He gave up three earned runs on six hits. Brandon would go on to have a seven-year Major League career, mostly with the Red Sox and Phillies. He retired after the 1973 season with a total of 28 wins and 37 losses. There were four home runs in the game. For Boston, Tony Conigliaro hit number 15 in the third inning, with two runners on, and Carl Yastrzemski hit his 21st in the seventh inning. In a losing cause for the Tigers, Willie Horton notched his 11th of the season in the second, and in the ninth inning center fielder Mickey Stanley hit his 5th of the 1967 season. Red Sox center fielder Reggie Smith went three-for-four in the game and scored two runs. The loss for Detroit went to their starter Joe Sparma (9-3). Attendance at Fenway was 28,237. Boston was now 45-40 for the season. This win was the third in a ten-game winning streak for the Red Sox. The loss dropped the Tigers to an identical record of 45 wins and 40 losses.

By July 29, with over one-half the season complete, both defending league champions occupied eighth place in their respective leagues. The American League Baltimore Orioles were 44-53 and the National League Los Angeles Dodgers were 45-54. On Saturday, July 29, the Cardinals shut out the Atlanta Braves 6-0 to improve their record to 60 wins and 40 losses. There were 35,243 fans at Atlanta Stadium to see their Braves take the loss. Left-hander Steve Carlton (9-6) pitched eight innings for the win. Carlton gave up five hits, walked four, and struck out five, before reliever Joe Hoerner came in to pitch the ninth for St. Louis. The Cardinals produced three home runs in the game by first baseman Orlando Cepeda, his 18th, catcher Tim McCarver, his 9th, and right fielder Roger Maris, his 8th of the season. Atlanta used four pitchers in the game, with the loss being charged to starter Tony Cloninger (3-6), who surrendered five runs in his three innings pitched. At this point, the second place Chicago Cubs were 57-43 and trailed the Cardinals by three games.

At Busch Stadium in St. Louis a crowd of 49,093 was gathered on Saturday, August 12, as the Cardinals defeated the San Francisco Giants 3 to 2. There were no home runs in the game. The line score read 3 runs, 7 hits, 2 errors for St. Louis and 2 runs, 10 hits and no errors for San Francisco. The Giants took an early lead with two unearned runs off starter Steve Carlton in the top of the first inning. The Cardinals came from behind with one run in the home half of the first inning and then scored two lead runs in the sixth. The Giants were held scoreless for the last eight innings of the game. Center fielder Curt Flood and first baseman Orlando Cepeda each had two hits and drove in a run for the Cardinals. One of Flood's hits was his first triple of the season. The winning pitcher for St. Louis was Jack Lamabe (1-6), who worked seven innings, gave up only three hits, and had six strikeouts. The loss for the Giants was charged to the veteran Lindy McDaniel (1-5). McDaniel gave up the two lead runs in the sixth during his four and two-third innings pitched. The Cardinals had now won 70 and lost 44, which extended their league lead to eight and one-half games over the second place Atlanta Braves.

INTERLUDE - ORLANDO CEPEDA

Orlando Cepeda was born in Ponce, Puerto Rico on September 17, 1937. He began his Major League Baseball career in 1958 with the San Francisco Giants, and was named National League Rookie of the Year at the age of 21. Over a seventeen-year span, mostly with the Giants, Cardinals, and Braves,

Cepeda, a right-handed power hitter, accumulated 379 home runs, with an overall .297 batting average. In the twelve seasons from 1957 through 1968, Cepeda hit 284 home runs with a batting average of .303. Cepeda was with several excellent San Francisco teams from 1958 until he was traded to the Cardinals on May 8, 1966. His time with St. Louis extended through the end of the 1968 season. Then in the off-season, he was traded to the Atlanta Braves. His performance on the field in the 1967 season for the Cardinals earned him the 1967 National League MVP Award. Cepeda played with Atlanta from 1969 into the 1972 season. Then, he was briefly with Oakland, Boston, and Kansas City, before retiring as an active player following the 1974 season.

Cepeda appeared in the 1962 World Series with San Francisco and the 1967 and 1968 World Series with St. Louis. Overall in nineteen World Series games, he had a batting average of .171 and hit two home runs, which were both in the 1968 Series against Detroit. In All-Star game competition, Cepeda made appearances in nine games. He had only one base hit in 27 at bats for an average of .037. He also walked once, was hit by a pitch once, and grounded into three double plays.

In the American League, the pennant race was very close with the Minnesota Twins ahead of the White Sox by one and one-half games as of Wednesday, August 16. On that day Minnesota defeated the California Angels by 5 to 1 with the Twins scoring all five of their runs in the top of the first inning. Following this game, the Twins had won 65 games and lost 50. There were no home runs in the game. The winner was right-hander Dean Chance (16-8), who fanned ten Angels' hitters and scattered nine hits and four walks over nine complete innings pitched. The loser for the Angels was Jim McGlothlin (10-5), who gave up all five Twins' runs in his two-third innings pitched as the starter. McGlothlin would go on to finish the 1967 season for the Angels with 12 wins, 8 losses, and a 2.96 earned run average. As visitors, the Twins made the most of only six hits in the game. First inning hits included the 26th double of the year for second baseman Cesar Tovar, the 11th double for center fielder Ted Uhlaender, and the 6th triple of the year for shortstop Zoilo Versalles. The Twins were held scoreless the remaining eight innings of the game on only two hits.

The Cardinals continued solid play and picked up their 80th win against 49 losses on Sunday, August 27, over the Dodgers at Dodger Stadium by 6 to 2. In second place now were the Cincinnati Reds at 70-60, which trailed the Cardinals by ten and one-half games. The Cardinals outhit the Dodgers by eleven to eight in a game in which neither team managed a home run. St. Louis scored five runs in the third inning off losing pitcher Claude Osteen (15-13), who was relieved after two and two-third innings. For the Cardinals, the winning pitcher was 24-year-old Nelson Briles (9-5). Briles went eight innings, gave up two runs on seven hits, and struck out six. Briles would go on to have a Major League career which lasted for fourteen years through the 1978 season. He compiled a record of 129 wins, 112 losses, with an earned run average of 3.44 runs per game. In a losing cause, Dodgers' right fielder Ron Fairly hit safely four times in four times at bat during the game. Fairly's batting average for L.A. during 1967 dropped to .220 for the season, down from .288 in the previous year. As of August 27, both the Dodgers and the Baltimore Orioles still remained in eighth place in their respective leagues. Baltimore was now 57-69 and Los Angeles had a record of 59 wins and 68 losses.

By September 11, the St. Louis lead over the second place San Francisco Giants was ten and one-half games and, as the Cardinals (90-55) defeated the Philadelphia Phillies 5 to 1, the days of the season were running out. The game was played at Busch Stadium in St. Louis before 18,390 fans. Nine total bases on balls by the Philadelphia pitchers helped lengthen the game to 3 hours and 1 minute. The Phillies scored a single run in the top of the second, but St. Louis countered with three in the fourth, one in the seventh, and one in the eighth to pick up the win. Nelson Briles (12-5) pitched the complete game win. He gave up eight hits and struck out six for the Cardinals. The losing pitcher for Philadelphia was left-hander Chris Short (7-10), who lasted three and two-third innings and surrendered the go-ahead runs to the Cardinals in the fourth. There were no home runs in the game, but the Cardinals did have eleven base hits. Leading the hit parade for St. Louis were Tim McCarver, 4 hits, Julian Javier, 3 hits, and Curt Flood, 2 hits, which included his 20th double of the season.

The Cardinals won game number 100 versus 60 losses by 3 to 1 on the road at Atlanta on Saturday, September 30. They had 3 runs, 7 hits and 1 error against 1 run, 3 hits and 2 errors for the Braves. With the pennant already decided, the game took only 1 hour and 54 minutes and attendance was a sparse 5,604. The winner for St. Louis was Dick Hughes (16-6). In nine innings, Hughes gave up one run on three hits and had six strikeouts. The losing pitcher for Atlanta was 23-year-old rookie Jim Britton (0-2). Even though he lost, Britton only allowed seven hits and three runs in eight innings on the mound. There were no home runs in the game. A highlight for St. Louis was left fielder Lou Brock's three hits in four at bats. Brock also scored two of the runs for the Cardinals and recorded his 52nd stolen base of the season. The Cardinals would complete the regular season the next day with another win finishing ten and one-half games in front of second place San Francisco at 91-71.

The pennant race in the American League continued to be undecided down to the very last day of the season. Boston, Minnesota and Detroit all had identical records of 91 wins and 70 losses with one game remaining. On Sunday, October 1, it was the Minnesota Twins playing at Boston and the Tigers hosting the Angels at Detroit. Detroit lost to California by a score of 8 to 5, so the winner between the Twins and the Red Sox would claim the pennant. The Twins picked up single runs in the first and third innings to take a 2-0 lead. Then the Red Sox rallied with five big runs in the bottom of the sixth and went on for a 5 to 3 win for the American League pennant. The winning pitcher in this crucial game for Boston was Jim Lonborg (22-9). Lonborg worked all nine innings, gave up seven hits, four walks, and had five strikeouts. Only one of the Twins' three runs against him was earned, due to errors by Carl Yastrzemski, in left field, and by first baseman George Scott. The losing pitcher for Minnesota was Dean Chance (20-14). Chance pitched five shutout innings but then was pounded for all five Boston runs in the sixth. The Red Sox had twelve hits to seven for Minnesota, including a four-for-four performance with two runs batted in from left fielder Carl Yastrzemski. There were no home runs in the game. There were only two extra base hits, including the 31st double of the season for Yastrzemski, and the 34th double of the year for Minnesota right fielder Tony Oliva. Attendance at Fenway Park numbered 35,770 for this deciding contest, which was played in 2 hours and 25 minutes. This final dramatic game of the American League 1967 season, played at Fenway, was keyed by the heroic performances by the Red

Sox team, and especially, by their star players Carl Yastrzemski and pitcher Jim Lonborg.

Carl Yastrzemski of the Boston Red Sox was the American League batting champion with an average of .326. He was followed by Frank Robinson of the Baltimore Orioles at .311, and Detroit's Al Kaline with .308. In home runs, Harmon Killebrew of the Minnesota Twins tied for the lead with Yastrzemski at 44. Frank Howard of the Washington Senators finished third with 36. Yaz also led the league with 121 runs batted in, followed by Killebrew with 113, and Frank Robinson with 94. League champions, the Boston Red Sox, led in the hitting statistical categories with a .255 batting average, 158 home runs, and 722 total runs scored.

In individual pitching, Jim Lonborg of Boston and Earl Wilson of Detroit each won 22 games, followed by Dean Chance of Minnesota with 20. The pitcher with the lowest earned run average was Joel Horlen of the Chicago White Sox at 2.06. His White Sox teammate Gary Peters finished second with 2.28 runs per game. Lonborg recorded 246 strikeouts to lead the league, followed by Sam McDowell of Cleveland with 236, and Dean Chance with 220. Chicago White Sox pitchers had the lowest combined team earned run average with 2.45 runs per game, and allowed the fewest hits with 1,197. The Cleveland Indians' pitching staff finished the year with the most strikeouts at 1,189.

Roberto Clemente of the Pittsburgh Pirates won the National League batting crown with .357, which was well ahead of Tony Gonzalez of the Philadelphia Phillies at .339, and Matty Alou of the Pirates at .338. Finishing fourth was the Cardinals' Curt Flood with .335. In home runs, the leader was Henry Aaron of the Atlanta Braves with 39, followed by Jimmy Wynn of Houston with 37. Willie McCovey of the Giants and the Cubs' Ron Santo were next, each with 31. Orlando Cepeda of the St. Louis Cardinals topped the runs batted in list with 111, followed closely by Clemente, 110, Aaron, 109, and Wynn, with 107. Team batting was led by the Pittsburgh Pirates with an average of .277. The Atlanta Braves hit the most home runs with 158, and the Chicago Cubs led the league in total runs scored with 702.

There were two twenty-game winners in the National League. Mike McCormick of San Francisco led with 22, and Fergie Jenkins of the Chicago

Cubs won 20. Pitcher Phil Niekro of the Atlanta Braves posted the lowest ERA with 1.87. Jim Bunning and Chris Short both of Philadelphia were next with 2.29 and 2.39, respectively. In strikeouts, Bunning led with 253, followed by Jenkins with 236, and Gaylord Perry of the Giants at 230. In overall pitching, the San Francisco Giants had the lowest team earned run average with 2.92, and allowed the fewest hits with 1,283. The Cincinnati Reds' pitching staff recorded the most strikeouts with 1,065.

It almost seemed like Carl Yastrzemski personally willed the Boston Red Sox to the American League pennant, so his selection as Most Valuable Player was no surprise. The Junior Circuit Rookie of the Year honors went to Rod Carew of the Minnesota Twins. At the age of 22, Carew mainly played second base and batted .292 in 137 games. Orlando Cepeda of the pennant winning Cardinals became the National League MVP. Rookie of the Year honors went to a young pitcher, Tom Seaver of the New York Mets. For the tenth place Mets, Seaver, at age 23, won 16 games and lost 13, with an earned run average of 2.76. 1967 was the first season that baseball recognized a separate Cy Young Award winner in both leagues. The American League winner was Jim Lonborg of Boston and the National League Award went to Mike McCormick of the San Francisco Giants.

The 1967 World Series featured the National League champion St. Louis Cardinals against the Boston Red Sox, the surprise and unlikely winner of the American League pennant on the final day of the regular season. The Red Sox were making their first appearance in the Series since 1948. Before the start of the season, the Cardinals had added outfielder Roger Maris to their roster in a trade with the Yankees. Boston had barely won a close American League pennant race, and were bolstered by the outstanding season of outfielder Carl Yastrzemski.

The World Series would open with games one and two scheduled at Fenway Park in Boston. It had been many years since much attention had been focused on Fenway, which the Red Sox opened in 1912. Fenway's very first game was on April 20, 1912, just a few days following the Titanic disaster. The ceremonial first pitch was thrown by Boston Mayor John F. Fitzgerald, President Kennedy's maternal grandfather. Fenway is located near Kenmore Square in Boston just south of the Massachusetts Turnpike. The most celebrated feature of Fenway Park is its left field wall, aptly known as the

Green Monster. Fenway is one of the smallest parks in baseball and tends to favor hitters at the expense of pitchers. The Green Monster is 37 feet tall and varies in its distance from home plate, from 310 feet to 315 feet. The other outfield dimensions in Fenway are also relatively short. The outfield has odd angles which make it a unique setting in which to watch a game. The 1967 World Series would put Boston and Fenway Park on center stage for the enjoyment of a national audience. The stage was beautifully set. Key players in the Series were expected to be as follows.

CATCHER - St. Louis, Tim McCarver, 26, and Boston, Elston Howard, 38. McCarver was in his fifth season as the regular catcher for St. Louis. He batted .295 with 14 home runs in 138 games. Howard, the former Yankee, was traded to the Red Sox midway through the 1967 season. He had a batting average of only .147 for the Red Sox in 42 games. Advantage goes to St. Louis.

FIRST BASE - St. Louis, Orlando Cepeda, 30, and Boston, George Scott, 23. In his second season with St. Louis, Cepeda played in 151 games and had 25 home runs with a batting average of .325. Scott had been with Boston for two full years. In an improved second season he batted .303 and hit 19 home runs in 159 games. Cepeda was a veteran player formerly with San Francisco. Advantage to St. Louis.

SECOND BASE - St. Louis, Julian Javier, 31, and Boston, Jerry Adair, 31. Javier had been with the Cardinals since 1960. In 1967 he had 14 home runs and batted .281 in 140 games. Adair, formerly of the Orioles, was in 89 games for Boston in 1967, during which he averaged .291. Rated only with a slight advantage for the Cardinals.

SHORTSTOP - St. Louis, Dal Maxvill, 28, and Boston, Rico Petrocelli, 24. Maxvill began his career with the Cardinals in 1962. He had an average of .227 in 152 games. Petrocelli began with the Red Sox in 1963. He hit .259 and had 17 home runs in 142 games. With Petrocelli's power, the edge is with Boston.

THIRD BASE - St. Louis, Mike Shannon, 28, and Boston, Joe Foy, 24. Shannon was a veteran of the World Series three years earlier. In 130 games in 1967 he hit 12 home runs with a .245 batting average. Foy was in his second year with Boston. He finished with a .251 batting average and 16 home runs in 130 games. A slight edge leans to the Cardinals, based on experience.

LEFT FIELD - St. Louis, Lou Brock, 28, and Boston, Carl Yastrzemski, 28. Brock batted .299 with 21 home runs in 159 games. This was his fourth consecutive season with at least 12 home runs. He had been with the Cardinals since 1964 and was a real threat as a base runner, with 52 stolen bases. Yastrzemski had been with the Red Sox beginning in 1961 and had been in double figures in home runs each year. While leading Boston to the pennant, he batted .326 and hit 44 home runs, with 121 RBI in 161 games. Because of his stellar performance in 1967, the advantage must go to Boston.

CENTER FIELD - St. Louis, Curt Flood, 29, and Boston, Reggie Smith, 22. Flood was an experienced veteran outfielder who had been a regular with St. Louis since 1958. He averaged .335 in 134 games and generally batted second in the order behind the speedy Brock. Smith was in his first full season with Boston. In 158 games he hit 15 home runs with a batting average of .246. Advantage is with St. Louis.

RIGHT FIELD - St. Louis, Roger Maris, 33, and Boston, Jose Tartabull, 29. Maris was traded from the Yankees to the Cardinals after the 1966 season. In 1967 Maris appeared in 125 games, and hit 9 home runs with a .261 batting average. Tartabull, born in Cuba, was in his second year with Boston, after starting with Kansas City in 1962. In 115 games his batting average was .223. The Cardinals have the edge because of experience.

STARTING PITCHING - For St. Louis: Bob Gibson, 32, won 13, lost 7. Nelson Briles, 24, won 14, lost 5. Dick Hughes, 29, won 16, lost 6. For Boston: Jim Lonborg, 25, won 22, lost 9. Jose Santiago, 27, won 12, lost 4. John Wyatt, 32, won 10, lost 7. The hard throwing Gibson led the way, giving St. Louis a competitive edge in pitching.

MANAGERS - St. Louis, Red Schoendienst, 44, and Boston, Dick Williams, 38. Schoendienst became manager of the St. Louis Cardinals beginning with the 1965 season. He had been a Major League player from 1945 through 1963 with the Cardinals, Giants, and Braves. Williams was in his first year as manager of the Red Sox. He had a career as a Major League player from 1951 through 1964 with the Dodgers, Orioles, Indians, Athletics, and Red Sox.

St. Louis won 101 and lost 60 to finish in first place in the National League by ten and one-half games. The Cardinals had a winning record each month. Their best month was August, with 21 wins and 11 losses. They only had a losing record against Pittsburgh, with 7 wins and 11 losses. Boston eked out the American League pennant by one game over Minnesota and Detroit. The Red Sox won 92 and lost 70. They were strongest in the second half of the season. Starting on July 1, Boston won 55 and lost 36. They fared the best against Cleveland with 13-5 and the worst against Minnesota with 7-11. The Red Sox had 27 wins and 28 losses in games decided by one run.

The first game of the 1967 World Series took place on Wednesday, October 4, at Fenway Park in Boston. The game turned out to be a low scoring pitcher's duel between the Cardinals' Bob Gibson and Jose Santiago of the Red Sox. Both teams picked up a single run in the third inning, with the Boston run coming on a solo home run by pitcher Santiago. Then the Cardinals scored the winning run in the top of the seventh for a 2 to 1 win in the opener. Left fielder Lou Brock keyed the Cardinals' offense with four hits in four at bats in the game, along with two stolen bases. Right fielder Roger Maris notched both runs batted in for St. Louis. The line score was 2 runs, 10 hits, no errors for St. Louis and 1 run, 6 hits and no errors for the Red Sox. Bob Gibson (1-0) went all the way to earn the win for the Cardinals. He struck out ten in his nine innings pitched. The loss went to Boston starter Jose Santiago (0-1), who allowed ten hits and two walks in seven innings.

The second game was played the next day. Boston evened the Series with a 5-0 one-hit shutout by starter Jim Lonborg (1-0) and two home runs by left fielder Carl Yastrzemski. The Cardinals prevailed in game three at Busch Stadium in St. Louis on Saturday, October 7, with a 5 to 2 win behind the pitching of Nelson Briles (1-0). After three games, the Cardinals led the Series by two games to one. The formidable Bob Gibson was scheduled to pitch for St. Louis in the fourth game on Sunday.

In the fourth game Bob Gibson (2-0) allowed the Red Sox only five hits in a 6-0 Cardinals win in which he had six strikeouts. St. Louis jumped to an early lead with four runs in the bottom of the first inning followed by two more in the third inning. Boston starter Jose Santiago (0-2) retired only two batters in the first inning before giving way to relief help. There were no home runs in the game. The Cardinals had four doubles by Roger Maris, Orlando

Cepeda, Julian Javier, and Lou Brock. Maris and Tim McCarver each drove in two of the six St. Louis runs. In a losing cause, Carl Yastrzemski had two hits including one double for the Red Sox. The time of the game was a crisp 2 hours and 5 minutes with 54,575 Busch Stadium fans in attendance.

In the fifth game on Monday, October 9, the Red Sox picked up a 3 to 1 win and forced the Series back to Boston for a sixth game. Red Sox starter Jim Lonborg (2-0) threw a three-hitter, which was marred only by a ninth inning solo home run by the Cardinals' Roger Maris. Back at Fenway, the Red Sox needed one more win to force a seventh game. On Wednesday, October 11, they prevailed over St. Louis in an 8 to 4 slugfest, which featured four Red Sox home runs and a win in relief by pitcher John Wyatt (1-0). Boston home runs were hit by Carl Yastrzemski, Reggie Smith, and two by shortstop Rico Petrocelli.

For the seventh and deciding game on Thursday, October 12, the pitching matchup was Bob Gibson for St. Louis, against Jim Lonborg for Boston. Both had already won two games in the Series. The Cardinals took a 4-0 lead with two runs in the third inning, and two more in the fifth. Pitcher Bob Gibson homered in the fifth for one of the Cardinals' tallies. After the Red Sox came back with one run in the fifth, St. Louis finished off Lonborg with three runs in the sixth, on a three-run home run by Julian Javier, to make the score 7 to 1. Boston scratched for one more run in the eighth inning off Gibson to make the final score Cardinals 7, Red Sox 2. Gibson (3-0) worked all nine innings, allowed three hits, and struck out ten. In six innings, the loser, Jim Lonborg (2-1) gave up six earned runs on ten hits and struck out three. Other highlights in the deciding game for St. Louis were two hits in three at bats for Roger Maris, and two hits in four at bats, plus three stolen bases for left fielder Lou Brock. Maris led the Series with seven runs batted in, and Brock finished the Series with a total of seven stolen bases.

Overall it was a well-played and entertaining World Series, with the favorite St. Louis winning the championship of Major League Baseball for the second time in four years. The Cardinals narrowly outhit the Red Sox by a .223 to .216 average and outscored them 25 runs to 21 for the Series. The Red Sox did hit eight home runs in the Series, including three by Yastrzemski, compared to five by St. Louis. No Cardinal player hit more than one. Leading hitters for St. Louis were Lou Brock at .414, Roger Maris at .385, and Julian

Javier at .360. Carl Yastrzemski batted .400 in the Series for Boston. The St. Louis pitching staff ERA was 2.66 for the Series, with Boston posting one of 3.39 runs per game. Bob Gibson was by far the dominant pitcher. Gibson had three wins in three complete games and a 1.00 earned run average. Nelson Briles was the winner of the other game for the Cardinals, and had an ERA of 1.64 in eleven innings pitched. Jim Lonborg of Boston won two games, lost one, and finished with a 2.63 ERA in 24 innings in the Series.

1967 World Series Summary

Game 1	At Boston	Cardinals 2, Red Sox 1
Game 2	At Boston	Red Sox 5, Cardinals 0
Game 3	At St. Louis	Cardinals 5, Red Sox 2
Game 4	At St. Louis	Cardinals 6, Red Sox 0
Game 5	At St. Louis	Red Sox 3, Cardinals 1
Game 6	At Boston	Red Sox 8, Cardinals 4
Game 7	At Boston	Cardinals 7, Red Sox 2

St. Louis wins the World Series by 4 games to 3.

1968 Season

The Year of the Pitcher

O pening day in St. Louis on Wednesday, April 10, at Busch Stadium for the World Series champion Cardinals was against the Atlanta Braves. Opposing pitchers on the celebratory occasion were Pat Jarvis of the Braves and Bob Gibson for St. Louis. In the top of the second inning, Atlanta scored an unearned run on an error by Cardinals' left fielder Lou Brock and took a 1-0 lead. The lead stood up, with Jarvis on the mound, until the eighth inning when the Cardinals tied the score at one run each. Then the Cardinals won the opener with another run in the ninth to make the final score Cardinals 2, Braves 1. The line score read 2 runs, 7 hits, 1 error for the Cardinals and 1 run, 3 hits and 1 error for Atlanta. In a no-decision, Gibson pitched seven innings, gave up three hits, and had an unusual no strikeouts. The winner in relief was Ray Washburn (1-0), who pitched the eighth and ninth innings for St. Louis. Although Jarvis (0-1) pitched eight and one-third innings and surrendered only two runs, he ended up with the opening day loss. In an eight-year career in the Major Leagues, nearly all with Atlanta from 1966 through 1973, Jarvis won 85 and lost 73 with an ERA of 3.58. There were no home runs in the game. First baseman Orlando Cepeda and shortstop Dal Maxvill both had key doubles for the Cardinals in their late-inning rally. The first four batters in the Braves lineup, which included right fielder Henry Aaron and catcher Joe Torre, all failed to get a hit in four at bats. The Busch Stadium crowd of 34,740 witnessed a successful beginning to the Cardinals 1968 season.

The Cardinals won ten of their first fourteen games in the spring of 1968. On Friday, April 26, they squeezed by the Pittsburgh Pirates 2 to 1 for their 10th win against 4 losses. At this point in the early season, the Cardinals were two games in front of the second place Los Angeles Dodgers. The game was played at Busch Stadium before a crowd numbering 39,866. Both St. Louis runs were the result of solo home runs. Orlando Cepeda hit his 4th of the year, and Tim McCarver, his 1st, which was the winning run scored in the

185

last of the seventh inning. Pittsburgh outhit the Cardinals seven to five in the game. The Pirates' only run was driven in by first baseman Donn Clendenon in the fourth. Bob Gibson (1-1) was the winning pitcher for St. Louis. He scattered the Pirates' seven hits and struck out five in the complete game win. The loser for Pittsburgh was starter Bob Veale (0-3), who went seven innings, struck out seven, but surrendered the two homers hit by Cepeda and McCarver. Veale would go on to finish the 1968 season for the Pirates with 13 wins, 14 losses, and an ERA of 2.05 in 245 innings pitched.

In another game against Pittsburgh at Forbes Field on May 15, the Cardinals won number 20 against 10 losses by a score of 1-0. The complete game winner was left-hander Steve Carlton (4-1), who gave up four hits, walked only one, and struck out six. The only run of the game was scored on a fourth inning homer by Cardinals' second baseman Julian Javier, his 1st of the season. The loser for the Pirates was Steve Blass (1-1). Blass went six innings and allowed eight hits including the game winner. Blass would go on to complete an excellent year on the mound for Pittsburgh. He won 18, lost 6, and had an earned run average of 2.12 runs per game. In a ten-year Major League career ending in 1974, all with Pittsburgh, Blass won 103 games and lost 76 with an ERA of 3.63. The league lead for St. Louis was now three and one-half games over the Giants and four full games over the Atlanta Braves.

In early June, the pennant race in the American League was starting to take shape with the Detroit Tigers, at 30-17, with a three game lead over Baltimore and a four game edge over the Cleveland Indians. On June 2, The Yankees played at Detroit in a Sunday doubleheader. The Yankees edged the Tigers 4 to 3 in a close first game. In the second game, the Tigers won for the 30th time by 8 to 1, before a crowd of 43,912. After the Sunday split, the Yankees had won 22 and lost 26 so far in the season. The second game was scoreless until the Tigers came up with a six-run inning in the last of the fifth. Then the Tigers added two in the seventh, and the Yankees managed only the single tally in the top of the ninth inning. Detroit southpaw John Hiller (3-1) went all the way for the win. Hiller allowed six hits and four bases on balls. The only home run in the game was a grand slam in the fifth inning by Tigers' center fielder Mickey Stanley, his 3rd of the season. New York committed two errors in the field, so only three of the eight Detroit runs were earned. The loss for the Yankees went to starter Steve Barber (0-1), who lasted six and two-third innings and was roughed up by the Tigers for eight hits and four walks.

At Dodger Stadium in Los Angeles on June 4, the Dodgers, behind Don Drysdale, shut out the Pittsburgh Pirates 5-0. Drysdale (7-3) was in the middle of a historic streak of 58 and two-third consecutive scoreless innings, which broke the existing Major League record. In this win against the Pirates, he allowed only three hits, walked none, and had eight strikeouts. One of the three Pirates' hits was by Maury Wills, the former Dodgers' speedster, who was now with Pittsburgh. The Dodgers scored three runs in the fourth inning, one in the sixth, and one more in the stretch half of the seventh. The single run in the sixth was a solo home run by first baseman Wes Parker, his 2nd of the season. In a nine-year Major League career, all with the Dodgers from 1964 through 1972, Parker averaged .267 and hit 64 home runs. The losing pitcher for Pittsburgh was veteran Jim Bunning (3-6), who worked the first five innings of the game and allowed the three Dodgers' runs in the fourth inning. Los Angeles improved its record to 27-26 and the Pirates dropped to 19-26 at this point of the season. It is worth noting that Don Drysdale's consecutive scoreless innings streak was attracting a lot of media attention. Drysdale's name was mentioned in congratulatory terms by Bobby Kennedy in his brief speech in downtown Los Angeles after winning the 1968 California Primary Election, just a few minutes before he was tragically shot and fatally wounded.

Over the next twelve days, Detroit won ten out of thirteen games to improve their record to 40 wins and 20 losses. On Friday, June 14, at Comiskey Park in Chicago, the Tigers defeated the White Sox 6 to 5 in a fourteen inning marathon which lasted 4 hours and 12 minutes. The White Sox scored first with three runs in the first inning on a three-run home run by first baseman Tommy McCraw, his 7th of the season. Chicago added another run in the second, but then the Tigers tied the game at four runs each in the fifth inning. Detroit starting pitcher Earl Wilson homered for the Tigers with two on base to produce three of the four runs that tied the game. This was the 2nd of the 7 home runs Wilson would hit in the 1968 season. In his eleven-year Major League career, Wilson hit 35 home runs in 740 times at bat. The game remained deadlocked at four runs each until the thirteenth inning when each team scored a single run. Finally in the fourteenth inning, third baseman Don Wert delivered the game winning home run, his 7th of the year, to put the Tigers in the lead 6 to 5. Detroit had nine hits in the game, compared to eight for the White Sox. Detroit catcher Bill Freehan finished with three hits in six at bats. The two clubs combined used a total of ten pitchers in the game. The winner for the Tigers was John Hiller (5-1), who pitched the last two innings and allowed only two bases on balls. The loss for Chicago was charged to right-hander Bob Priddy (0-3). Priddy pitched the last two innings and surrendered the game winning home run. The win put Detroit into a six and one-half game lead over Baltimore and a seven and one-half game lead over the Cleveland Indians. The loss dropped the White Sox into ninth place in the American League with a won-lost record of 24-31.

Detroit continued to set the pace in the American League as the season approached its halfway point. After 77 games, the Tigers had won 50 and lost 27. Win number 50 came on Tuesday, July 2, at home against the California Angels in a close 3 to 1 ballgame. The Angels outhit the Tigers seven to five. Detroit managed two runs in the first inning, driven in by left fielder Willie Horton, and one run in the seventh. There were two home runs in the game. Detroit shortstop Tom Matchick hit his 1st of the season in the seventh to extend the Tigers lead, and in the eighth, shortstop Jim Fregosi hit his 7th of the year for the Angels' only run. Earl Wilson (6-5) pitched the complete game win for Detroit and struck out nine in the process. For California, the loss went to 23-year-old rookie Tom Murphy (2-1). Over six innings, Murphy gave up two runs, four hits, and walked one. At this point, Detroit was eight and one-half games ahead of the second place Cleveland Indians. Meanwhile in the National League, the St. Louis Cardinals maintained a lead of seven and one-half games over both Atlanta and the San Francisco Giants.

Strong pitching dominated the 1968 All-Star game which was played on Tuesday, July 9, at the Astrodome, the home of the Houston Astros. This was the first All-Star game to be held indoors in a domed stadium. The attendance was 48,321. There were no home runs in the game, which was won by the National League 1-0. The only run in the game was scored in the first inning by Willie Mays, who scored from third base as Willie McCovey hit into a double play with no one out. The National League had five hits to only three by the American League. The winning pitcher was National League starter Don Drysdale of the Los Angeles Dodgers and the loser was starter Luis Tiant of the Cleveland Indians.

On Saturday, July 20, the Cardinals shut out the New York Mets at Busch Stadium by 2-0. This was win number 60 for St. Louis against 33 losses. In a well-pitched game by both teams, the Cardinals scored a single run in both the seventh and eighth innings for the win. There were no home runs in the game. There was one triple in the eighth by the Cardinals' right fielder Roger Maris, his 2nd of the season. Pitching all the way to pick up the win was Ray Washburn (8-3). Washburn scattered eight Mets' hits and struck out six for the game. Washburn would go on to finish the season with 14 wins, 8 losses, and an ERA of 2.26 runs per game. The loss for the Mets went to right-hander Dick Selma (8-5), who allowed one run and seven hits over his seven innings pitched. In a losing cause for New York, center fielder Cleon Jones had three hits in four at bats and would go on to end the season with a .297 average in 147 games. This win increased the St. Louis lead over the Atlanta Braves, with 50 wins and 43 losses, to ten full games.

By the end of July, the St. Louis lead had expanded even more, to fourteen and one-half games over Cincinnati and to fifteen games over Atlanta. On July 31, the Cardinals edged the Philadelphia Phillies by a score of 3 to 2 at Connie Mack Stadium in Philadelphia. This was the Cardinals' 70th win against only 36 losses. Once again there were no home runs in the game as base hits were a scarce commodity. St. Louis starting pitcher Nelson Briles (13-7) picked up the complete game victory. In nine innings, Briles allowed two runs, seven hits, walked three, and had four strikeouts. The loser for the Phillies was left-hander Woodie Fryman (11-11), who worked seven innings and gave up three runs on seven hits by St. Louis. The Cardinals used only nine players in the ballgame. Leading the Cardinals on offense were left fielder Lou Brock and center fielder Curt Flood. Each had two hits and scored a run in the contest.

INTERLUDE - LOU BROCK

Lou Brock was born June 18, 1939, in El Dorado, Arkansas. He was a left-handed hitting outfielder who played Major League Baseball from 1961 through 1979. He broke in with the Chicago Cubs, but then was traded to the St. Louis Cardinals on June 15, 1964. His arrival to the Cardinals in 1964 was an important factor in the team's improvement in the second half of the season, which led to the National League pennant. In his nineteen-year career, Brock accumulated 3,023 hits for an overall batting average of .293. He had 486 doubles, 141 triples, and 149 home runs. He was best known for his speed and outstanding ability as a base runner and stolen base artist. He finished his career with a total of 938 stolen bases.

In the twelve years from 1957 through 1968, Brock stole 334 bases, with a high of 74 for the 1966 season. Although he was not known for being a home run hitter, Brock possessed occasional power. He hit 70 home runs for the Cardinals from 1964 through 1968, with a peak of 21 in 1967. Brock was a key member of the St. Louis Cardinals' World Series winning teams of 1964 and 1967, and of the St. Louis National League champion team of 1968. In 21 World Series games, he had a total of 34 hits, including four home runs for a batting average of .391. He stole fourteen bases in World Series competition, seven in 1967 and seven in 1968, and was caught stealing only twice. Brock batted .375 with two stolen bases in five All-Star game appearances for the National League.

The Athletics had relocated from Kansas City to Oakland beginning with the 1968 season. They were an improving team and on Thursday, August 15, they hosted the Yankees at the Oakland Alameda County Coliseum. There was no score in the game through four innings. In the bottom of the fifth inning, Oakland took a 4-0 lead with home runs by catcher Jim Pagliaroni, his 5th, and 22-year-old right fielder Reggie Jackson, his 22nd home run of the season. Jackson was in his first full year with the Athletics, and would finish the year with 29 home runs. Oakland shortstop Bert Campaneris notched his 17th double of the year and drove in one of the four runs. Then in the sixth inning, New York scored three runs on a three-run home run by first baseman Mickey Mantle, his 15th of the year. Mantle was 37-years old and in his final season as a player. He would hit three more home runs to finish with 18 for the season and 536 for his career. That was the extent of the scoring for the game. New York had eleven hits to only four for Oakland, but the final outcome was an Oakland win by 4 to 3. The winning pitcher for Oakland was John "Blue Moon" Odom (11-8). He worked six innings, allowed three runs on eight hits, and had seven strikeouts. The Athletics used three additional pitchers over the last three innings, with a save going to Lew Krausse, his 4th of the season. The loss for the Yankees went to starter Mel Stottlemyre (15-10), who surrendered four runs and struck out six batters in six innings pitched. After this game, Oakland was 62-57 and New York was 54-61.

INTERLUDE - BERT CAMPANERIS

Bert Campaneris was born in Cuba on March 9, 1942, and first played Major League Baseball in 1964 at the age of 22 for the Kansas City Athletics. Although he was not a prolific home run threat, in 1964 he became one of only five players in Major League history to hit two home runs in his very first game. Over a nineteen-year career which ran through the 1983 season, Campaneris was one of the most active base stealers in baseball. He completed his career with a lifetime total of 649 stolen bases. He accumulated 2,249 career hits including 313 doubles, 86 triples, 79 home runs, and finished with an overall batting average of .259.

In the five years from 1964 through 1968, Campaneris accumulated 230 stolen bases, which ranks fourth overall in the twelve-year period from 1957 through 1968. His number increased each year, up to 62 stolen bases for the 1968 season. A few years later in his career, Campaneris was the shortstop on the Oakland Athletics' World Series winning teams of 1972, 1973, and 1974.

On August 19, St. Louis defeated the Phillies at Philadelphia for their 80th win against 45 losses. This win was a classic 2-0 two-hitter by Cardinals' ace Bob Gibson (18-5), who also struck out eleven. The Cardinals scored one in the second inning, one in the eighth, and had a total of ten hits. The loss for Philadelphia went to starter Woodie Fryman (11-12), who pitched only two innings and allowed the winning run scored in the second inning. Phillies' reliever John Boozer came on to work six innings, allowing seven hits and the Cardinals' run in the eighth inning. There were no home runs in the game. Offensive highlights for St. Louis included left fielder Lou Brock reaching 35 stolen bases for the year and three hits in four at bats for 27-year-old center fielder Ron Davis, who drove in both St. Louis runs. In a relatively brief career, mostly with the Houston Astros, Davis had a total of 199 base hits and a batting average of .233. After 125 games, the Cardinals remained solidly in control of the National League race with a lead of thirteen and one-half games over the Cincinnati Reds at 64-56.

INTERLUDE - BOB GIBSON

Bob Gibson was born on November 9, 1935, in Omaha, Nebraska. He broke into the Major Leagues in 1959 with the St. Louis Cardinals and had a seventeen-year playing career exclusively with the Cardinals through the 1975 season. When he was at his best, he was an overpowering right-handed strikeout pitcher, who was known for his extremely competitive spirit. He accumulated 251 wins, 174 losses, 56 shutouts, 3,117 strikeouts, and a 2.91 earned run average during his career. From 1961 through 1974, Gibson had a streak of at least eleven wins per season. He won 20 or more games five times, including the years 1965, 1966, 1968, 1969, and 1970. In 1968, which is sometimes referred to as the year of the pitcher, he won 22 games, lost 9, and posted an extremely low earned run average of 1.12 in 304 innings pitched. Gibson also recorded thirteen shutouts and was named the National League Most Valuable Player.

During the years from 1957 through 1968, Gibson won 147 games. Gibson pitched well in the 1964, 1967, and 1968 World Series for St. Louis. Overall in World Series play, he won 7 games, lost 2, and had an ERA of 1.89 in 81 innings pitched. He had 92 strikeouts in World Series competition. Gibson also appeared in six All-Star games, in which he pitched eleven innings with an ERA of 3.27.

Over in the American League, the Detroit Tigers reached win number 90 with an 8 to 3 decision over the Minnesota Twins on Friday, September 6, at Tiger Stadium. This extended the Tigers record to 90-52 which was nine games ahead of second place Baltimore. In the first inning, Detroit jumped on Twins' starting pitcher Jim Kaat (12-11) for four runs. Three of these first inning runs resulted from a home run by Detroit left fielder Willie Horton, his 32nd of the season. Horton drove in a total of five runs in the ballgame. The Tigers also picked up two runs in the fourth inning, two more in the seventh, and coasted to the win. Twenty-four-year-old right fielder Graig Nettles hit his first career home run in the top of the second inning for the Twins. This was the first of 390 lifetime home runs for Nettles, in a career that was mostly with the New York Yankees. The winning pitcher for Detroit was Denny McLain (28-5). At the age of 24, McLain was having what would be the best year of his career in baseball. In this complete game, McLain gave up three runs on nine hits, and had twelve strikeouts.

On Friday, September 20, with the American League pennant already assured, Detroit reached a milestone with the team's 100th win of the season over the Washington Senators by a score of 6 to 3. The game took place at D.C. Stadium before a small crowd of only 5,929 fans. The Senators had a 3-0 lead after five innings and a 3 to 2 lead after seven innings, but the Tigers came from behind with four runs in the top of the eighth inning for the win. The line score was 6 runs, 12 hits, no errors for Detroit and 3 runs, 4 hits and no errors for Washington. Mickey Lolich (16-9) was the winner for the Tigers. Lolich pitched seven complete innings, gave up three runs, three hits, walked seven, and struck out nine. Reliever Pat Dobson came on to pitch the last two innings to earn his 7th save of the year for Detroit. The loss in relief for Washington was charged to Bob Humphreys (4-7), who was responsible for all four Tigers' runs in the eighth inning. In his nine-year Major League career, mostly with the Senators, Humphreys won 27 and lost 21, with an ERA of 3.36 runs per game. Detroit had four home runs in the game. Center fielder Jim Northrup hit two, his 20th and 21st of the season, 34-year-old right fielder Al Kaline, his 10th, and reserve catcher Jim Price, his 3rd. Northrup had four runs batted in during the game and Kaline had a perfect four hits in four at bats. With eight games left on the schedule, the Detroit Tigers were World Series bound, having won 100 and lost 54, which was thirteen and one-half games in front of the second place Baltimore Orioles at 87-68.

INTERLUDE - AL KALINE

Al Kaline was born December 19, 1934, in Baltimore, Maryland. Kaline enjoyed a Major League Baseball career of twenty-two years entirely with the Detroit Tigers from 1953 through 1974. Overall, he accumulated 3,007 hits, 399 home runs, and a batting average of .297. In 1955 Kaline became the youngest player, at the age of 20, to win the American League batting title with an average of .340. He provided quiet and consistent leadership as a right-handed hitting outfielder to one of the more successful American League franchises. His career was fulfilled with the American League title and World Series win in 1968.

In the years from 1957 through 1968, Kaline had 1,782 hits, including 255 home runs, with a twelve-year batting average of .302. With 767 walks and 555 strikeouts, Kaline was one of only a few players with more walks than strikeouts. In six of the twelve years in this period, he batted for an average of .300 or better. His highest average was .327 in 1959 and the lowest was .278 in 1960. In his only World Series appearance in 1968, Kaline had 11 hits in 29 times at bat for a batting average of .379, including two home runs and eight runs batted in. In All-Star competition, Kaline managed 12 hits in 37 at bats for an average of .324. After his playing career ended, Kaline worked in radio and television broadcasting for the Detroit Tigers.

The last day of the 1968 regular season was Sunday, September 29. In the National League, the pennant race had also already been decided for several days. In the last game of the season, the St. Louis Cardinals swamped the Houston Astros 11 to 1 at Busch Stadium. The Cardinals scored nine big runs in the second inning to take command and outhit the Astros thirteen to seven for the game. In preparation for the World Series, the Cardinals used four pitchers in the game with the win going to starter Ray Washburn (14-8). Washburn went the minimum five innings required for the win and allowed just the one run on five hits. The only run for the Astros was a first inning home run by center fielder Jimmy Wynn, his 26th of the season. St. Louis second baseman Julian Javier hit his 4th homer of the year in the fourth inning to score the Cardinals' tenth run. The loss for Houston went to their starter 31-year-old Mike Cuellar (8-11), who left the game after just one and two-third innings pitched. The Cardinals ended the season with their second consecutive National League pennant and a record of 97 wins and 65 losses. Finishing second were the San Francisco Giants who were nine games behind at 88-74.

The 1968 World Series, which would open with the first game in St. Louis, was a reminder of the Series of 1934. Thirty-four years in the past, the Cardinals also matched up against the Detroit Tigers. The 1934 World Series went the full seven games, and the Cardinals won over Detroit by four games to three.

For the second year in a row, the leader in batting average for the American League was Carl Yastrzemski of the Boston Red Sox at .301. Yaz was the only American Leaguer to bat over .300. He was followed by Danny Cater of the Oakland Athletics with .290, and Tony Oliva of the Minnesota Twins with .289. Frank Howard of the Washington Senators was at the top in home runs with 44. Willie Horton of the Detroit Tigers was second with 36 and was closely followed by Ken Harrelson of the Red Sox with 35. Harrelson led the league in runs batted in with 109, just ahead of Frank Howard with 106. The Detroit Tigers' Jim Northrup came in third with 90. The Oakland Athletics finished with the highest team batting average at .240. League champion Detroit had the most home runs with 185 and also led the league with 671 runs scored.

Individual pitching honors belonged to Denny McLain of the Detroit Tigers with 31 wins, followed by Dave McNally of Baltimore with 22, and Mel Stottlemyre of the Yankees and Luis Tiant of the Cleveland Indians with 21 each. Tiant finished with the lowest earned run average of 1.60. He was followed by his Indians' teammate Sam McDowell with 1.81. McNally was third in ERA with 1.95, just ahead of McLain at 1.96 runs per game. McDowell led the league with 283 strikeouts, which just edged out Denny McLain with 280. Luis Tiant was third with 264. In team pitching, the staff of the Cleveland Indians led in earned run average with 2.66, in fewest hits allowed with 1,087, and in strikeouts with 1,157.

The National League batting title was won by Pete Rose of the Cincinnati Reds who batted .335. He was followed by brothers Matty Alou of Pittsburgh and Felipe Alou of Atlanta, with .332 and .317, respectively. In home runs, Willie McCovey of the San Francisco Giants led with 36, and was followed closely by Dick Allen of the Phillies with 33. Ernie Banks of the Chicago Cubs finished third with 32. McCovey had the most runs batted in with 105. Teammates Ron Santo and Billy Williams of the Chicago Cubs ended with 98 each. In team batting, the Cincinnati Reds finished with the best average of .273. The Reds also scored the most runs with 690. The Chicago Cubs hit the most home runs with 130.

In individual pitching, Juan Marichal of the Giants led with 26 wins. Next were Bob Gibson of St. Louis with 22, and Fergie Jenkins of the Chicago Cubs at 20. Gibson easily finished with the lowest earned run average with 1.12. Bobby Bolin of San Francisco had 1.99, and Bob Veale of Pittsburgh ended at 2.05 runs per game. Gibson was also first in the National League with 268 strikeouts, followed closely by Jenkins with 260. The Los Angeles Dodgers' Bill Singer struck out 227 to finish third. The St. Louis Cardinals had the lowest team ERA with 2.49. New York Mets' pitchers gave up the fewest hits at 1,250. The most strikeouts recorded were by the Houston Astros' pitchers with a total of 1,021.

Postseason awards in the American League went to pitchers Denny McLain of the Detroit Tigers for Most Valuable Player, and to Stan Bahnsen of the New York Yankees for Rookie of the Year. McLain also took home the Cy Young Award. Bahnsen, 24-years old in 1968, won 17 games, lost 12, and compiled an ERA of 2.05 in 267 innings pitched. His career may never have quite equaled his rookie experience, but in sixteen years through the 1982 season for six different teams, Bahnsen won 146, lost 149, and had a 3.60 earned run average. The National League Most Valuable Player and Cy Young Award went to Bob Gibson of St. Louis. The National League Rookie of the Year was Cincinnati Reds' 21-year-old catcher Johnny Bench. In his first full season with the Reds, Bench hit .275 with 15 home runs. In seventeen years with Cincinnati through the 1983 season, Bench would finish his career with 389 home runs and a .267 batting average.

The most notable players set to compete against each other in the 1968 World Series by position were the following. The St. Louis Cardinals team lineup was much the same as the previous year, except they were all one year older.

CATCHER - Detroit, Bill Freehan, 27, and St. Louis, Tim McCarver, 27. Freehan was in his sixth season with Detroit. In 155 games he hit 25 home runs and batted .263. The offensive production was down for McCarver from his 1967 statistics. In 128 games he hit 5 home runs and had a batting average of .253. Both were tested veteran ballplayers. The advantage to Detroit is slight.

FIRST BASE - Detroit, Norm Cash, 34, and St. Louis, Orlando Cepeda, 31. Cash had been with Detroit since 1960. For nine years in a row, he had hit at least 18 home runs. In 127 games Cash hit 25 home runs with an average of .263. Cepeda was in his third year with the Cardinals and his offensive numbers were down from the previous two years. In 1968 he had a batting average of .248 with 16 home runs in 157 games. Again, both were experienced players with the edge leaning to Detroit.

SECOND BASE - Detroit, Dick McAuliffe, 29, and St. Louis, Julian Javier, 32. McAuliffe began his career with the Tigers in 1960. For seven consecutive seasons he had hit at least 12 home runs. In 1968 he had 16 home runs and batted .249 in 151 games. Javier had been with the Cardinals since 1960 and this would be his second World Series. In 139 games he had a batting average of .260 with 4 home runs. The two are rated even.

SHORTSTOP - Detroit, Mickey Stanley, 26, and St. Louis, Dal Maxvill, 29. Stanley had been with Detroit starting in 1964. In 153 games he batted .259 and hit 11 home runs. Maxvill, in his second full year as the Cardinals' regular shortstop, had a batting average of .253 in 151 games. No advantage to either team.

THIRD BASE - Detroit, Don Wert, 30, and St. Louis, Mike Shannon, 29. Wert had broken in with Detroit in 1963. He averaged only .200 but did hit 12 home runs in 150 games. In the previous five years, his lowest average had been .257. In 156 games Shannon batted .266 and hit 15 home runs. These numbers were increased from his previous season. A slight advantage for St. Louis.

LEFT FIELD - Detroit, Willie Horton, 26, and St. Louis, Lou Brock, 29. Horton had started playing with Detroit in 1963. He hit 36 home runs and averaged .285 in 143 games. This would be the third World Series for Brock. In 159 games he batted .279 with 6 home runs and 62 stolen bases. Both players had competing strengths with no advantage to either team.

CENTER FIELD - Detroit, Jim Northrup, 29, and St. Louis, Curt Flood, 30. Northrup was in his third year as a regular outfielder for the Tigers. In 154 games he hit 21 home runs with an average of .264. Flood had a batting average of .301 with 5 home runs in 150 games for St. Louis. Both are strong players. Rated even.

RIGHT FIELD - Detroit, Al Kaline, 34, and St. Louis, Roger Maris, 34. Kaline had been a member of the Detroit Tigers going all the way back to 1953. He was an icon for the city of Detroit. He was finally in the World Series for the first time. In 1968 he was limited to 102 games but hit 10 home runs and finished with a .287 batting average. This was Maris' second World Series playing for St. Louis and his seventh Series overall. He had already announced his retirement from baseball, so this would be his last one. In 1968 Maris was limited to 100 games. In his final season he hit 5 home runs and sported a batting average of .255. Both Kaline and Maris could rise to the occasion. Rated even.

STARTING PITCHING - For Detroit: Denny McLain, 24, won 31, lost 6. Mickey Lolich, 28, won 17, lost 9. Earl Wilson, 34, won 13, lost 12. For St. Louis: Bob Gibson, 33, won 22, lost 9. Nelson Briles, 25, won 19, lost 11. Ray Washburn, 30, won 14, lost 8. With Gibson's success in two prior World Series for St. Louis, it is hard to go against the Cardinals. However, with the phenomenal season by McLain the two pitching staffs are declared even.

MANAGERS - Detroit, Mayo Smith, 53, and St. Louis, Red Schoendienst, 45. Smith was in his second year as manager of the Detroit Tigers. He was briefly with the Philadelphia Athletics during the 1945 season as a player. Schoendienst was in his second World Series as manager of St. Louis.

INTERLUDE - RED SCHOENDIENST

St. Louis Cardinals manager Red Schoendienst had a history as a player that went back to 1945 when he broke in with the Cardinals at the age of 22. Schoendienst was born in Germantown, Illinois on February 2, 1923. He was with St. Louis from 1945 until midway through the 1956 season, when he was traded to the New York Giants. Then on June 15, 1957, Schoendienst was traded to the Milwaukee Braves. In 1957 he led the National League in hits with 200 and appeared in the 1957 and 1958 World Series with Milwaukee. His time with the Braves ended after the 1960 season. In 1961, 1962, and very briefly in 1963, he was back with St. Louis, where he ended his playing career. In his nineteen-year career, Schoendienst, primarily a second baseman, accumulated 2,449 hits for a .289 lifetime batting average. He was an excellent contact hitter who could put the ball in play and avoid striking out. He hit only 84 home runs in his career, but drew 606 walks compared to only 346 strikeouts.

In the two October Classics with Milwaukee in 1957-1958 and one with the Cardinals in 1946, Schoendienst had 21 hits in 78 at bats for an average of .269. In his appearances in nine All-Star games, he had four hits, including a game-winning home run in the fourteenth inning of the 1950 All-Star game at Comiskey Park in Chicago. Following his playing career, Schoendienst was manager of the St. Louis Cardinals from 1965 through 1976.

Detroit ran away with the American League by twelve full games and finished at 103-59. The Tigers had consistently winning months all season long. July was their worst month at 17-12. They also consistently won against all the other teams in the League. They went 13-5 against California, Chicago, and Oakland. St. Louis won in the National League by nine games with 97 wins and 65 losses. The Cardinals played their best baseball in June and July, when they were a combined 46-15. Against both Atlanta and Houston, the Cardinals were 13-5, but against San Francisco their record was 8 wins and 10 losses. St. Louis won in shutouts 30 times.

The Series began at Busch Stadium in St. Louis on Wednesday, October 2. The pitching matchup featured both clubs' best -- Denny McLain for Detroit and Bob Gibson for St. Louis. There were only eleven hits in the game, five for Detroit and six for St. Louis. Gibson (1-0) was at his best and hurled a complete game 4-0 win over the Tigers, allowing five hits, one walk, and recording seventeen strikeouts, a new World Series record. McLain (0-1) pitched five innings and gave up three runs in the bottom of the fourth inning on run scoring singles by Mike Shannon and Julian Javier. In the seventh inning, the Cardinals added a fourth run on a Lou Brock solo home run off Detroit reliever Pat Dobson. The Cardinals' team speed was also evident in the game with stolen bases by Brock, Javier, and center fielder Curt Flood. Coming on to pitch a scoreless eighth inning for the Tigers, was 38-year-old reliever Don McMahon, who had earlier pitched for the Milwaukee Braves in the 1957 and 1958 Fall Classics.

In game two, played the next day, Detroit squared the Series at one win apiece behind the pitching of left-hander Mickey Lolich (1-0), with an 8 to 1 victory. The Tigers outhit the Cardinals thirteen to six in the game. Then the Series shifted north to Tiger Stadium in Detroit for the next three ballgames. In game three on Saturday, October 5, the Cardinals outhit Detroit thirteen to four to win by a score of 7 to 3. Catcher Tim McCarver hit a three-run homer in the fifth inning for the game winning blow for St. Louis. Starting pitcher Ray Washburn (1-0) was the winner for the Cardinals. After three games, St. Louis led the Series two games to one.

The Cardinals then took a commanding three games to one lead in the Series on Sunday, October 6, with a lopsided win over the Tigers in game four by a score of 10 to 1. The line score read 10 runs, 13 hits, no errors for St. Louis and 1 run, 5 hits and 4 errors for Detroit. Bob Gibson (2-0) won for the second time in the Series with another complete game win and ten strikeouts.

Detroit could at least take some solace in knowing that they scored one run off him in the fourth inning on a home run by center fielder Jim Northrup. The loser for Detroit was starter Denny McLain (0-2), who lasted only two and two-third innings before departing. The Tigers used six pitchers in the game. The Cardinals had two solo home runs hit by left fielder Lou Brock in the first inning and then by pitcher Bob Gibson in the fourth. Brock also stole one base to bring his 1968 Series total up to seven so far. Four games into the Series, it was fair to say that none of the games had exactly been nail biters. Detroit faced an elimination game going into game five.

In the fifth game at Tiger Stadium on Monday, October 7, the Cardinals assumed a lead by scoring three runs in the top of the first inning. That was all they would score in the game. Detroit came from behind with two runs in the fourth and then three more in the seventh inning to produce a 5 to 3 win, which sent the Series back to St. Louis. Detroit starter Mickey Lolich (2-0) went all nine innings for the win. There were 53,634 fans in the stands to see the Tigers, nearly on the brink of elimination, finally win one of the three games in their own park. Game six back in St. Louis on Wednesday, October 9, proved to be an easy win for the Tigers behind pitcher Denny McLain (1-2). The Tigers scored two runs in the second and ten big runs in the third inning and went on for a 13 to 1 win which evened the Series. For the second year in a row the Series would be extended to a full seven games.

On Thursday, October 10, the seventh game pitching matchup was Mickey Lolich for Detroit, who was pitching with two days of rest, and Bob Gibson of St. Louis. Both would be going for their third win of the Series. After six complete innings, there was no score in the game. In the seventh, the Tigers took a 3-0 lead and added an insurance run in the top of the ninth to make it 4-0. Two of the Detroit runs were driven in by Jim Northrup, and one each by Bill Freehan and Don Wert. In the last of the ninth, third baseman Mike Shannon homered for the Cardinals, but it was too late. The final score was 4 to 1 and the Tigers would take the World Series trophy back to Detroit for the first time since 1945. In nine innings, Lolich (3-0) gave up five hits, walked three, and struck out four. Gibson (2-1) in nine innings as the loser surrendered four runs, eight hits, one walk, and struck out eight. Even with everything on the line, the game was the quickest of the seven Series games, taking only 2 hours and 7 minutes.

It was an entertaining World Series that probably could have gone either way. Detroit outscored St. Louis 34 runs to 27, but St. Louis batted .255 compared to .242 for the Tigers. For Detroit, Norm Cash hit .385, Al Kaline, .379, and Willie Horton, .304. Kaline and Jim Northrup each hit two home runs. For St. Louis, Lou Brock hit .464 and Tim McCarver and Julian Javier each batted .333. Brock and Orlando Cepeda each hit two home runs for the Cardinals. The three games won by Mickey Lolich were key for Detroit, as well as their tenacious comeback in game five. In 27 innings pitched, Lolich had an earned run average of 1.67 and 21 strikeouts. Gibson won two games but ultimately lost in the seventh. In 27 innings, he struck out 35 and also had a 1.67 ERA. In team pitching, the Detroit staff ERA finished at 3.34 compared to 4.65 for St. Louis. Only the fifth game and the seventh game were decided by a margin of three or fewer runs. The Tigers won both. The other two games that Detroit won were by a total margin of nineteen runs. The Cardinals' team ERA was thus inflated by extra runs scored by the Tigers, which they did not really need to win.

1968 WORLD SERIES SUMMARY

Game 1	At St. Louis	Cardinals 4, Tigers 0
Game 2	At St. Louis	Tigers 8, Cardinals 1
Game 3	At Detroit	Cardinals 7, Tigers 3
Game 4	At Detroit	Cardinals 10, Tigers 1
Game 5	At Detroit	Tigers 5, Cardinals 3
Game 6	At St. Louis	Tigers 13, Cardinals 1
Game 7	At St. Louis	Tigers 4, Cardinals 1

DETROIT WINS THE WORLD SERIES BY 4 GAMES TO 3.

In the American League, the years from 1965 through 1968 saw four different teams win the pennant, following several years of domination by the Yankees. Figure 3 shows that during this period five American League teams won more than half of their games. In order these were the Detroit Tigers,

57.3%; Minnesota Twins, 55.7%; Baltimore Orioles, 55.5%; Chicago White Sox, 51.5%; and Cleveland Indians, 50.9%. The ranking of the remaining clubs was Boston Red Sox, 48.1%; California Angels, 47.3%; New York Yankees, 46.8%; Washington Senators, 43.9%; and Kansas City/Oakland Athletics, 42.9%. The relatively low ranking of the Red Sox indicates just how much their 1967 American League win was an unexpected upset.

In the National League, seven of the ten teams managed to win more than half of their games during this four season stretch. As illustrated by Figure 3, these were the San Francisco Giants, 56.7%; St. Louis Cardinals, 55.9%; Pittsburgh Pirates, 52.9%; Los Angeles Dodgers, 52.6%; Cincinnati Reds, 51.9%; Philadelphia Phillies, 51.0%; and Milwaukee/Atlanta Braves, 50.8%. Of these seven teams, the Giants ranked first and were very consistent from year to year but did not win a National League pennant. This leaves three teams of a significantly lower rank. In order they are the Chicago Cubs, 46.7%; Houston Astros, 42.9%; and New York Mets, 38.6%. These three were also the three lowest ranking National League clubs from the five season 1960-1964 period.

INTERLUDE - ALL-STAR GAMES

The very first Major League Baseball All-Star game was held at Comiskey Park in Chicago on July 6, 1933, and the tradition continued during the years from 1957 through 1968. For four years, from 1959-1962, two All-Star games were held instead of one. The American League won both the 1957 and 1958 games by a margin of one run each. After the 1958 game, the Junior Circuit led in total victories in the Series with 15 games to 10. Of the eight games played from 1959-1962, the National League came away with wins in five games, the American League won twice, and the second game staged in 1961 at Fenway Park in Boston had to be ended in a 1-to-1 tie, called after nine innings because of rain. Then beginning in 1963, the National League won six All-Star games in a row. The 1966, 1967, and 1968 games reflected the newer trend in baseball of well-pitched games with fewer runs scored. The cumulative score for these three games was National

League 5 and American League 2. After 1968, the All-Time All-Star game series stood at 21 victories for the National League, 17 victories for the American League, and one game ending in a tie.

INDIVIDUAL LEADERS

⌒つ

Figures 4 through 8 show the top ten individual leaders for the twelve-year period in the statistical categories of home runs, hits, stolen bases, pitching wins, and strikeouts. The following comments attempt to highlight some noteworthy statistical achievements of the players who are included on one or more of these lists.

The three players with the most home runs were Henry Aaron of the Braves with 444, Willie Mays of the Giants with 435, and Harmon Killebrew of the Twins with 388. Killebrew led the group in home run frequency with a home run every 13.0 times at bat. Mickey Mantle of the New York Yankees was second with 14.2. Mantle also tended to either walk or strike out the most frequently. Mantle walked one time for every 4.3 times at bat and also struck out once every 4.6 times at bat. His twelve-season totals were 1,209 walks and 1,132 strikeouts. Together, he either walked or struck out once for every 2.2 at bats. Mantle and Rocky Colavito of the Indians were the only two out of the group with more walks than strikeouts. Four of the top ten home run hitters batted for an overall average of greater than .300 for the period. These were Aaron at .315, Mays at .309, with Frank Robinson of the Orioles, and Orlando Cepeda of the Giants both at .303. Roger Maris ranked tenth in home runs for the twelve-year period with 275. His home run frequency of one home run every 18.5 times at bat was ninth among the group. His batting average of .260 ranked tenth behind Killebrew, who hit for an average of .263. Only Aaron and Mays in the group exceeded 2,000 hits for the period.

The top three leaders in hits for the twelve-year period were Henry Aaron with 2,272, Willie Mays with 2,104, and Roberto Clemente of the Pittsburgh Pirates with 2,094. Clemente, with a batting average of .316, had the highest average of the group. Henry Aaron had the most doubles of the period with 386, and Clemente hit the most triples with 111. Willie Mays and Frank

Robinson were co-leaders in the frequency of extra-base-hits, with one every 7.9 times at bat. Players that made the top ten hits list but were not on the home runs list were Clemente, Vada Pinson of the Reds, Luis Aparicio of the White Sox, Ken Boyer of the Cardinals, Al Kaline of the Tigers, and Brooks Robinson of the Orioles. Detroit's Al Kaline was the only player in the group with more walks than strikeouts, 767 walks and 555 strikeouts. Ernie Banks of the Chicago Cubs, made both lists with 381 home runs and 1,858 hits. Shortstop Luis Aparicio finished seventh on the hits list with 1,833. He was much more of a singles hitter, with only 63 home runs and one extra-base-hit for every 18.1 times at bat. Aparicio also struck out the least, with one strikeout recorded for every 13.9 times at bat. The list included six National League players, three from the American League, and one player, Frank Robinson, who was in both Leagues during the period.

In stolen bases, the individual leaders were Maury Wills of the Dodgers with 502, Luis Aparicio with 431, and Lou Brock of the Cardinals with 334. Willie Mays, Henry Aaron, and Frank Robinson were also in the stolen bases top ten, finishing tied for sixth, eighth, and tenth, respectively. They are the only three players included in all three top ten lists. Although 1964 was his first season, Bert Campaneris of the Athletics finished fourth in stolen bases over the period with 230. He accomplished this in only 2,663 times at bat, whereas, the other nine were all at bat well over 4,000 times. In the percentage of attempted stolen bases which were successful, the leader was Aaron at 80.0%. Second was Aparicio at 78.6%, and third was Campaneris at 76.9%. All ten players on the list were successful at least seventy percent of the time with Tony Taylor of the Phillies in tenth place with exactly 70.0%. Vada Pinson of the Reds, who is also included among the top ten in hits, placed fifth in stolen bases with 221. Willie Davis of the Dodgers tied with Mays for sixth place with 216 base thefts and is not included on the other two lists.

In pitching wins for the 1957 through 1968 period, the top three leaders were Don Drysdale of the Dodgers with 199, Jim Bunning of the Tigers/Phillies with 188, and Larry Jackson of the Cardinals/Cubs with 183. Measured in terms of winning percentage, the three best were Juan Marichal of the Giants at .688, Whitey Ford of the Yankees at .667, and Sandy Koufax of the Dodgers at .665. Drysdale, Bunning, and Jackson all pitched 3,000 or more innings. The most innings pitched by one of the others was 2,394 innings by Camilo Pascual of the Twins. In other measures of pitching effectiveness, Koufax was the leader with 0.74 hits per inning. Bob Gibson of the Cardinals ranked second at 0.82. Marichal had the highest ratio of 3.64 strikeouts per walk, followed by both Bunning and Koufax at 3.07. Marichal completed the twelve-year period with the lowest earned run average of 2.63 runs per game, followed closely by Koufax at 2.70, and Ford at 2.75. Two other pitchers on the list were Warren Spahn of the Braves with 160 wins in sixth place, and Milt Pappas of the Orioles with 150 wins in ninth place. By 1957, Spahn was already in the latter stages of his pitching career. His ERA for the period was 3.25, which placed eighth, and he had the lowest ratio of 1.85 strikeouts per walk.

The leading pitchers in strikeouts over the twelve years were Jim Bunning with 2,422, Don Drysdale with 2,407, and Sandy Koufax with 2,336. These were the only three with over 2,000 strikeouts for the period. Bob Gibson was fourth at 1,850, and Camilo Pascual was fifth at 1,798. Bunning and Drysdale pitched over 3,000 innings each, but Koufax reached the top three because of his high strikeout ratio of 9.45 per nine innings. Two pitchers were in the strikeouts top ten who were not in the top ten in pitching games won. These were Jim Maloney of the Cincinnati Reds, who ranked eighth with 1,483, and Sam McDowell of the Cleveland Indians, who tied Whitey Ford for ninth place with 1,384 strikeouts. Both Maloney and McDowell started their careers later in the period and worked fewer than 2,000 innings each for the period. McDowell led all ten with the highest ratio of 9.54 strikeouts per nine innings pitched. Maloney was third in this ranking with a ratio of 8.22.

INTERLUDE - HENRY AARON

A standout ball player of this era was Henry Aaron of the Milwaukee and then Atlanta Braves. Aaron was born in Mobile, Alabama on February 5, 1934. He broke in with the Milwaukee Braves in 1954 at the age of 20. He remained a fixture in Milwaukee through 1965 and then moved south to Atlanta with the Braves, starting with the 1966 season. Aaron remained in Atlanta through the 1974 season, and then returned to Milwaukee as a member of the Milwaukee Brewers for his last two years in 1975 and 1976. For 23 years he was one of the most able and consistent home run hitters in baseball history. In his career, Aaron accumulated 755 home runs, 3,771 hits, and finished with a batting average of .305. Aaron broke the record held by Babe Ruth for most career home runs when he hit home run number 715 in Atlanta on April 8, 1974. It was a truly significant moment in American history when Aaron, a black man, broke this record in the heart of the deep South and was overwhelmingly and enthusiastically cheered by the Atlanta crowd.

In the twelve years from 1957 through 1968, Aaron hit 444 home runs, with a high of 45 in 1962 and a low of 24 in 1964. His batting average in those years ranged from a low of .279 in 1966 to a high of .355 in 1959. His average was over .300 in nine of the twelve years. Aaron led the Braves to two National League pennants in 1957 and 1958, and the World Series win in 1957. In 1957 he was selected as the National League Most Valuable Player. In 1959 the Braves finished the regular season tied with the Dodgers for the National League pennant, but then narrowly lost in a two game playoff. In his fourteen World Series games, Aaron hit .364 with three home runs. His playing longevity allowed him to participate in 24 All-Star games, in which he had a batting average of .194 with 2 home runs.

INTERLUDE - MICKEY MANTLE

Mickey Mantle was born October 20, 1931, in Spavinaw, Oklahoma. Later, the Mantle family moved to Commerce, Oklahoma where he grew up and attended school. Mantle played eighteen years with the New York Yankees from 1951 through 1968. Widely considered the greatest switch-hitter in baseball history, he hit 536 lifetime home runs with a batting average of .298. He was the recipient of the American League Most Valuable Player Award three times in 1956, 1957, and 1962. In 1956, he was the winner of the triple crown by leading the American League in all three categories of home runs, runs batted in, and batting average. He exceeded 40 or more home runs four times in his career with 52 in 1956, 42 in 1958, 40 in 1960, and 54 in 1961. In the twelve seasons from 1957 through 1968, Mantle ranked sixth in home runs with 363 and batted for an average of .292.

Mantle played throughout much of his career with chronic injury to and pain in his legs. He had been initially injured while running in the outfield after a fly ball in the 1951 World Series. Mantle played in twelve World Series as a member of the Yankees, with the first in 1951 and the last in 1964. In every one of those October Classics, Mantle managed at least one base hit. In 65 games, he had 59 hits in 230 at bats for a batting average of .257. He hit eighteen home runs in World Series play, including three each in 1956, 1960, and 1964. Over the years, Mantle made appearances in sixteen All-Star games. He hit two home runs, one each in 1955 and 1956, and overall had an All-Star game average of .233.

When many young people who grew up in the fifties and sixties thought about baseball, the first thing that came to mind was the image of Mickey Mantle, the New York Yankees great home run hitter. He was always in the World Series, the greatest spectacle at the time in all of sports, wearing uniform number 7. Mantle died in 1995 at the age of 64. Near the time of his death, Mantle made appearances openly admitting the role that many years of alcoholism had played in the decline of his health. In a moving eulogy at his funeral, sports commentator Bob Costas spoke of Mantle in terms of not being a "role model," but of always being a "hero" to an entire generation of baseball fans like himself.

INTERLUDE - ROGER MARIS

This historical narrative has had a cast of hundreds, but if it has one central character, it is Roger Maris. As discussed in the opening chapter, I chose to write specifically about the twelve years from 1957 through 1968, because those were the twelve seasons that Maris played in Major League Baseball. Maris was born in Hibbing, Minnesota on September 10, 1934. Maris grew up and attended school in Fargo, North Dakota, where I was born. The twelve-year period was also the time of my years in school, grades one through twelve. 1968 was the final year before baseball permanently split its two leagues into divisions. Baseball would never again be quite the same.

In his baseball career from 1957 through 1968, Maris hit 275 home runs, which ranked tenth for the twelve-year period. He accumulated 1,325 hits, homered once for every 18.5 times at bat, and averaged .260. His team was in the World Series seven times, five with the Yankees and two with the Cardinals. The Yankees took home the Series prize in 1961 and 1962, and the Cardinals won it all in 1967. In World Series competition, Maris hit six home runs, five for the Yankees and one for St. Louis. He averaged .217 in 152 at bats. His finest Fall Classic, arguably, was in 1967 with the Cardinals. Maris had ten hits, including one home run, seven runs batted in, and batted .385. In the years when there were two All-Star games, from 1959 through 1962, he appeared in seven out of the eight. He had two hits, including one double, and three bases on balls, with an average of .105.

Roger Maris passed away from cancer in 1985 at the age of 51. In the years since Maris played baseball, there have been three other players who have surpassed the single-season home run mark of 61. They have all been in the National League. In the over 100-year history of the American League, there have been only two players who have reached 60 in a single-season. These are Yankees left-handed right fielders Babe Ruth in 1927, with 60, and Roger Maris, with 61 in 1961. Maris still remains the American League's all-time, single-season home run champion.

BASEBALL HALL OF FAME

The National Baseball Hall of Fame was established to preserve memories of the game of baseball and to honor retired players who have excelled in the game. Voting for members is done by the Baseball Writers Association of America (BBWAA) and is based on the player's record, playing ability, integrity, sportsmanship, character, and contributions to the team or teams on which the player played.

Most of the players that have been presented in the interludes portions of this narrative are members of the Baseball Hall of Fame, either through election by the BBWAA or through a separate selection process by a special

Veterans Committee of the Hall of Fame. Selection from among the eligible candidates is a subjective process involving the exercise of a collective judgment by those individuals responsible for making the selection.

Two extremely important and highly successful players from the twelve-year period from 1957 through 1968 have not yet been selected for the Hall. These are Roger Maris and Maury Wills. Although Maris and Wills both had relatively short Major League Baseball careers as players, they both managed record-breaking individual achievements and were key contributors on successful ball clubs during the era. Maris played with the Yankees and Cardinals in seven World Series and his team was victorious in three of them in 1961, 1962, and 1967. Wills was in the World Series four times with the Los Angeles Dodgers. The Dodgers won three of them in 1959, 1963, and 1965. For ten consecutive seasons from 1959 through 1968, either Maris or Wills played in the World Series. In 1963 their respective teams faced each other in a memorable October Classic swept by the Dodgers in four games.

It remains uncertain whether Maris and Wills will ultimately receive this recognition. All I can do in this book is narrate the history of those twelve years of baseball. Their influence on the baseball fields of play speaks for itself.

1957 - 1968

TEAM SUMMARIES

Figure 9 is a summary composite of figures 1, 2 and 3, presented earlier. It shows the total regular season games won and lost by each team for the entire twelve-year period. The New York Yankees were best in the American League by winning 56.4% of their games. In the National League, the San Francisco Giants came in first with 54.8%. Figure 10 recaps the Major League Baseball attendance each year from 1957 through 1968. The Milwaukee Braves had the highest attendance for both 1957 and 1958. The leader from 1959 through 1966 was the Los Angeles Dodgers. The leaders in 1967 and 1968 were the St. Louis Cardinals and Detroit Tigers, respectively. The National League had greater attendance than the American League in each year, except for 1961 when, because of American League expansion, 807 American League games were played compared to only 616 National League games.

In this chapter, I present a brief recap of the twelve-year highlights for each of the then existing twenty baseball franchises. They are presented in reverse order, in an alternating league format, with the least successful teams first, and the most successful teams presented at the end. This section also includes a summary recap of the games I covered as well as comments about home attendance and other significant factors regarding franchise history. In previous chapters of this narrative, I have described fourteen games in each season to provide a flavor of how the seasons progressed. Even though I was not at them in a literal sense, I can rightly claim that I was, indeed, present ever so much in spirit. Because of my interest and love for the game and my deep appreciation for the young men who went out on the fields of play, it is very much like I was always there watching intently.

National League - New York Mets - Won 394 and Lost 737 - 34.8%.

The New York Mets were a National League expansion team and began play in 1962. After four years in New York City without National League

213

baseball, the Mets filled the void left by the departure of the Dodgers and Giants. In five out of seven years, the Mets lost over 100 games. Their best year of the period was in 1968 with 73 wins and 89 losses. The lovable Casey Stengel was a saving grace for the Mets in their beginnings. He was their manager from 1962 through midway into the 1965 season. Even the improvement the Mets exhibited in 1968 could not have predicted their amazing rise to a National League pennant and World Series win the very next year in 1969. Members of the 1968 Mets who greatly contributed in 1969 included position players Tommie Agee, Bud Harrelson, and Cleon Jones plus pitchers Jerry Koosman and Tom Seaver.

In my tour of baseball, I saw the Mets in eight games, all losses, including three games in their inaugural season of 1962. After two years of home games at the old Polo Grounds, the Mets began play in a new ballpark named Shea Stadium starting with the 1964 season. This new venue contributed to good attendance, with over 1.5 million fans seeing Mets' home games each year from 1964 through 1968.

American League - Washington Senators - Won 773 and Lost 1,132 - 40.6%.

The Senators were the least successful of all the American League franchises during the twelve-year period. The original Senators franchise moved to greener pastures and became the Minnesota Twins following the 1960 season. When the American League expanded to ten teams in 1961, Washington was awarded one of the two expansion teams and kept the same Washington Senators identification. Several members of the future Minnesota Twins team began their careers in Washington, including pitchers Jim Kaat, Camilo Pascual, and Pedro Ramos plus position players Bob Allison, Earl Battey, Harmon Killebrew, Jim Lemon, and Zoilo Versalles. The expansion Senators franchise lost 100 or more games in each of its first four years from 1961 through 1964 and then improved to a combined 282-361 in the years from 1965 through 1968. In 1968 outfielder Frank Howard led the American League in home runs with 44.

Over the years, I was in attendance at nine Senators games in which their record was 1-8. The only win took place in August 1960 over the Detroit Tigers at Griffith Stadium. In twelve years in Washington, the team's attendance never climbed above the one million mark. The highest total was

770,868 achieved during the 1967 season. The second Senators franchise also abandoned the nation's capital and became the Texas Rangers, based in Dallas-Fort Worth, beginning in the 1972 season.

National League - Houston Astros - Won 474 and Lost 658 - 41.9%.

The other National League expansion franchise was established in Houston in 1962. The team was originally called the Houston Colt 45s. In 1965 the team moved into baseball's first ever domed stadium to escape the Texas heat and changed its name to the Houston Astros. The ballpark became known as the Astrodome. Although the team managed to avoid a 100 loss season in its first seven years, success on the field of play was hard to come by. Houston's two best years were 1966 and 1968 with identical records of 72 wins and 90 losses.

In the six games I attended over seven years, the team had two wins and four losses. A close 2 to 1 loss to the Giants at San Francisco on September 30, 1962, allowed the Giants to end the regular season tied with the Dodgers in the National League race. Compared to its first three years of existence, the attendance at home games dramatically improved with the opening of the Astrodome. In 1965 the Astros drew 2,151,470 fans to see games in the brand new, air conditioned indoor ballpark. Attendance remained good for the remaining three years of the period. Years later starting in the 2013 season, the Houston Astros were reassigned from the National League to the American League, in order to balance the two Major Leagues at fifteen teams each.

American League - Kansas City/Oakland Athletics - Won 796 and Lost 1,111 - 41.7%.

After Philadelphia origins, the Athletics called Kansas City home for thirteen seasons, from 1955 through 1967. In thirteen years in Kansas City, the team never once played .500 ball. The closest was a record of 73-81 in 1958. After the 1967 season, the team moved west to Oakland, California to become the second team in the Northern California Bay area. In it's very first year as the Oakland Athletics, the team won 82 games and lost 80. The team was building a foundation which would result in three consecutive World Series championships in 1972, 1973, and 1974. By the time of its last year in Kansas City, the Athletics had already secured many of the players which would soon lead their resurgence, including Catfish Hunter, Bert Campaneris, Joe Rudi, Sal Bando, and Reggie Jackson.

In my travels, I was on hand for eight games with the Athletics. The team won 2 and lost 6, including an August 1968 win over the Yankees in Oakland. The game featured home runs by both Mickey Mantle for the Yankees and Reggie Jackson for Oakland. Prior to being traded to New York, Roger Maris was with Kansas City for part of the 1958 season and all of 1959. Maris hit 35 home runs while wearing a Kansas City uniform, 19 in 1958, and 16 in 1959. The team's highest home attendance for the twelve-year period was 963,683 in 1959.

National League - Chicago Cubs - Won 851 and Lost 1,052 - 44.7%.

Out of the National League teams in existence in 1957, the Cubs finished with the eighth best overall record for the twelve-year period. However, they did play winning baseball for three years -- 1963 (82-80), 1967 (87-74), and 1968 (84-78). Then in 1969, they made a serious run but finished second to the Mets in the National League East race. Ernie Banks, the popular shortstop and first baseman, was the National League Most Valuable Player for both 1958 and 1959. In 1964 pitcher Larry Jackson, who ranked third in wins over the twelve-year period, had the best year of his career with 24 wins and 11 losses.

My itinerary included ten Chicago Cubs ballgames during which the Cubs only had 1 win against 9 losses. The losses included two against the Pittsburgh Pirates in 1960 and two against the San Francisco Giants in 1962. Attendance at Wrigley Field averaged 802,000 fans per season and improved at the end of the period to 977,226 in 1967, and 1,043,409 in 1968. The beautiful Wrigley Field was a major asset to the Cubs' franchise. Because of the growing interest in baseball history and nostalgia, it has remained so as the years have gone by.

American League - Los Angeles Angels - Won 614 and Lost 679 - 47.5%.

The Los Angeles Angels were the second American League expansion team that started with the 1961 season. In 1962, in only their second year of existence, the Angels finished in third place behind New York and Minnesota, with 86 wins and 76 losses. In 1964 Angels right-hander Dean Chance went 20-9. He was recognized as the best pitcher in baseball and won the Cy Young Award. In the early years, the Angels struggled somewhat with the team's identity. From 1962 through 1965, the team played its home games at Chavez Ravine, the home ballpark of the Los Angeles Dodgers. In 1966 the team changed its name to the California Angels and moved to a newly constructed stadium in Anaheim, California, not far from Disneyland. Even so, the Dodgers continued to outrank the Angels in prestige, attendance, and success on the field.

Attendance for the Angels increased to 1,400,321 in 1966, with the opening of Anaheim Stadium. It remained above the one million mark for both 1967 and 1968. The Angels lost all eight of their games that I attended. In subsequent years, the Angels' franchise has taken advantage of its Southern California and City of Angels roots to become a highly successful baseball enterprise both on and off the field.

National League - Philadelphia Phillies - Won 906 and Lost 996 - 47.6%.

The Philadelphia Phillies are mainly remembered in this period for a late September collapse which prevented them from winning the 1964 National League pennant. Even with this failure, the Phillies had improved considerably from a record of 47 wins and 107 losses in 1961, last in the National League. In 1958 the Phillies also finished in last place with a record of 69-85, however, their center fielder Richie Ashburn led the league in hits with 215 and batting average with .350. Ashburn was one of the "Whiz Kids" from the Philadelphia pennant winning season of 1950. Jim Bunning, one of the best pitchers of the era, spent four complete seasons in Philadelphia, from 1964 through 1967. His four-year record was 74 wins and 46 losses.

Attendance at Philadelphia over the twelve-year period averaged 932,000 per season, with a peak of 1,425,891 in 1964. Over the years, the Phillies compiled a record of 4 wins and 12 losses in the games I attended. I was present for two wins in 1964, including a win over the Dodgers on September 20, just before their season fell apart and they embarked on their infamous ten game losing streak. Despite this adversity, the Philadelphia Phillies are definitely here to stay. The "Phillies" nickname, in use since the team joined the National League in 1883, is the oldest continuously used nickname in professional sports.

American League - Boston Red Sox - Won 913 and Lost 996 - 47.8%.

The Red Sox actually had a winning record in four of the twelve years in the period -- 1957, 1958, 1967, and 1968. In 1967 they defeated the Twins on the last day of the season to win the American League pennant. In the 1967 World Series, Boston extended St. Louis to seven games, before losing out to the pitching of Bob Gibson. Early in the period, the Red Sox featured hitting stars Ted Williams, Jackie Jensen, and Pete Runnels. Carl Yastrzemski replaced Williams in left field in 1961. He eventually grew into a player who could largely inspire Boston's 1967 season with a triple crown performance. Eight years later, in 1975, catcher Carlton Fisk would hit a classic home run, with the aid of his body language, hitting the foul pole in left field to win a World Series game. However, the team would again lose the Series in seven games.

I was fortunate to be at Fenway on September 28, 1960, to see Red Sox outfielder Ted Williams homer against the Baltimore Orioles in his final time at bat. Overall I was on hand for 5 Red Sox wins and 11 losses. Three of the wins came in the pennant winning year of 1967 over Kansas City, Detroit, and Minnesota. Like the Cubs, the Red Sox benefited from the historic legacy provided by playing its home games at Fenway Park. Through all the ups and downs over the twelve-year period, Boston averaged 1,076,000 fans in attendance.

National League - Pittsburgh Pirates - Won 984 and Lost 919 - 51.7%.

The highlight for Pittsburgh by far was the 1960 World Series win over the Yankees with the dramatic seventh game walk-off home run by second baseman Bill Mazeroski. Other Pirates recognized with awards in 1960 were Cy Young winner Vern Law, and National League Most Valuable Player and batting champion shortstop Dick Groat. Pittsburgh was one of seven elite teams that could claim a World Series championship in the twelve-year period. A member of the Pirates won the National League batting title in six of the twelve years from 1957 through 1968. Right fielder Roberto Clemente won four titles in 1961, 1964, 1965, and 1967. Also, Matty Alou was batting champion for the 1966 season. In an unusual occurrence in May 1959, Harvey Haddix pitched a perfect game for twelve complete innings only to lose the game to Milwaukee in the thirteenth inning.

In six of twelve years, the Pirates attracted over one million fans to see its games at Forbes Field, including a peak of 1,705,828 in 1960. Over the years, I was an observer at 22 Pittsburgh games, out of which the Pirates won 10 and lost 12. I saw eight wins in the pennant winning year of 1960 with five of them played at Forbes Field, which was home to the Pirates starting in 1909. It was subsequently replaced by Three Rivers Stadium in downtown Pittsburgh in the middle of the 1970 season.

INTERLUDE - ROY FACE

Pittsburgh Pirates' relief pitcher Roy Face saved three games in the 1960 World Series. He also pitched effectively for the Pirates up through the 1968 season. Face was born on February 20, 1928, in Stephentown, New York. Face began his pitching career for the Pirates in 1953, and beginning in 1958 was used exclusively in relief. He was one of the earliest pitchers in the National League to specialize in the relief role. In the twelve years from 1957 through 1968, Face had 177 saves with a 3.03 earned run average. He also won 77 games, lost 65, and pitched 934 innings with 606 strikeouts and only 234 walks. In the three seasons from 1958 through 1960, Face had 33 wins, 11 losses, and 54 saves. Then after an off-year in 1961, his best year may have been in 1962 with 8 wins, 7 losses, 28 saves, and an ERA of 1.88 runs per game. Face threw a hard forkball as his best pitch and was widely considered the most effective and consistent reliever in the National League during this era.

American League - Cleveland Indians - Won 963 and Lost 945 - 50.5%.

The Cleveland Indians, with eighteen more wins than losses, were for both leagues the team with a record closest to the .500 mark for the entire period. In 1966 the Indians won their first ten games in a row to start the season. Typically, the team finished the year five months later with exactly 81 wins and 81 losses. One genuine charismatic baseball star that started the era with the Indians was outfielder Rocky Colavito. After the 1959 season, in which the Indians had gone 89-65, Colavito, the American League co-leader in home runs, was traded to Detroit for batting champion Harvey Kuenn. Colavito would later return to Cleveland in 1965 and hit a total of 190 home runs in his two stretches with the Indians, which extended over all or part of eight seasons. Roger Maris spent his rookie year of 1957 with Cleveland. Then, he was traded to Kansas City early in the 1958 season. At the start of his Major League career, Maris hit 23 home runs in a Cleveland Indians' uniform.

Attendance at Indians' home games climbed above one million for only one year out of twelve. This was in 1959, as the Tribe finished in second place, only five games behind the White Sox. Municipal Stadium in Cleveland was a large multi-purpose stadium located on the Lake Erie lakefront. It was known as a pitcher's ballpark, and over the years the Indians did have some excellent pitching. As recently as 1954, the Indians had won the American League pennant with a team featuring established veteran pitchers Bob Lemon, Bob Feller, and Early Wynn. In my tour of the Major Leagues, I was watching in the stands for two Indians wins, in 1959 and 1966, and eight losses.

National League - Cincinnati Reds - Won 1,001 and Lost 901 - 52.6%.

The Cincinnati Reds finished first in the National League in 1961 following three years of playing under .500 ball in 1958-1960, and then lost the World Series to the Yankees in five games. Outfielders Frank Robinson, 1961 National League Most Valuable Player, and Vada Pinson led the Reds until Robinson's departure for Baltimore after the 1965 season. In 1963, a young second baseman named Pete Rose arrived on the scene as National League Rookie of the Year. For a time, from 1953 through 1958, the team changed its official nickname to Redlegs to avoid association with Communism. However, the name never caught on and was quietly changed back to the much simpler and colorful Reds.

In twelve years in the games I attended, Cincinnati won six and lost eight. Early in the 1967 season, the Reds treated me to four consecutive wins over the Astros, Phillies, Cardinals, and Dodgers to start the year. Over the years, attendance at Crosley Field in Cincinnati grew increasingly sporadic with the team averaging 885,000 fans per year. Crosley was replaced by Riverfront

Stadium in downtown Cincinnati in time to be the stage for the Reds' World Series championship teams of 1975 and 1976.

American League - Minnesota Twins - Won 692 and Lost 601 - 53.5%.

The Washington franchise relocated to Minnesota and assumed a brand new identity as the Minnesota Twins beginning with the 1961 season. In eight years the Twins had five winning seasons. The Twins finished second to the Yankees in both 1962 and 1963. In their best year of 1965, the team won 102 and lost 60, to win the American League pennant and put an end to five straight years of League domination by the Yankees. In that year Twins shortstop Zoilo Versalles was voted American League Most Valuable Player. In the twelve-year period, Harmon Killebrew was third overall with 388 home runs. Cuban-born pitcher Camilo Pascual was seventh in games won with 158 and fifth in strikeouts with 1,798. Another native Cuban player, Tony Oliva, won batting titles in 1964 and 1965 and led the American League in hits in those two years and in 1966. In 1967, the Twins came close to a second pennant but lost to the Boston Red Sox at Fenway Park on the last day of the season.

In eight years I was fortunate to be in attendance for ten Minnesota wins and five losses, including seven wins during the 1965 campaign. The Minnesota Twins appealed to a large market area including not only the Twin Cities and greater Minnesota, but also North Dakota, South Dakota, plus portions of Iowa, Montana, and Wisconsin. The Twins drew over one million fans each year to suburban Metropolitan Stadium from 1961 through 1968, with an average of 1,331,000. Metropolitan Stadium was the home of Twins baseball through the 1981 season. The real estate on which it was located eventually became the Mall of America, one of the largest indoor shopping malls in the United States.

National League - St. Louis Cardinals - Won 1,027 and Lost 875 - 54.0%.

The bright red Cardinals' motif made St. Louis one of baseball's most colorful and magnificently displayed franchises. In nine out of twelve years the Redbirds played above .500 ball. In the process they captured three National League titles and World Series victories in 1964, over the Yankees, and 1967, over the Boston Red Sox. In 1957, the Cardinals won 87 games and finished the season in second place, eight games behind Milwaukee. In 1963, the final season played by Stan Musial, they challenged the Dodgers by winning 93 games, before again finishing second, six games out. Third baseman Ken Boyer was National League 1964 Most Valuable Player and contributed a clutch grand slam home run at Yankee Stadium in the World Series. The strong right-handed pitching of Bob Gibson was instrumental in all three pennant years of 1964, 1967, and 1968. In 1967 and 1968, St. Louis provided the setting for right fielder Roger Maris to finish his baseball career, as he contributed to two National League pennants and one World Series championship. Other significant position players for St. Louis in those years included 1967 MVP Orlando Cepeda, Lou Brock, Tim McCarver, and Curt Flood.

In twelve years, St. Louis averaged 1,287,000 fans in attendance at its home games. I was present over the years for Cardinals games totaling 18 wins and 4 losses, including 6 wins in 1967 and 7 wins in 1968. Cardinals' games were broadcast on radio station KMOX in St. Louis, which reached many states all over the USA. The Cardinals were an extremely popular team over a wide geographic region.

INTERLUDE - CURT FLOOD

Curt Flood was born January 18, 1938, in Houston, Texas. Flood was the primary center fielder with the St. Louis Cardinals for twelve seasons from 1958 through 1969. He won seven Gold Glove Awards in his career as an outfielder and was a lifetime .293 hitter. In the Cardinals' three pennant winning years of 1964, 1967, and 1968, Flood batted .311, .335, and .301, respectively. Flood is perhaps most known for his challenge to baseball's reserve clause in a legal action that went all the way to the U.S. Supreme Court, following his being traded to the Philadelphia Phillies after the 1969 season. Although his case was not successful, his challenge to Major League Baseball ownership interests helped pave the way for free agency for Major League Baseball players in the years that followed.

American League - Detroit Tigers - Won 1,023 and Lost 888 - 53.5%.

Two seasons stand out for Detroit from the rest. The first was 1961, during which the Tigers set the American League pace in the first half of the season, and eventually won 101 games and lost 61. They ended the season in a strong second place, eight games behind New York. The other season was 1968, during which the Tigers captured the American League pennant by going 103-59 and beat the Cardinals in the World Series in seven games. Pitcher Denny McLain won 31 games in the 1968 regular season and in the World Series, left-hander Mickey Lolich was credited with three wins over the Cardinals. In 1959, Harvey Kuenn won the batting title of the American League, with .353, as did Norm Cash in 1961, with .361. A consistent influence through all this period for the Tigers was their right fielder Al Kaline, who individually placed ninth in hits with a 1,782 twelve-year total.

I attended seventeen Detroit games of which the Tigers won 10 and lost 7. I saw 5 wins in 1961 and 5 more in 1968. Attendance in Detroit fell below one million fans only in 1963 and 1964. The Tigers' twelve-year total in the American League was second only to the New York Yankees. Detroit led both leagues in 1968 by drawing attendance of 2,031,847.

National League - Milwaukee/Atlanta Braves - Won 1,031 and Lost 875 - 54.1%.

The Milwaukee Braves won National League pennants in 1957 and 1958, and the World Series in 1957. The Braves maintained strong teams all the way through the club's tenure in Milwaukee up through the end of the 1965 season. The Braves were led by, arguably, the most outstanding hitter of the period, right fielder Henry Aaron, and third baseman Eddie Mathews. Aaron was National League Most Valuable Player for 1957. Although he was nearing the end of his baseball career, left-hander Warren Spahn led the Braves in pitching and ranked sixth in games won for the period. The strong Milwaukee teams of the late fifties had an outstanding supporting cast including catcher Del Crandall, first baseman Joe Adcock, shortstop Johnny Logan, outfielders Bill Bruton and Wes Covington, plus pitchers Lew Burdette, Bob Buhl, and Don McMahon.

The Braves led the Major Leagues in attendance in both 1957 and 1958, but after 1961 attendance began a decline that persisted until the team's final year

223

in Milwaukee in 1965. In Atlanta the club attracted over one million fans in each year from 1966 through 1968. After the move, the Braves continued to have strong hitting, with Aaron leading the league in home runs in 1966 and 1967, and Felipe Alou leading in hits in 1966 and 1968. Over the years, I witnessed nineteen Braves games, including 7 wins and 12 losses. The wins all were in the three-year 1957-1959 period.

American League - Baltimore Orioles - Won 1,026 and Lost 880 - 53.8%.

In 1954 the St. Louis Browns franchise relocated to Baltimore to become the Orioles. After three losing seasons, from 1957 to 1959, the breakout year for the Orioles was 1960 with 89 wins and 65 losses. They finished second to the Yankees and, from then on, Baltimore was a team on the rise. After serious challenges made towards a pennant in 1961, 1964, and 1965, the Orioles won it all in 1966, including a World Series sweep over the Dodgers. The big factor in their success was the acquisition of outfielder Frank Robinson from the Cincinnati Reds prior to the start of the 1966 season. He teamed up with third baseman Brooks Robinson, 1964 American League Most Valuable Player, to create an offensive punch second to none in 1966. Frank was 1966 MVP and triple crown winner. The Orioles seemed able to find good young pitching, including Milt Pappas, who was part of the Robinson trade with the Reds, and Jim Palmer, who was the winner of a World Series game in 1966 as a rookie.

Attendance at Baltimore over the twelve-year period proved to be very disappointing with an average of only 954,000 fans per year. In my travels, I saw the Orioles win 13 games and lose 10, including five wins in 1964 and six wins in 1966. At the end of the period, Baltimore was still playing good ball and would go on to three straight American League pennants in 1969, 1970, and 1971, plus a World Series crown in 1970.

National League - Brooklyn/Los Angeles Dodgers - Won 1,036 and Lost 873 - 54.3%.

The Los Angeles Dodgers won three World Series championships in 1959, 1963, and 1965. The Dodgers' teams were characterized by strong pitching and speed on the bases. Leading in pitching was the left- and right-handed combination of Sandy Koufax and Don Drysdale. Their outstanding record of achievement speaks for itself. On the bases of the National League, ran shortstop Maury Wills and outfielders Willie Davis and Tommy Davis. Wills was National League Most Valuable Player in 1962, followed by MVP Sandy Koufax in 1963. The Dodgers franchise had relocated from Brooklyn following the 1957 season. The Dodgers led the way in the integration of Major League Baseball while still in Brooklyn, with the first African American player, Jackie Robinson, in 1947. The Dodgers dominated the National League from 1947 through 1956 by winning six pennants in those ten years. It was with an extremely long, rich, and successful baseball tradition that the Brooklyn Dodgers moved to Los Angeles.

Once the Dodgers made the move to Los Angeles, the team dominated the attendance figures in both leagues. Over the twelve-year period, the Dodgers averaged 2,078,000 fans per season. For eight consecutive years, from 1959 through 1966, the team led both leagues in home attendance. When the team first moved to Los Angeles, the Dodgers played home games at the Los Angeles Memorial Coliseum from 1958 through the 1961 season. The Coliseum is basically a football stadium located in the University Park area of the city. The shape of the stadium was extremely ill-suited to baseball because a portion of the left field fence was only 251 feet from home plate. The Dodgers' home games moved to Dodger Stadium, also referred to as Chavez Ravine, beginning with the 1962 season. It is located near downtown Los Angeles, at the convergence of several freeways. In twelve seasons of baseball, I was on hand for 20 Dodgers' wins and 7 losses. Six of the wins were in the 1962 season, which was the year of the dramatic playoff loss to the Giants.

American League - Chicago White Sox - Won 1,050 and Lost 862 - 54.9%.

The White Sox played winning American League baseball for eleven years before falling to 67-95 in the 1968 season. The highlight was 1959, with the White Sox winning the American League pennant by five games over the Cleveland Indians. From 1963 through 1965 the team finished second each season with 94, 98, and 95 wins, respectively. The 1959 team was dubbed the Go-Go Sox and was led by the speed and defense of shortstop Luis Aparicio and second baseman Nellie Fox. Aparicio was among the leaders in hits and stolen bases for the entire twelve-year period. Later on,

225

the White Sox of the sixties continued to rely on pitching. Two of their best were Gary Peters and Joel Horlen.

In games I attended, the White Sox won 11 and lost 9, with five of the wins during the 1959 pennant winning campaign. In twelve years, attendance at Comiskey Park averaged 1,133,000 per season. In the last three years of the period, as the team's prospects dimmed somewhat, attendance dropped to under one million per year. Mostly due to the club's relatively superior success on the field, in ten out of the twelve years, the White Sox outdrew their North Side rival Chicago Cubs. The home of the White Sox in Chicago was Comiskey Park, located at 35th Street and Shields Avenue on the city's South Side. Comiskey was a pitcher friendly park with large outfield dimensions, and the White Sox generally adopted a style of play which took advantage of pitching, speed, and defense.

INTERLUDE - HOYT WILHELM

Hoyt Wilhelm was a knuckleball-throwing relief specialist who, in the 1957 through 1968 period, pitched mostly for the Orioles and the Chicago White Sox. In his entire career which ran from 1952 through 1972, Wilhelm won 143, lost 122, and had 227 saves with an earned run average of 2.52 runs per game. Wilhelm was born on July 26, 1922, in Huntersville, North Carolina. From 1957 through 1968, Wilhelm was 88-83 with 155 saves and a 2.26 ERA. Wilhelm was with the White Sox for six full years from 1963 through 1968. In those six seasons, Wilhelm pitched 675 innings, was credited with 98 saves, and posted an earned run average of 1.92 runs per game. In those innings, he allowed 465 hits which computes to an extremely low 0.69 hits per inning. Early in his career, from 1952 through 1956, Wilhelm had pitched for the New York Giants. After moving over to the Junior circuit, he became the era's premier example of a relief pitching specialist in the American League.

National League - New York/San Francisco Giants - Won 1,044 and Lost 862 - 54.8%.

Although the Giants only won the one National League pennant in 1962, in twelve years they won the most games of all the National League clubs with 1,044, equal to 54.8%. Only in 1957, the last year the team was based in New York, did the Giants finish below .500, with a record of 69-85. The Giants ended the period with four straight second place finishes from 1965 through 1968. Center fielder Willie Mays was second to only Henry Aaron in both home runs and base hits. Pitcher Juan Marichal placed fourth in games won and sixth in strikeouts. San Francisco fans may never forget the last play of the World Series in 1962, as a hard line drive hit by Willie McCovey found Bobby Richardson's glove for out number three to retire the side.

National League figures for the period showed that attendance data for the Giants was second, trailing only the Dodgers. Overall attendance in the eleven years in San Francisco averaged 1,439,000 per season. In the games I attended, the Giants won 16 and lost 8. In a game played at County Stadium in Milwaukee on April 30, 1961, Willie Mays knocked out four home runs. In their pennant winning year of 1962, I saw the Giants in action for five wins against only one loss.

American League - New York Yankees - Won 1,076 and Lost 832 - 56.4%.

From 1957 through 1964, the New York Yankees managed a winning season each year and won every pennant except for their one off-year of 1959. They won the World Series three times in 1958, 1961, and 1962. In 1960, they mostly outplayed the Pittsburgh Pirates in the Series, but lost game seven in dramatic fashion. Yankee Stadium was the scene of the Mickey Mantle and Roger Maris home run chase, in which Maris finally surpassed Babe Ruth with home run number 61 on the last day of the 1961 season. New York's most dominant pitcher in the period, especially in 1961, was southpaw Whitey Ford. Other notable pitchers for the Yankees were Bob Turley, Ralph Terry, Don Larsen, and Al Downing. A list of other position players for the Yankees reads like classic baseball. Players like Yogi Berra, Elston Howard, Bill Skowron, Bobby Richardson, Tony Kubek, and Hank Bauer all seemed present at the game's creation. In many games, one or more of these players was instrumental in putting numbers on the board for another Yankees' win. In the last four years of the period, the Yankees experienced an inevitable decline to a four-year mark of 302-343. Roger Maris, number 9, was dealt to the Cardinals which revived his career for two more good years in 1967 and

1968. Mickey Mantle, number 7, retired at the end of the 1968 season at the age of 37 with 536 career home runs.

In my tour of Major League Baseball, I was drawn to 42 Yankees games, the most of any Major League team, in which the Bronx Bombers won 30 and lost 12. In attendance, the Yankees exceeded the one million mark in all twelve years of the period. Average home attendance was 1,395,000 per season, with a peak of 1,747,725 fans in 1961.

BASEBALL THEN AND NOW

Earlier in this narrative, I laid the groundwork for some historical perspective by mentioning that the 1957-1968 period were the last years before baseball split the two leagues into divisions and lengthened the postseason. I also described the evolution of the single-season baseball records for home runs and stolen bases which were vanquished by Roger Maris and Maury Wills. Since 1968, Major League Baseball has gradually expanded from twenty to thirty teams. Over the years, attendance at games has steadily increased. Average seasonal home attendance per team increased in the American League from 1.153 million in 1960, to 1.563 million in 1980, and 2.289 million in 2010. In the National League, the comparable numbers are 1.335 million in 1960, 1.760 million in 1980, and 2.563 million in 2010. Most fans seem to have a splendid time at the ballparks and that is the most important thing.

The game was played in 2012 in much the same way compared to 1968. A comparison of the numbers needed to lead the American and National Leagues in the statistics of home runs, hits, batting average, stolen bases, pitching wins, strikeouts, earned run average, and complete games is shown in Figures 11 and 12. The offensive categories twelve-year averages don't seem that much different. Recently, it has taken a little more offensive production to be a league leader. However, in the pitching statistics there is a noticeable difference. In the past, it took roughly twenty complete games by a starting pitcher to lead the league. Recently, it is extremely rare for a pitcher to reach even ten in a single-season. Starting pitchers are not kept in close games nearly as much as before and the use of relief pitching specialists has become increasingly important. The leading earned run average numbers are higher than previously was the case, and the leading pitcher in wins typically has one or two fewer victories in a season.

WORDS ABOUT SOURCES

I have been a lifelong fan of Major League Baseball. Many of the games that are described in this narrative, I remember either from reading about them in a newspaper or sports magazine, listening to them on the radio, or watching them on television. This is true especially of the World Series games which have always attracted nationwide media attention. My parents took me to my very first Major League Baseball game I ever attended at Comiskey Park in Chicago on August 1, 1958, which is one of the games presented for the 1958 season. Over the years, I have enjoyed reading books and periodicals about many of the players from the 1957 through 1968 era.

The best source I have found for a wealth of information and extensive detail about baseball history is *www.baseball-almanac.com*. It has individual player's statistics by individual seasons and career, plus box scores of nearly every Major League game played since they began being published. This also includes box scores of World Series and All-Star games. This source of information is very well presented. It has for each team and season the results of scheduled games and cumulative record of the teams day-by-day as each year progressed. This web site was the primary source of information about all of the regular season games, All-Star games and individual player's statistics.

For World Series games, I also used *"The Sporting News Official World Series Records - 1903-1982."* This publication contains box scores of all World Series games and a brief article about each individual World Series, which provides background information about the teams, players, managers, and commentary about the games.

I wish to express my sincere thanks to the above-named sources of information. They offered a clear and concise presentation of the myriad of data, which I needed for this historical narrative. I tried very hard to be extremely careful in naming the players, describing the baseball games and seasons, and quoting the statistics about those players, games, and seasons. The narrative includes references to over 500 individual players, managers, or other personalities. If I have made any misstatements of fact or made any flawed interpretations in describing anything in this narrative, then the responsibility for the errors is solely mine.

Major League Baseball
Statistics and Charts: 1957-1968

◡◠

AMERICAN LEAGUE BASEBALL
Team Results: 1957, 1958 and 1959

AMERICAN LEAGUE	1957		1958		Two-Year Total		1959	
	Won	Lost	Won	Lost	Won	Lost	Won	Lost
Baltimore Orioles	76	76	74	79	150	155	74	80
Boston Red Sox	82	72	79	75	161	147	75	79
Chicago White Sox	90	64	82	72	172	136	94	60
Cleveland Indians	76	77	77	76	153	153	89	65
Detroit Tigers	78	76	77	77	155	153	76	78
Kansas City Athletics	59	94	73	81	132	175	66	88
New York Yankees	98	56	92	62	190	118	79	75
Washington Senators	55	99	61	93	116	192	63	91
Totals	614	614	615	615	1229	1229	616	616

Figure 1 ~ A two-year total of 1957 and 1958 is presented to illustrate the success of the Braves and the Yankees. In 1959 pennants were won by the Dodgers and White Sox. The year is presented by itself.

∽ NATIONAL LEAGUE BASEBALL ∽
Team Results: 1957, 1958 and 1959

NATIONAL LEAGUE	1957		1958		Two-Year Total		1959	
	Won	Lost	Won	Lost	Won	Lost	Won	Lost
Brooklyn/ L.A. Dodgers	84	70	71	83	155	153	88	68
Chicago Cubs	62	92	72	82	134	174	74	80
Cincinnati Reds	80	74	76	78	156	152	74	80
Milwaukee Braves	95	59	92	62	187	121	86	70
New York/S.F. Giants	69	85	80	74	149	159	83	71
Philadelphia Phillies	77	77	69	85	146	162	64	90
Pittsburgh Pirates	62	92	84	70	146	162	78	76
St. Louis Cardinals	87	67	72	82	159	149	71	83
Totals	616	616	616	616	1232	1232	618	618

Figure 1 ∼ A two-year total of 1957 and 1958 is presented to illustrate the success of the Braves and the Yankees. In 1959 pennants were won by the Dodgers and White Sox. The year is presented by itself.

AMERICAN LEAGUE BASEBALL
Team Results: 1960 through 1964

AMERICAN LEAGUE	1960 Won	1960 Lost	1961 Won	1961 Lost	1962 Won	1962 Lost	1963 Won	1963 Lost	1964 Won	1964 Lost	Total Won	Total Lost	Percent
Baltimore Orioles	89	65	95	67	77	85	86	76	97	65	444	358	55.4%
Boston Red Sox	65	89	76	86	76	84	76	85	72	90	365	434	45.7%
Chicago White Sox	87	67	86	76	85	76	94	68	98	64	450	352	56.1%
Cleveland Indians	76	78	78	83	80	82	79	83	79	83	392	409	48.9%
Detroit Tigers	71	83	101	61	85	76	79	83	85	77	421	380	52.6%
Kansas City Athletics	58	96	61	100	72	90	73	89	57	105	321	480	40.1%
Los Angeles Angels	-	-	70	91	86	76	70	91	82	80	308	338	47.7%
Minnesota Twins	-	-	70	90	91	71	91	70	79	83	331	314	51.3%
New York Yankees	97	57	109	53	96	66	104	57	99	63	505	296	63.0%
Washington Senators	73	81	61	100	60	101	56	106	62	100	312	488	39.0%
Totals	616	616	807	807	808	808	808	808	810	810	3,849	3,849	

Figure 2 ~ In the American League, the Yankees won the pennant each year from 1960 through 1964.

234

NATIONAL LEAGUE BASEBALL
Team Results: 1960 through 1964

NATIONAL LEAGUE	1960 Won	1960 Lost	1961 Won	1961 Lost	1962 Won	1962 Lost	1963 Won	1963 Lost	1964 Won	1964 Lost	Total Won	Total Lost	Total Percent
Chicago Cubs	60	94	64	90	59	103	82	80	76	86	341	453	42.9%
Cincinnati Reds	67	87	93	61	98	64	86	76	92	70	436	358	54.9%
Houston Colt 45s	-	-	-	-	64	96	66	96	66	96	196	288	40.5%
Los Angeles Dodgers	82	72	89	65	102	63	99	63	80	82	452	345	56.7%
Milwaukee Braves	88	66	83	71	86	76	84	78	88	74	429	365	54.0%
New York Mets	-	-	-	-	40	120	51	111	53	109	144	340	29.8%
Philadelphia Phillies	59	95	47	107	81	80	87	75	92	70	366	427	46.2%
Pittsburgh Pirates	95	59	75	79	93	68	74	88	80	82	417	376	52.6%
San Francisco Giants	79	75	85	69	103	62	88	74	90	72	445	352	55.8%
St. Louis Cardinals	86	68	80	74	84	78	93	69	93	69	436	358	54.9%
Totals	616	616	616	616	810	810	810	810	810	810	3,662	3,662	

Figure 2 ~ Five separate National League teams each won one pennant.

AMERICAN LEAGUE BASEBALL
Team Results: 1965 through 1968

AMERICAN LEAGUE	1965 Won	Lost	1966 Won	Lost	1967 Won	Lost	1968 Won	Lost	Total Won	Lost	Percent
Baltimore Orioles	94	68	97	63	76	85	91	71	358	287	55.5%
Boston Red Sox	62	100	72	90	92	70	86	76	312	336	48.1%
Chicago White Sox	95	67	83	79	89	73	67	95	334	314	51.5%
Cleveland Indians	87	75	81	81	75	87	86	75	329	318	50.9%
Detroit Tigers	89	73	88	74	91	71	103	59	371	277	57.3%
K.C./Oakland Athletics	59	103	74	86	62	99	82	80	277	368	42.9%
L.A./California Angels	75	87	80	82	84	77	67	95	306	341	47.3%
Minnesota Twins	102	60	89	73	91	71	79	83	361	287	55.7%
New York Yankees	77	85	70	89	72	90	83	79	302	343	46.8%
Washington Senators	70	92	71	88	76	85	65	96	282	361	43.9%
Totals	810	810	805	805	808	808	809	809	3,232	3,232	

Figure 3 ~ Four different American League teams won a pennant in 1965 through 1968.

NATIONAL LEAGUE BASEBALL
Team Results: 1965 through 1968

NATIONAL LEAGUE	1965 Won	1965 Lost	1966 Won	1966 Lost	1967 Won	1967 Lost	1968 Won	1968 Lost	Total Won	Total Lost	Percent
Chicago Cubs	72	90	59	103	87	74	84	78	302	345	46.7%
Cincinnati Reds	89	73	76	84	87	75	83	79	335	311	51.9%
Houston Astros	65	97	72	90	69	93	72	90	278	370	42.9%
Los Angeles Dodgers	97	65	95	67	73	89	76	86	341	307	52.6%
Milwaukee/Atlanta Braves	86	76	85	77	77	85	81	81	329	319	50.8%
New York Mets	50	112	66	95	61	101	73	89	250	397	38.6%
Philadelphia Phillies	85	76	87	75	82	80	76	86	330	317	51.0%
Pittsburgh Pirates	90	72	92	70	81	81	80	82	343	305	52.9%
San Francisco Giants	95	67	93	68	91	71	88	74	367	280	56.7%
St. Louis Cardinals	80	81	83	79	101	60	97	65	361	285	55.9%
Totals	809	809	808	808	809	809	810	810	3,236	3,236	

Figure 3 ~ The Dodgers and Cardinals each won two National League pennants in this four year period.

MAJOR LEAGUE BASEBALL
Home Run Leaders: 1957-1968 Totals

	Rank	Home Runs	At Bats	Hits	Doubles	Triples	At Bats per HR	Walks	Strikeouts	At Bats per Walk	At Bats per SO	Batting Average
Aaron, Henry	1	444	7,210	2,272	386	59	16.2	752	837	9.6	8.6	.315
Mays, Willie	2	435	6,816	2,104	344	86	15.7	851	888	8.0	7.7	.309
Killebrew, Harmon	3	388	5,047	1,325	185	17	13.0	917	1,081	5.5	4.7	.263
Banks, Ernie	4	381	6,789	1,858	306	61	17.8	554	899	12.3	7.6	.274
Robinson, Frank	5	380	6,431	1,951	375	54	16.9	865	952	7.4	6.8	.303
Mantle, Mickey	6	363	5,158	1,508	208	29	14.2	1,209	1,132	4.3	4.6	.292
Colavito, Rocky	7	353	6,172	1,637	270	17	17.5	902	832	6.8	7.4	.265
Mathews, Eddie	8	322	5,903	1,580	235	48	18.3	973	1,044	6.1	5.7	.268
Cepeda, Orlando	9	284	5,793	1,755	313	24	20.4	398	875	14.6	6.6	.303
Maris, Roger	10	275	5,101	1,325	195	42	18.5	652	733	7.8	7.0	.260

Figure 4

Illustration of the powerful left-handed batting swing of Roger Maris. After his career with the Yankees ended, Maris helped the St. Louis Cardinals compete in the World Series in 1967 and 1968. In his twelve-year baseball career, Maris hit 275 home runs and still remains as the single-season American League home run champion.

MAJOR LEAGUE BASEBALL
Hits Leaders: 1957-1968 Totals

	Rank	Hits	At Bats	Batting Average	Doubles	Triples	Home Runs	At Bats per EBH	Walks	Strikeouts	At Bats per Walk	At Bats per SO
Aaron, Henry	1	2,272	7,210	.315	386	59	444	8.1	752	837	9.6	8.6
Mays, Willie	2	2,104	6,816	.309	344	86	435	7.9	851	888	8.0	7.7
Clemente, Roberto	3	2,094	6,618	.316	297	111	172	11.4	441	859	15.0	7.7
Robinson, Frank	4	1,951	6,431	.303	375	54	380	7.9	865	952	7.4	6.8
Pinson, Vada	5	1,881	6,335	.297	342	96	186	10.2	409	831	15.5	7.6
Banks, Ernie	6	1,858	6,789	.274	306	61	381	9.1	554	899	12.3	7.6
Aparicio, Luis	7	1,833	7,120	.257	256	74	63	18.1	479	512	14.9	13.9
Boyer, Ken	8	1,814	6,296	.288	259	64	238	11.2	636	878	9.9	7.2
Kaline, Al	9	1,782	5,905	.302	312	44	255	9.7	767	555	7.7	10.6
Robinson, Brooks	10	1,779	6,388	.278	313	53	172	11.9	477	614	13.4	10.4

Figure 5 ~ Extra base hits (EBH) are doubles + triples + home runs.

MAJOR LEAGUE BASEBALL
Stolen Bases Leaders: 1957-1968 Totals

	Rank	At Bats	Hits	Batting Average	Walks	Strikeouts	Stolen Bases	Caught Stealing	SB%
Wills, Maury	1	5,710	1,636	.287	393	527	502	165	75.3%
Aparicio, Luis	2	7,120	1,833	.257	479	512	431	117	78.6%
Brock, Lou	3	4,249	1,211	.285	253	831	334	112	74.9%
Campaneris, Bert	4	2,663	704	.264	167	335	230	69	76.9%
Pinson, Vada	5	6,335	1,881	.297	409	831	221	84	72.5%
Davis, Willie	6	4,549	1,208	.266	209	552	216	76	74.0%
Mays, Willie	7	6,816	2,104	.309	851	888	216	69	75.8%
Aaron, Henry	8	7,210	2,272	.315	752	837	208	52	80.0%
Taylor, Tony	9	5,703	1,468	.257	445	839	182	78	70.0%
Robinson, Frank	10	6,431	1,951	.303	865	952	174	63	73.4%

Figure 6

MAJOR LEAGUE BASEBALL
Pitching Wins Leaders: 1957-1968 Totals

	Rank	Wins	Losses	Winning %	Complete Games	Shutouts	Innings	Hits	Hits per Inning	Earned Runs	Walks	Strikeouts	Strikeouts per Walk	ERA
Drysdale, Don	1	199	157	55.9%	164	48	3,270	2,918	0.89	1,064	811	2,407	2.97	2.93
Bunning, Jim	2	188	141	57.1%	141	40	3,115	2,748	0.88	1,054	788	2,422	3.07	3.05
Jackson, Larry	3	183	167	52.3%	145	36	3,000	2,942	0.98	1,109	707	1,571	2.22	3.33
Marichal, Juan	4	170	77	68.8%	170	37	2,250	1,917	0.85	658	449	1,635	3.64	2.63
Koufax, Sandy	5	161	81	66.5%	135	38	2,224	1,655	0.74	667	760	2,336	3.07	2.70
Spahn, Warren	6	160	110	59.3%	157	26	2,284	2,173	0.95	824	574	1,061	1.85	3.25
Pascual, Camilo	7	158	126	55.6%	124	36	2,394	2,133	0.89	855	791	1,798	2.27	3.21
Ford, Whitey	8	156	78	66.7%	91	30	2,161	1,947	0.90	661	626	1,384	2.21	2.75
Pappas, Milt	9	150	111	57.5%	96	32	2,243	2,060	0.92	839	640	1,324	2.07	3.37
Gibson, Bob	10	147	97	60.2%	138	38	2,209	1,810	0.82	698	766	1,850	2.42	2.84

Figure 7

242

᙮MAJOR LEAGUE BASEBALL᙮
Strikeouts Leaders: 1957-1968 Totals

	Rank	Strikeouts	Innings	Hits	Walks	Strikeouts per Walk	Strikeouts per 9 Inn.	Wins	Losses	ERA
Bunning, Jim	1	2,422	3,115	2,748	788	3.07	7.00	188	141	3.05
Drysdale, Don	2	2,407	3,270	2,918	811	2.97	6.62	199	157	2.93
Koufax, Sandy	3	2,336	2,224	1,655	760	3.07	9.45	161	81	2.70
Gibson, Bob	4	1,850	2,209	1,810	766	2.42	7.54	147	97	2.84
Pascual, Camilo	5	1,798	2,394	2,133	791	2.27	6.76	158	126	3.21
Marichal, Juan	6	1,635	2,250	1,917	449	3.64	6.54	170	77	2.63
Jackson, Larry	7	1,571	3,000	2,942	707	2.22	4.71	183	167	3.33
Maloney, Jim	8	1,483	1,623	1,322	685	2.16	8.22	122	75	3.12
Ford, Whitey	9	1,384	2,161	1,947	626	2.21	5.76	156	78	2.75
McDowell, Sam	10	1,384	1,305	985	686	2.02	9.54	71	66	2.96

Figure 8

American League Baseball
Team Results: 1957 through 1968

AMERICAN LEAGUE	1957-1958		1959		1960-1964		1965-1968		Total		
	Won	Lost	Won	Lost	Won	Lost	Won	Lost	Won	Lost	Percent
Baltimore Orioles	150	155	74	80	444	358	358	287	1,026	880	53.8%
Boston Red Sox	161	147	75	79	365	434	312	336	913	996	47.8%
Chicago White Sox	172	136	94	60	450	352	334	314	1,050	862	54.9%
Cleveland Indians	153	153	89	65	392	409	329	318	963	945	50.5%
Detroit Tigers	155	153	76	78	421	380	371	277	1,023	888	53.5%
K.C./Oakland Athletics	132	175	66	88	321	480	277	368	796	1,111	41.7%
L.A./California Angels	0	0	0	0	308	338	306	341	614	679	47.5%
Minnesota Twins	0	0	0	0	331	314	361	287	692	601	53.5%
New York Yankees	190	118	79	75	505	296	302	343	1,076	832	56.4%
Washington Senators	116	192	63	91	312	488	282	361	773	1,132	40.6%
Totals	1,229	1,229	616	616	3,849	3,849	3,232	3,232	8,926	8,926	

Figure 9

NATIONAL LEAGUE BASEBALL
Team Results: 1957 through 1968

NATIONAL LEAGUE	1957-1958		1959		1960-1964		1965-1968		Total		
	Won	Lost	Won	Lost	Won	Lost	Won	Lost	Won	Lost	Percent
Chicago Cubs	134	174	74	80	341	453	302	345	851	1,052	44.7%
Cincinnati Reds	156	152	74	80	436	358	335	311	1,001	901	52.6%
Houston Astros	0	0	0	0	196	288	278	370	474	658	41.9%
Los Angeles/Brk. Dodgers	155	153	88	68	452	345	341	307	1,036	873	54.3%
Milwaukee/Atlanta Braves	187	121	86	70	429	365	329	319	1,031	875	54.1%
New York Mets	0	0	0	0	144	340	250	397	394	737	34.8%
Philadelphia Phillies	146	162	64	90	366	427	330	317	906	996	47.6%
Pittsburgh Pirates	146	162	78	76	417	376	343	305	984	919	51.7%
San Francisco/N.Y. Giants	149	159	83	71	445	352	367	280	1,044	862	54.8%
St. Louis Cardinals	159	149	71	83	436	358	361	285	1,027	875	54.0%
Totals	1,232	1,232	618	618	3,662	3,662	3,236	3,236	8,748	8,748	

Figure 9

 ∽ MAJOR LEAGUE BASEBALL ∽
Attendance Data: 1957 through 1968

	AMERICAN LEAGUE	NATIONAL LEAGUE	Total	Highest Team	
1957	8,196,218	8,819,601	17,015,819	2,215,404	Milwaukee Braves
1958	7,296,034	10,164,596	17,460,630	1,971,101	Milwaukee Braves
1959	9,149,454	9,994,525	19,143,979	2,071,045	Los Angeles Dodgers
1960	9,226,526	10,684,963	19,911,489	2,253,887	Los Angeles Dodgers
1961	10,163,016	8,731,502	18,894,518	1,804,250	Los Angeles Dodgers
1962	10,015,056	11,360,159	21,375,215	2,755,184	Los Angeles Dodgers
1963	9,094,847	11,382,227	20,477,074	2,538,602	Los Angeles Dodgers
1964	9,235,151	12,045,190	21,280,341	2,228,751	Los Angeles Dodgers
1965	8,860,764	13,581,136	22,441,900	2,553,577	Los Angeles Dodgers
1966	10,166,738	15,015,471	25,182,209	2,617,029	Los Angeles Dodgers
1967	11,336,923	12,971,430	24,308,353	2,090,145	St. Louis Cardinals
1968	11,317,387	11,785,358	23,102,745	2,031,847	Detroit Tigers
Total	114,058,114	136,536,158	250,594,272		

Figure 10

Major League Baseball
Leaders in Offense - Numbers Comparison: 1957 - 1968 compared to 2001-2012

	HOME RUNS				HITS				BATTING AVERAGE				STOLEN BASES			
	American League		National League		American League		National League		American League		National League		American League		National League	
	1957-1968	2001-2012	1957-1968	2001-2012	1957-1968	2001-2012	1957-1968	2001-2012	1957-1968	2001-2012	1957-1968	2001-2012	1957-1968	2001-2012	1957-1968	2001-2012
Year 1	42	52	44	73	196	242	200	206	.388	.350	.351	.350	28	56	38	46
Year 2	42	57	47	49	187	209	215	206	.328	.349	.350	.370	29	41	31	48
Year 3	42	47	46	47	198	215	223	212	.353	.326	.355	.359	56	55	27	65
Year 4	40	43	41	48	174	262	190	221	.320	.372	.325	.362	51	59	50	70
Year 5	61	48	46	51	193	221	208	199	.361	.331	.351	.335	53	62	35	60
Year 6	48	54	49	58	209	224	230	204	.326	.347	.346	.344	31	58	104	64
Year 7	45	54	44	50	183	238	204	216	.321	.363	.326	.340	40	50	40	78
Year 8	49	37	47	48	217	213	211	204	.323	.328	.339	.364	57	50	53	68
Year 9	32	39	52	47	185	225	209	203	.321	.365	.329	.342	51	70	94	61
Year 10	49	54	44	42	191	214	218	197	.316	.359	.342	.336	52	68	74	52
Year 11	44	43	37	39	189	213	209	207	.326	.344	.357	.337	55	49	52	61
Year 12	44	44	36	41	177	216	210	194	.301	.330	.335	.336	62	49	62	44
Average	44.8	47.7	44.4	49.4	191.6	224.3	210.6	205.8	.332	.347	.342	.348	47.1	55.6	55.0	59.8

Figure 11

MAJOR LEAGUE BASEBALL

Pitching Leaders - Numbers Comparison: 1957 - 1968 compared to 2001-2012

	WINS				STRIKEOUTS				EARNED RUN AVERAGE				COMPLETE GAMES			
	American League		National League		American League		National League		American League		National League		American League		National League	
	1957-1968	2001-2012	1957-1968	2001-2012	1957-1968	2001-2012	1957-1968	2001-2012	1957-1968	2001-2012	1957-1968	2001-2012	1957-1968	2001-2012	1957-1968	2001-2012
Year 1	20	21	21	22	184	220	188	372	2.45	3.05	2.66	2.49	16	8	18	6
Year 2	21	23	22	24	179	239	225	334	2.01	2.26	2.47	2.32	19	7	23	8
Year 3	22	22	21	21	201	207	242	266	2.19	2.22	2.83	2.34	17	9	21	8
Year 4	18	21	21	20	201	265	246	290	2.67	2.61	2.70	2.27	15	5	18	9
Year 5	25	21	25	22	221	238	269	216	2.40	2.86	3.02	1.87	22	5	21	7
Year 6	23	19	25	16	206	245	232	216	2.21	2.77	2.54	2.98	18	6	22	6
Year 7	24	20	25	19	202	239	306	240	2.33	3.01	1.88	2.54	18	7	22	4
Year 8	20	22	24	22	217	231	250	265	1.65	2.54	1.74	2.53	15	9	22	7
Year 9	21	19	26	19	325	269	382	261	2.18	2.16	2.04	2.24	18	9	27	4
Year 10	25	21	27	21	225	233	317	231	1.98	2.27	1.73	2.30	19	7	27	9
Year 11	22	24	22	21	246	250	253	248	2.06	2.40	1.87	2.28	18	11	20	8
Year 12	31	20	26	21	283	239	268	230	1.60	2.56	1.12	2.53	28	6	30	5
Average	22.7	21.1	23.8	20.7	224.2	239.6	264.8	264.1	2.14	2.56	2.22	2.39	18.6	7.4	22.6	6.8

Figure 12

Made in the USA
Middletown, DE
11 June 2015